Joe Hockey served as Australia's Ambassador to the United States of America in Washington, DC from January 2016 to January 2020. He was responsible for Australia's relationship with the USA during the final year of President Obama's tenure and the first three years of President Trump's term. Hockey was previously Treasurer of Australia and served as a frontbencher for sixteen of his nineteen years as a Member of Australian Parliament. He is founding partner and president of Bondi Partners and is based in both Sydney and Washington, DC.

Leo Shanahan is an award-winning journalist, writer and corporate consultant. He is the recipient of the News Award for Scoop of the Year and the National Press Club Financial Journalism global and economic award, and has twice been a finalist nominated for the Walkley Award for business journalist of the year. He has most recently held positions as the media editor of *The Australian* and chief business reporter for Sky News.

JOE HOCKEY

DIPLOMATIC

JOE HOCKEY

DIPLOMATIC

A Washington Memoir
with Leo Shanahan

HarperCollins*Publishers*

HarperCollins*Publishers*

Australia • Brazil • Canada • France • Germany • Holland • Hungary
India • Italy • Japan • Mexico • New Zealand • Poland • Spain • Sweden
Switzerland • United Kingdom • United States of America

First published in Australia in 2022
by HarperCollins*Publishers* Australia Pty Limited
Level 13, 201 Elizabeth Street, Sydney NSW 2000
ABN 36 009 913 517
harpercollins.com.au

A catalogue record for this book is available from the National Library of Australia.

ISBN 978 1 4607 5951 6 (paperback)
ISBN 978 1 4607 1314 3 (ebook)

Cover design by Darren Holt, HarperCollins Design Studio
Front cover image by mbell / Getty Images
Back cover image © Gregg Delman
Typeset in Sabon LT Std by Kirby Jones
Printed and bound in Australia by McPherson's Printing Group

MIX
Paper from
responsible sources
FSC® C001695

We engage in public life to make our community better, safer and more prosperous. Our family are conscripts to this cause, not volunteers like us.

This book is dedicated to my wife, Melissa, and our children, Xavier, Adelaide and Ignatius. It would never have happened without them.

To my extended family, friends, fellow Australians and fellow Americans, this is also for you.

CONTENTS

PROLOGUE

Landing in America and the evolution of the
Australia–United States relationship

The first time I flew into the United States was aboard Pan Am Airlines. There was some irony about that. It was the end of 1988, and I was completing my article clerkship with an undistinguished London law firm. They were ambulance chasers: they loved litigation, and played tough against big corporations. They were suing Pan Am over the recent Lockerbie disaster, and were sending me to Washington, DC for the case. But they wanted me to take the cheapest flight. So there I was, arriving in the United States on Pan Am, with the task of serving papers on Pan Am.

Donald Trump would soon purchase a failing airline called the Eastern Air Lines Shuttle. As with everything else in his life, he would rebrand it in his unique way: with gold, gaud and glitz. While I missed my chance to fly the 'Trump Shuttle', as he soon rebranded it, his name conjured up all the unique imagery of the 1980s.

I landed in New York and then flew to Washington, DC a few days later. It wasn't my first trip to the USA but it was my first visit to the East Coast. And having grown up in Sydney on a healthy diet of Americana that stretched from Disney to McDonald's, I felt somewhat at home.

Australia in the 1970s had embraced all things American. In a short time, the speed and excitement of Uncle Sam, from television and food to music and toys, became all-pervasive. America was what Australia would look like in ten years' time. Some of it we loved, like disco music and fast food. Some of it was amusing, like bringing an American NFL footballer over to play Rugby League. Sadly, Manfred Moore wasn't the next big thing; indeed, these days we send Rugby League players to the NFL with an equal rate of success.

Some of what we imported from America was just scary. The United States seemed to be the world headquarters for gun-related crime. The *Dirty Harry* movies and a feast of shows like *Adam-12*, *Starsky and Hutch*, *Kojak* and *The Streets of San Francisco* told us that the United States was a rough place. It seemed that the biggest security threat to America was American citizens.

On my first night in New York, my suspicions were confirmed. After the arduous trans-Atlantic flight, I found myself in midtown and wandered into a pizzeria for a 'piece of pie'. While I waited for my slice, a guy walked in wearing a hoodie and carrying a black Adidas sports bag. Completely unprovoked, the shop owner jumped over the register and, in a singular, speedy manoeuvre, grabbed the guy by the throat and pinned him against the wall. 'Think you're going to rob my shop?' he screamed into the stranger's terrified face. He took the black bag off the would-be customer and ripped it open – only to reveal gym clothes. Unperturbed, the proprietor tossed the bag and the innocent man out onto the sidewalk, warning him never to return.

I stood there, stunned. I'd been to some tough towns over the years, including a mid-war Beirut, but I'd never seen a respectable-looking guy threatened and thrown out of a shop for carrying a gym bag. Perhaps America really needed vigilantes like Batman and Superman to keep the pizza shops safe.

* * *

That America is different from Australia is self-evident. But such is the depth of the relationship and cultural similarities between the two countries, Australians can be lulled into thinking we're more or less the same.

Unlike Australia, though, the modern United States was born of two wars: the War of Independence and the Civil War. And that has made America fundamentally different from us. States' rights, gun control, race relations and the whole notion of American freedom and nationhood should be understood through the prism of the bloody wars Americans have fought with each other over these issues.

The War of Independence was initially fought over tax. A surprisingly large number of Americans supported Britain's running (read: taxing and controlling) the unruly New World colony. According to the prominent historian Robert Calhoon, up to one in five Americans were loyal to Mother England. It wasn't a simple matter.

Australia, by contrast, won its 'independence' by coming of age. The British decided they should handle us like an unruly teenager. Given that the white settlers of Australia were convicts, and that we lived a long way away, independence by mutual agreement was acceptable to both sides.

The impact of the next great battle of US history is far more complex. More Americans died in the Civil War than in every other modern war combined. More than 500,000 Americans were killed, from a population the size of modern-day Australia's. It was a brutal war fought over economics and slavery. There remain today many demons in the American psyche, which are reflected in the ongoing tense race relations. They have found expression in the decapitation of Confederate statues, in the 'history wars' and in the widening gap between rich and poor.

Despite these inherent differences between the United States and Australia, the two nations have a long and friendly history. It's a bit like a successful marriage: we like each other a lot, we are not identical and do not always agree; however, we have shared our lives over many years. We are loyal to each other and we really enjoy each other's company.

During our '100 Years of Mateship' – a phrase I coined as ambassador – soldiers from the United States and Australia have fought and died together in every major war since World War I. The Battle of Hamel in 1918 was the first time many US soldiers saw combat on the Western Front. They did so alongside Australian soldiers, and under the command of the great Australian military leader General Sir John Monash.

The strength of the relationship was solidified in World War II, and especially by the Allied victory in the Battle of the Coral Sea. There the combined American and Australian naval force stopped a potential Japanese occupation of Port Moresby, at the expense of many young American lives. The threat to Australia during World War II also inspired Prime Minister John Curtin's famous foreign policy pivot away from Britain and towards the United States.

However, Australia was never going to understand America fully until we unleashed ourselves from Britain, because we still tended to look at the United States through British eyes. Even after the USA was hugely instrumental in helping save Australia during World War II, Britain maintained its political and cultural dominance. Despite Curtin's declaration in late 1941 that 'Australia looks to America', this was not the point at which the relationship between Australia and the United States was recast. While Curtin's statement was a major step, the tipping point was Vietnam.

It was in Vietnam in 1962 that Australia stood with the United States in a pivotal Cold War conflict – and the United Kingdom wasn't there. It was the first time we'd gone into a war without British involvement. The famous 1966 declaration with which Prime Minister Harold Holt showed Australia's support for President Lyndon B. Johnson – 'All the way with LBJ' – was not well received among left-wingers and Empire conservatives, but it was a foreign policy statement that redefined Australia's outlook for the second half of the twentieth century.

Then there was the advent of a cultural and commercial wave from America that would define what 'modern' living looked like. American popular culture and goods had a profound impact on Australia in the late 1960s, and into the 1970s and '80s. Growing up in suburban Sydney at this time, I became aware of the enormous variety of new US consumable goods that had begun to flood our supermarket shelves. (Not to mention the supermarket itself, a US innovation.)

The cultural similarities meant American commercial concepts assimilated easily, and the changing economy led to a surge in investment in Australia by US companies. For better or for worse, America also introduced our suburbs to a form of materialism typified by fast-food chains such as Pizza Hut and Kentucky Fried Chicken. Newly imported tech like the colour television brought American culture directly into our homes. US television productions such as *Mister Ed* and *Flipper* came with a flair that made Australian and British programs, all largely produced and exported by the BBC, look drab and dated.

By the 1970s, Australia's political relationship with the United States had begun to evolve as well. While there has been a view that the government of Gough Whitlam was not popular with the Nixon administration (boosting conspiracy theories about the CIA being involved in Whitlam's 1975 dismissal), the pair were in sync on foreign policy when it came to China. The two leaders actually had a great deal in common when it came to foreign policy, despite Whitlam's (correct) decision to pull Australia out of the Vietnam War, and the supposedly frosty relationship between him and Nixon. In opening Australia up to China, Whitlam was following the lead of the US president.

The bombing of the Hilton Hotel in Sydney in 1978 woke Australia up to global terrorism. We became aware that we were not immune from the threats and global pressures which, until that point, we had seen as the problems of other nations. We were no longer immune from the horror of terrorism, and we would increasingly look to the United States for help and advice on how to deal with the growing threat.

The opening-up of Australia to the US capital markets in the 1980s meant a flood of new investment in the Australian economy, and established closer financial ties between the two countries. The opening-up of the banking system and the floating of the Australian dollar by the government of Prime Minister Bob Hawke and Treasurer Paul Keating were pivotal to this.

Although a modern prime minister, Malcolm Fraser, who led the government between 1975 and 1983, had a distinctly British tinge in his foreign policy outlook. Rather, it was the relationship between Bob Hawke and President George H.W. Bush that formed the backbone of the modern US–Australian alliance. It sent a message to both countries that, regardless of party political differences, what we had in common far outweighed any disagreements.

While the great global political relationship of the 1980s was between two conservatives – Prime Minister Margaret Thatcher of the United Kingdom and President Ronald Reagan of the United States – Labor Prime Minister Hawke understood how Australia could contribute. The fall of the USSR at the end of the decade meant there was a role for Australia as both a liberal-democratic leader in the Pacific and a key ally of the United States.

Hawke saw that President Bush, who succeeded Reagan in 1989, was a leader with whom he could forge a genuinely warm relationship, one that would cross the political divide between the Labor Party and the Republican Party. 'Golf course diplomacy' played a role, with much of the relationship cemented on the putting green.

The Democrat Bill Clinton, too, was a good supporter of Australia and the alliance. His relationship with prime ministers Paul Keating and John Howard was reasonably strong, and he visited Australia on several occasions. However, Clinton wanted to stay out of the 1999 East Timor conflict, which did not impress

John Howard, who had to work particularly hard to get Clinton's support for an international peacekeeping force, which, in a first, Australia led.

The relationship changed again, and most profoundly, during the administration of President George W. Bush (son of former President George H.W. Bush), with whom Prime Minister Howard was much more comfortable. Theirs was a unique friendship forged during the terrorist attacks of 11 September 2001 in the United States; by chance, Howard was in Washington, DC on that awful day.

On 10 September 2001, Howard had met President George W. Bush for the first time, at an event to mark the fiftieth anniversary of the ANZUS Treaty. On the morning of 11 September, Howard was giving a press conference at the Willard Hotel as a hijacked plane flew into the Pentagon. Journalists could see smoke rising at the Pentagon from the lobby window, and Howard's security detail had picked up an explosion on their radios. Howard was bundled away from the Willard and taken to the bunker at the Australian Embassy; he and his wife, Janette, would ultimately spend the night at a secret location and were later brought to the ambassadorial residence.

And so, just days after celebrating its fiftieth anniversary, Howard invoked the ANZUS Treaty for the first time. This treaty, first signed in 1951, was intended to be a security pact for the Pacific region between Australia, New Zealand and the USA. No Australian would have contemplated that the first invocation of the mutual defence treaty would be in response to a direct attack on America, rather than Australia. But Howard's immediate and unconditional show of support meant he and Bush were bonded like no other Australian and American leaders before them.

On Wednesday, 12 September, Howard attended a special session of Congress, accompanied by Janette and Australian Ambassador Michael Thawley, and heard motions condemning the attacks and discussions about America's response. The speaker of the House of Representatives highlighted the attendance of Howard and the Australian delegation, the lone visitors to the gallery that day. Everyone in the chamber rose to their feet to provide a long and emotional salute to Howard. At that moment, America really needed its mates, and we were first in line.

Australia's military commitment to a second war in the Persian Gulf in a little over a decade, and then to further conflict in Afghanistan, deepened the defence relationship between the two nations. But the domestic politics were far from straightforward. Ever since the debacle of Vietnam, both sides of politics in Australia had been at pains to ensure bipartisan support for our troops. But the second Iraq War had many critics. It created division in my own electorate of North Sydney. The Labor Party was hopelessly divided on the conflict, and the situation was particularly difficult for the party's leader, Simon Crean.

Simon is a good man, and he struggled with the internal disunity of his team. The fact that the war became another point of division between the Labor Right and the Labor Left further weakened Crean's leadership. The discord ultimately led to the rise of Mark Latham to the party's leadership. Unlike any other ALP leader since the 1970s, Latham openly questioned the utility of Australia's relationship with the United States. (Latham back then was a far cry from the Donald Trump–supporting, One Nation state MP we see today.) It was a major foreign policy blunder, and fed into a perception in the electorate that Latham in government would pose a massive risk to Australia's stability.

Despite these pressures, the Australia–USA relationship continued to evolve under Howard and Bush, leading to a free trade agreement in 2005. This was an opportunity for both countries to 'change the channel' from the military relationship and the failures in Iraq to a deeper and broader economic partnership.

My experience is that political leaders like to change the topic when they are stuck talking about something as unpopular as the second Iraq War. Pardon the pun, but the failure to find actual weapons of mass destruction led to the advent of a weapon of mass *distraction* in the Australia–United States Free Trade Agreement. Part of this deal saw the creation of the new E-3 visa, which would give tens of thousands of Australians the opportunity to work and live in the United States.

Today, instead of rushing off to London after school or university, young Australians can think about taking the opportunity to live, work and travel in America. Many more Americans have also taken the opportunity to come and live in Australia. Why not? It's just like Southern California – and, unlike most Californians, we like Americans! Australia remains the only country to have the E-3 visa category available to its citizens, despite (as I would learn as ambassador) the protestations of America's other close allies, including the always influential Republic of Ireland.

After the extraordinary partnership between Howard and Bush, the relationship between President Barack Obama and Prime Minister Kevin Rudd was not notably warm. One major reason for this was because Rudd portrayed himself as a Sinophile. In my view, Rudd was asking Australians to choose between our closest ally, the United States, and our new largest trading partner, China. The problem was that Rudd didn't have the Australian people behind him. People were curious about China, and could see a lot of good for both our culture and the broader economy in fostering a closer engagement, but there was always a level of caution. Although they didn't go 'all the way' with Rudd on China, the Australian community instinctively knew that the opening-up of China was good for its people, for the Australian economy and for the region.

I first went to China with my parents in 1978. I was just thirteen years old, and it was only the second Western tour group to visit since the Cultural Revolution came to an end with the death of Mao Zedong. When I became Australia's treasurer, I was a supporter of Chinese companies in Australia. At one point I allowed China's biggest state-owned enterprise, the energy behemoth State Grid Corporation, to take a stake in two Australian energy companies. This created some tension with the Americans, especially after I blocked US agricultural giant Archer Daniels Midland's takeover bid for GrainCorp (which didn't happen for its own reasons).

Still, the suspicions of many Australians about Beijing's intentions in Australia have been justified in recent years. We will never have a more important or closer ally in the Pacific than the United States because of the strength of our economic ties, the importance of our military relationship and our cultural similarities. China simply cannot replicate all of these elements – at least, not in the foreseeable future.

The relationship between Rudd's successor, Prime Minister Julia Gillard, and President Obama was warm, but she was never really an internationalist. Her focus was necessarily on domestic politics: her minority government was always just one or two votes away from falling over. It was a tumultuous period.

When the Gillard government did lose power, Australia's new Liberal Prime Minister Tony Abbott surprised many people with his keen interest in foreign affairs. And no one, it turned out, was more surprised than Barack Obama.

Before Abbott's first visit to Washington, DC, the then Australian ambassador, Kim Beazley, was told by Obama confidants that the president was wary of the new prime minister. Obama had been briefed that Abbott was a traditionalist and a monarchist, and that he certainly did not believe in climate change. So Obama was anticipating a frosty encounter when he first met Abbott, in June 2014. But the new prime minister surprised the US president when he arrived at the Oval Office. 'Everyone who walks into this office comes to ask you for something,' Abbott said. 'I'm coming into this office to say: How can I help you?' Obama hadn't been prepared for any warmth, and was disarmed. Apparently, no one ever goes into the Oval Office and offers to help. Some good agreements were made that day, especially around the placement of US marines in Darwin – known as the Force Posture. Abbott's approach allowed him to develop a relationship with Obama that, while never warm, could have been a lot worse.

There were risks on both sides. When, during the G20 meeting in Brisbane in November 2014, President Obama gave without warning a speech about climate change, and Australia's supposed lack of action, that upset and embarrassed the Abbott government. Our relationship with the Obama administration became more challenging, as Abbott himself made clear. Just as the president wouldn't like a foreign leader going to Washington and giving him a lecture on policy, our prime minister was not pleased when a visiting leader focused in this way on what was a hugely divisive domestic political issue among Australians.

Despite this, the people-to-people contact between Americans and Australians had evolved by this point across politics and business. It had largely inoculated our nations against policy disagreements. A large and increasingly prominent number of Aussies were making their way in America. Our relationship was maturing.

But let's not get too carried away. Despite being our top ally, America is a tough partner. Just like my pizzeria-owning friend in New York, they don't hesitate to jump across the counter and make it clear who's in charge. During my time in politics, and especially as federal treasurer, I had a few encounters with this more abrasive brand of US diplomacy. Key among these was my decision to deny Archer Daniels Midland the opportunity to take over Australia's GrainCorp.

But nothing would quite prepare Australia (and the rest of the world) for the challenges of the Trump administration.

Much to my own surprise, I would find myself among that number of Aussies moving to the United States when I became our government's ambassador in Washington, DC. The bulk of my time in that role was during the extraordinary period of the Trump administration. I was given the sometimes bizarre but honestly thrilling challenge of putting up the best diplomatic fight possible for Australia's interests during one of the most historic and unpredictable presidencies in US history.

With the help of my team in Washington, I would write my own chapter in the history of one the greatest bilateral relationships in modern history: the alliance between the United States of America and Australia. In fact, it was more than a chapter; we would write a book.

CHAPTER 1

'A DUMB DEAL'

Trump and Turnbull's leaked phone call

My phone started to light up like a Christmas tree, buzzing and receiving texts with the kind of urgency that means something had to be going wrong.

It was 2 February 2017, at about 10 p.m., and I was at an official dinner at one of Washington's most famous networking restaurants, Cafe Milano in Georgetown. It was a small group of journalists, businesspeople, congressmen and congresswomen. There was an energy in the room and despite the strangeness of Trump's early weeks in office, there was a sense of excitement within his administration, a keenness to take on the challenges ahead. After all, new presidents are rare. A president like Donald Trump is even rarer.

Seated directly across the table from me that night was Devin Nunes, a Republican congressman and the chair of the House Intelligence Committee. While my own mobile phone was furiously vibrating with calls during dinner, I could see that Devin's phone was also going crazy.

I discreetly picked up and was informed by one of our staff that *The Washington Post* had a story detailing the recent disastrous phone call between President Trump and Prime Minister Malcolm Turnbull. My stomach (or what was left of it) sank. As I looked around at Devin and others in the room, I immediately recognised the ghostly 'oh shit' apparitions of members of the political class getting bad news.

Usually, the differences between Australia and the United States are kept behind closed doors, but I never would have thought details of a private conversation between the US president and the Australian prime minister would be published as the lead story of *The Washington Post*. 'That' phone call between Donald Trump and Malcolm Turnbull took the Australia–USA relationship to a new level – and it was closer to the basement than the penthouse.

I was appointed Australia's ambassador to the United States of America in the last year of the Obama administration, and throughout 2016 had witnessed the familiar but not particularly warm relationship between President Obama and Prime Minister Turnbull. Both men had a healthy love of detailed intellectual discourse – especially their own. Like two history professors discussing dialectic materialism, their conversation was eye-watering but hardly warm.

Despite this, Turnbull had managed to get Obama over the line for a refugee-swap agreement that would be an essential part of his border protection policy. Under the deal, the United States agreed to resettle up to 1200 refugees whom Australia had held offshore on Papua New Guinea's Manus Island and on Nauru. It was a big win for Australia, as many of the 1200 had been held for years and had been vetted as primarily economic refugees, but could not be allowed into Australia on well-established policy grounds. In return, Australia undertook to increase our overall refugee intake, including taking some people whom the United States could not accept for its own domestic political reasons.

The agreement was quietly struck between Obama and Turnbull at the beginning of 2016, but the leaders agreed to hold it back from the public until after the November presidential election. Obama feared that if Trump got wind of the deal, he'd furiously campaign against it, to his electoral advantage. As it turned out, Trump didn't need to know about the refugee deal to win the election, but Obama was certainly right about Trump coming out against it when he did find out. As soon as Trump was elected, many on the Australian side assumed the new president would honour the deal, even if he didn't like it.

Even so, no one expected that Trump's distaste for the deal would be written up on the front pages of *The Washington Post*. Nor did I expect to witness the lowest point in US–Australian relations since a Californian gunman started shooting at Victorian police in 1854 (the first shots in Australia's Eureka Stockade). Even more surprising was the news that it was my job to fix things.

After Donald Trump was sworn in as president in January 2017, Prime Minister Turnbull was most anxious to talk to him as soon as possible. Turnbull wanted the refugee deal honoured, and it was clear to me how important this was for him and his government. Characteristically, Turnbull would grab an issue and run hard with it. He'd be like a dog with a bone, not letting go until he got his way. That's Malcolm Turnbull. He wanted and needed this win, and it was a very big deal for him. The refugee agreement had helped take the heat out of the issue of refugees in Australian politics, and the Labor opposition didn't particularly want to make it a partisan one, lending their support to the Manus Island solution.

The underlying commitments of this refugee deal made by Australia and the United States were based on mutual respect and a long-term friendship. The problem for Malcolm Turnbull, and indeed for many other world leaders, was that Donald Trump had no regard for historical relationships. As far as Trump was concerned, he was starting with a clean slate.

Trump's engagement with other world leaders followed the pattern of his business relationships. If you had something Donald Trump wanted, then he would engage with you. If you had nothing he wanted or needed, then you were simply a new acquaintance. He only trusted people he knew personally, or whose reputation he respected. And one way he judged people was by measuring how much money they had. Malcolm had made lots of money in his business career and worked for a few billionaires in his time, so at least he was off to a good start.

The pair had already had one good phone conversation the previous November, when Trump was elected, which I had organised with a big helping hand from golfer Greg Norman. That first call had gone well, featuring a discussion about dealing with Kerry Packer – something both men knew about – and so our hopes were high for Malcolm's first interaction with President Trump.

We had managed to get a spot for our first official discussion on the day the president was speaking to other significant world leaders, so that was a win. But unfortunately for Malcolm, the call came at the end of the day, by which time Trump had already had a number of long and no doubt tiresome phone calls with world leaders.

Malcolm rang me before the phone call, and we prepped only for smooth sailing. But in the minutes ahead – unlike the UK ambassador, who had a secure line to listen in on the president's call with his prime minister – I just had to wait around and hope for the best. When Turnbull rang me straight after the conversation, he was shaken. His voice was quivering and he was clearly upset. The phone call had gone badly, the PM told me. He then gave me a full recount of the discussion. His recollection was very similar to what was subsequently leaked to *The Washington Post*.

As reported, the call was supposed to go for an hour, but Trump had ended the discussion after just twenty-five minutes. (He hadn't, however, hung up on Turnbull, as was reported.) Malcolm thought the refugee deal was now off the rails. Relations with the United States were now in bad shape, he felt, and were only going to get worse.

At various points after the disastrous conversation, Malcolm wanted to come to the United States to meet with Trump and try to repair the relationship. I advised him against it. There was a conga line of world leaders trying to see Trump, and all of them were fawning. Even President Xi Jinping travelled to Mar-a-Lago (which Trump liked to call the 'Southern White House') to pay homage to the new king. In my view, it would look terrible for a close ally like Australia to join that queue. We could do better.

Malcolm accepted that he would have to wait for the fury to pass, and we decided to hold our ground for a while. We talked regularly, almost daily. Each nomination, or speculated nomination, of a person to an administration position was a cause for intense speculation, not just in Australia but around the world. Donald Trump, of course, loved the limelight. He would marvel to his staff at how much media coverage he was receiving around the world. From Trump's perspective, all media was good media.

I recalled one of John Howard's pearls of political wisdom (number 464!) that the high point of your term in office is usually the day you are elected; it just goes downhill from there. Well, that was never truer than for Donald Trump. The critics took a few days after his election to detox from the sedatives they'd needed to cope with his victory. Then came the anger, the depression and the applications for Australian or Canadian visas. The sun still rose, and with it, each day, so too did the anxiety.

This all played out in the Australian media. It had a big impact on the politicians in Canberra, and on the public servants who supported them. Everything was up for grabs. Every aspect of the US–Australian relationship was suddenly thrown into the air by Donald Trump. Would we suffer tariffs? Would he tear up our Five Eyes intelligence relationship? How about our E-3 visas, or the green investment corridors for our business-to-business engagement? Every aspect of the decades-long relationship was questioned. Many expected that I and my embassy team had all the answers. We didn't.

A few hours before *The Washington Post* story broke on 2 February, Trump let fly with a rather prescient tweet: 'Do you believe it? The Obama administration agreed to take thousands of illegal immigrants from Australia. Why? I will study this dumb deal!' Trump's public cynicism at the deal gave us cause for concern, but we had not anticipated what would follow.

As I read the *Post*'s article that night in Georgetown, I realised it reflected the real phone call. Headlined 'This is the worst call by far', the *Post*'s lead read:

> *It should have been one of the most congenial calls for the new commander in chief – a conversation with the leader of Australia, one of America's staunchest allies, at the end of a triumphant week.*
>
> *Instead, President Trump blasted Australian Prime Minister Malcolm Turnbull over a refugee agreement and boasted about the magnitude of his electoral college win, according to senior U.S. officials briefed on the Saturday exchange. Then, 25 minutes into what was expected to be an hour-long call, Trump abruptly ended it.*
>
> *At one point, Trump informed Turnbull that he had spoken with four other world leaders that day – including Russian President Vladimir Putin – and that 'this was the worst call by far.'*

The story went into excruciating detail about Trump's objection to the refugee deal: it was 'the worst deal ever', he'd said. To my dismay, it appeared the newspaper even had the transcript. (That would be confirmed in the coming months, when the *Post* published the conversation, along with the transcript of another Trump phone call, with Mexican President Enrique Peña Nieto.)

Chairman Nunes and I immediately left the dinner. I started frantically working from my home office at the Australian ambassadorial residence, White Oaks.

I always felt the presence of ghosts in my study at the ambassador's residence. How would Kim Beazley, Andrew Peacock or Richard Casey have handled this situation? Other fearless ambassadors like Michael Thawley, Dennis Richardson and Owen Dixon would always have had the answers. The pressure, all of a sudden, was immense.

Things were now moving so quickly that I didn't have much time to war-game my responses. It was close to midnight, and we were coordinating with the White House on how the leak had occurred and our response to it. Despite the astonishing number of leaks coming out of the White House at that time, administration officials immediately claimed that Australia had leaked it to *The Washington Post*.

My shock quickly turned to indignation. 'Why would you even think Australia would leak a call like that?' I said. 'Are you so distrustful of your closest ally that you would think we'd want to blow up the relationship for the next four years?'

The truth of the situation dawned on those White House staff and Republican members of Congress at around the same time the sun rose over Washington. For the first time ever, a transcript of a presidential conversation with another world leader had been leaked by someone within their own administration. It was an unlawful leak of a leader's telephone call, with the intent of undermining the alliance between the United States and Australia. It also embarrassed both our prime minister and the US president.

The fact the leak had occurred spoke volumes about the administration's inability to hold sensitive information. The White House was leaking almost daily. It was understood that the DC establishment – mainly Democrats, but also many traditional Republicans – were deeply shaken by the election of Donald Trump. There were motivated leakers throughout the administration, both in the White House and in the broader civil service, and nothing was kept confidential. The institutions in Washington were like an underground movement against Donald Trump's presidency.

We never established exactly where the leak of the Trump–Turnbull conversation came from. After the story appeared in the *Post*, Malcolm even asked me if I'd leaked it! I told him it certainly wasn't me – I hadn't listened in on the conversation, and we didn't even have a transcript. Soon the PM accepted that the leak had to have come from the American side.

In fact, Turnbull himself was the only person who had taken extensive notes of the conversation. He always worried that someone would leak against him, so he took contemporaneous notes of most conversations. As it turned out, in this instance, he was right to do so. But what leaked was a word-for-word transcript, something none of us had.

The National Security Committee of the White House was one organisation with access to the conversation. And with over one hundred staff and myriad possible motivations, it was impossible to nominate a leaker.

Trump's tweet concerning the refugee deal earlier that day had indicated to many that the leak had come from the White House, as part of an attempt to scuttle the refugee deal – or at the very least put on record Trump's strident opposition to it. This theory ignores the possibility that Trump and the White House may have just been trying to get ahead of the story once they knew what the *Post* had. If it was leaked from the White House, it was a hopeless miscalculation.

The next morning, the *Post* story went around the world. It was big news with the Australian press, of course, but it was all over US media as well: Fox News, MSNBC and CNN were all running with it. Every galah had an opinion, but one thing was consistent, from the left-wing media to the right-wing media: no one could believe the way Donald Trump had spoken to the prime minister of Australia.

That Friday morning I went to the National Prayer Breakfast at the Hilton Hotel. It is a famous annual event. Every president since Eisenhower had addressed the annual gathering of political and religious leaders from around the world. Perhaps more than two thousand people attend each year. Sadly, it was outside this hotel in March 1981 that President Reagan was shot.

The Prayer Breakfast is an uplifting and bipartisan event. It's where presidents rise to the moment. They discuss values and faith. This event was noteworthy as Donald Trump's first address to the event. But it was an absolute shocker of a speech. Among other things, he talked about his TV ratings as host of *The Apprentice* and used the platform to attack his successor as host of the show, Arnold Schwarzenegger.

My enduring memory of the event was my discussion with the Israeli ambassador to the United States, Ron Dermer. He was one of the most important and controversial players in DC. Ron came up to me, shook my hand and said: 'Joe, welcome to the controversy club.' As I was coming out of the breakfast, a number of congressmen, congresswomen, senators and other diplomats approached me and expressed their shock at the revelations in the *Post*.

At about that time, Senator John McCain rang me on my mobile phone. McCain was a good friend, whom I'd first met in Davos, Switzerland, at the World Economic Forum. It was a global meeting with a lot of famous people fawning over each other – less an economics forum than a celebrity one. I felt out of place and so did John, who was standing by himself in a corner of the room trying to look busy with a briefcase. I went over and introduced myself. He couldn't have been more humble or gracious. We had a lengthy discussion over a cup of coffee, and were relieved that we shared a view of the event. He loved Australia and Australians. We were buddies.

That morning in Washington, John McCain was angry. And I mean really angry. 'This is outrageous, Joe,' he told me. 'You know, I'm embarrassed for my country. And I want to put out a media statement saying that I'm appalled at the behaviour of our president towards one of our closest allies. I fought with Australians in Vietnam. You've been loyal to us for as long as I can remember.'

I replied that we were indeed one of America's oldest allies, with a relationship that went back over one hundred years to the trenches of the Western Front.

'Absolutely,' McCain said. 'And you know, I'm going to put out a statement saying that. And I'm going to say I've rung the

Australian ambassador to express my anger about the treatment of Australia, and to express my full support for your country.'

After putting up a rather limp plea for him not to inflame the situation by putting out a statement like that, I then helped him draft it. As soon as the statement hit the media, I received an avalanche of phone calls from congressmen and congresswomen and senators from all sides expressing support. In total, I had over sixty phone calls and numerous emails.

John McCain was widely respected by his colleagues, and his immediate and firm intervention had an impact. Some representatives wanted to start a petition showing their support for Australia and its prime minister. All of them expressed their dismay, and apologised on behalf of their country. The only cohort who didn't contact me was comprised of Republican congressmen and congresswomen who didn't want to be seen to be going against Donald Trump. Privately, many still dropped me notes some time later.

By now it was around two o'clock in the afternoon, and I decided we needed to resolve the issue before the Australian media cycle began. I spoke to my deputy, Caroline Millar, a very accomplished and experienced career diplomat. We resolved to go to the White House and confront the administration directly on the issue.

This was a pretty big step, and would usually involve a lot of discussions back in Canberra. And all of Canberra seemed unhappy with our plans. There was opposition in the Department of Foreign Affairs and in the prime minister's office. Malcolm Turnbull himself was less than happy about it. Regardless, I resolved that we were going to the White House. Having been federal treasurer and chair of the G20, I was not easily intimidated by any political office. That's a very important qualification for an ambassador in Washington to have.

Our plan was, first, to express our disappointment directly to the White House. But in the shock of the aftermath of the leak, we realised, this was also our big opportunity to lock in the refugee agreement.

I began by ringing the president's chief of staff, Reince Priebus. He agreed to a 4 p.m. meeting in his office at the White House. Caroline and I walked over to 1600 Pennsylvania Avenue, not realising as we entered that we had been caught on camera by one of the seemingly permanent news crews camped outside the visitors entrance.

Sitting in the chief of staff's office with Priebus were two of Trump's key aides, chief strategist Steve Bannon and senior adviser (and son-in-law) Jared Kushner. I wasn't sure who was in charge, so I sat down and addressed all three of them. At that point we had what you would call in politics 'a full and frank discussion'. For about half an hour the officials continued to claim we had leaked the transcript, but by the end of the conversation they had accepted this wasn't the case.

When we turned to the refugee agreement itself, Bannon was typically defiant, saying it was 'a bad deal' – the exact phrase Trump had used in his phone call with Turnbull.

I was polite but forthright in my response. 'I accept it just doesn't fit with the president's narrative in the election campaign,' I said. 'But a deal is a deal. An agreement was done and was made with the Office of the President of the United States. We expect the deal to be honoured.'

Kushner was going in and out of the room during the discussion, and Priebus appeared increasingly sympathetic. When Priebus was briefly called into the Oval Office, I reminded Bannon of our long-term partnership with the United States – which, frankly, few in the Trump administration seemed to understand.

'We're not going to be bound by something Obama did,' Bannon said. 'Our people will never accept it.'

At that point, I made it clear that not only were they obliged to sign off on the agreement because of our undertaking with Obama, but also that I believed they owed me a favour. 'I reached out to your campaign and engaged with you before anyone else had the guts to do so,' I told Bannon. 'I first spoke with you guys nearly one year ago. Sam Clovis [a campaign co-chair] and Stephen Miller [a Trump adviser] came around to my house and we talked. I copped it in Australia for doing so. We were the first country in the world to engage with the Trump campaign. I did so because I know that a strong, successful United States is good for Australia.'

Reince Priebus already knew this, but Bannon didn't, and he seemed surprised.

'Second, let me explain to you the nature of the relationship.' And I spoke about the history of our nations' military and intelligence relationship and its importance.

'I was in the navy in the Pacific, I know how important you guys are,' Bannon responded.

Then Priebus piped up: 'Hey, Joe, what's your family history?'

I told him my father was a Palestinian refugee to Australia. He then started to talk to me about his family's Greek history, trying to establish common ground. Not long after that he was called away by the president again. This created space for Bannon and me to continue what was becoming a genial conversation, and I felt he was loosening up.

Then Reince came back into the room. 'Okay, where are we at?'

'Well, there are two things,' I said. 'One, we need you to commit to keep the agreement. There will be very significant implications for our relationship if we do not keep an agreement between the prime minister and the president of the United States.'

Bannon grumbled that he'd have to speak to the president about it.

'The second thing is we need to find a way to publicly rebuild the relationship,' I went on. 'Because it's not in your interests to have a massive deterioration in the alliance between Australia and the United States.'

They accepted that, and we agreed to work on something. In the end, we got the result we wanted and the deal was upheld. The deal even survived Turnbull's removal from office and successfully resettled up to one thousand people.

Amid the madness that followed the leaked phone call, I learnt an important lesson about the US–Australian relationship: its fate can't be undermined by the whims of a leader. It has incredibly strong foundations, built on shared values, mutual sacrifice and respect. The underlying affinity and affection that the American people and the Australian people have for one another is not a fiction. It's real, and it has the capacity to bring two clashing leaders together in a way that might not occur in any political system other than an open and transparent democracy.

That is the strength of a shared history and shared values. They do matter. Especially as it's always much easier to get over an argument with someone you really like.

CHAPTER 2

MR HOCKEY GOES TO WASHINGTON

Early life, leaving politics and heading to Washington

I'm sitting at my desk, about to sign away my political career. It's a Friday evening, 23 October 2015, and I'm in my electorate office in North Sydney. I'm sitting alone amid the emptiness of a brutal political landscape. Aside from a few packed boxes, the room that was my office as treasurer of Australia and the member for North Sydney is now almost bare. Pen in hand, I can't quite bring myself to sign the letter. I have to resign as the member for North Sydney after almost twenty years in the federal parliament.

I've been holding this pen for ten minutes. Once this letter is signed and sent to the Speaker of the House of Representatives, my lifetime ambition to lead my country is over. I confess it was heart wrenching. After a lot of reflection and a few tears, I sign the letter, put the pen down and quietly sigh. It is the end of my political career. I'd missed my shot to be prime minister.

* * *

My life in politics was always about serving Australia. That sense of service to my country was tied to what Australia had given my family. My father was born Richard Hockeduney. It was a shortened name from his father, Hagop Hockedunian, an Armenian from Aleppo in Syria. Dad was an Armenian Palestinian who migrated to Australia as a teenager. He was born in Bethlehem and grew up in Jerusalem. He arrived in Darwin on his twenty-first birthday, 3 September 1948. He was accompanied by his mother, Rose, and his brother, Jack. My father had Anglicised his name to Hockey while working in Jerusalem with the British Army, and when he moved to Australia he changed it permanently.

His history mirrors so many migrant success stories of that era. He worked hard and ended up establishing a very successful and comfortable life for his family. He used the opportunities afforded to him by a booming Australian middle class to their full extent.

His first store was a local corner shop in Bondi, which was then a working-class suburb. Dad had numerous entrepreneurial tricks to succeed in the delicatessen business. One was to put up a chalkboard outside the shop and deliberately misspell things he was selling, like 'Vegitmite Sandwitch 1 shilling'. Reading the sign, some old dear would walk into the shop to help the immigrant store owner spell 'Vegemite Sandwich'. With profuse thanks, he'd introduce himself: 'My name is Richard – what's your name? What can I get for you today?' As well as making a sale, he'd usually strike up a conversation and, with seamless ease, have a new customer for a regular weekly order.

But Richard's most important customer was the young woman who would later become my mum. He deserves high accolades for winning over Beverley Little.

Dad was only a shade over 150 centimetres tall. He probably suffered malnutrition as a child in the orphanage in which he spent many years of his early life (his father left when he was very young, and his mother couldn't afford to raise two children, so she put the youngest, Richard, into an orphanage for five years). In contrast, Beverley was a tall, beautiful blonde who had appeared on numerous magazine covers. Dad's best asset was his charm, and he worked it hard to win over the Bondi beauty.

It was that chance meeting in a Bondi delicatessen that prompted me, many years later, to name my business Bondi

Partners. The beachside suburb had given me a future, and I always wanted to round out that small business storyline.

Despite their initial meetings going well, my parents didn't actually get together until some years later. Beverley was warned off 'the wog' by her very Anglo-Saxon Protestant parents. She went on to marry another man.

After building up his Bondi business, Dad moved to Chatswood, in northern Sydney. He worked around the clock to save and buy the shop that housed his new delicatessen. It was on Victoria Avenue in the middle of Chatswood, prime real estate even in those days.

Some years later, by chance, my father met my mother again. This time Richard would not let Beverley get away. By now she had separated from her first husband and had three young children – Michael, Colin and Juanita – and Richard won her heart.

In those days divorce was particularly hard on women, who had little support from the legal system. Child support was rare. My father's paternal instincts kicked in. He'd never known his own father, and he could not leave Beverley and her children to fend for themselves. Richard pledged to raise Beverley's children as if they were his own. That was almost unprecedented in Dad's culture, but that was the sort of man he was. It's one of many reasons he has always been my hero.

Richard and Beverley were married in October 1963 in a registry office, and two years later I was born. My father named me after my grandfather, the father he never knew. He also named me after former Prime Minister Joseph Benedict Chifley, the great Labor leader whose immigration policies had made it possible for Richard to come to Australia in the first place. I suppose you could say politics was in me from day one.

After being urged by my mother to be more ambitious, Dad expanded his property portfolio after buying the building next door to his original shop. He eventually set up his own real estate agency. He and Mum worked incredibly hard to get the new business off the ground. In fact, all six in the family chipped in to make it work. On Saturdays when I was young my job was to sweep out the store and then put out the sandwich board saying we were open for business.

Suburban Australia was a pretty uncomplicated place in the 1970s. Everything was predictable – until change arrived, thanks to America. I remember the very first time we went out to dinner as a family. It was to the Anzac Club in North Sydney. We were served a prawn cocktail, roast beef on a servery and a bombe Alaska – whoosh! At the end of the meal, I asked if we could do this again. Mum replied that it was too expensive to keep going out to dinner – and that was that.

So, when McDonald's opened their very first Australian outlet in Yagoona, in south-western Sydney, it was an unreachable hamburger dream. I was convinced it would be years until I could visit, because they described their store as a 'restaurant'. I obviously made up for it in later life.

Our loyalties were pretty simple, because we usually had limited choices. You picked a side and stuck with it. In cars it was Ford or Holden. In footy (in Sydney at least) it was the Eastern Suburbs Roosters or the Manly Sea Eagles. Politics was simple – you were Liberal or Labor. You even had to take sides with rock bands – were you Skyhooks or Sherbert? So life was pretty uncomplicated – but it was also pretty dull.

Disruption, when it did arrive, came from America, and mainly through our television screens. Being the baby of the family by some margin, I grew up watching a lot of television. It really began my love affair with America. I still remember the day we got our first colour television (which was three years after everyone else). I grew up on the likes of *McHale's Navy*, *Hogan's Heroes* and *The Wonderful World of Disney*. The production quality was far superior to the Australian or British shows. In comparison, we had *Skippy the Bush Kangaroo*, who would bounce around with some kid interpreting the sound of the marsupial's grinding teeth as if it were speaking perfect French.

This is how the dialogue went:

Skippy 'speaks': [The sound of grinding teeth behind lips munching on a eucalyptus leaf for eight seconds.]

The kid interpreting: 'Oh, Skippy, a man is down by the edge of the river? He's unconscious and in need of help? He's a diabetic with a wooden leg?'

Don't get me wrong. American television had lots of fluent and articulate animals of its own, from Mr Ed and Francis the talking mule through to Flipper. Heck, let's not even get into *Sesame Street* or *The Muppets* (they weren't real?). In another life I may come back as a scriptwriter, although I fear I'd be stuck in the '70s.

As Mum and Dad's business succeeded, they started to enjoy a bit more leisure in their life. Travel became more affordable, and Dad, missing the cultural diversity of his early life, made up for it in the late 1970s and beyond. As the fourth child, and therefore the spoilt one, I was lucky enough to be dragged along on their belated honeymoon trips.

My parents became intrepid tourists. Their trips were interesting by the standards of the time, including places as varied as China and Lebanon. It was in 1979 that we first went to the United States. I'd always wanted to go to Disneyland – the influence of TV! – and I was over the moon when they were kind enough to take me.

Disneyland (and America generally) was much bigger than I expected. Everything was larger, from the cars to the hotel to the people to the soft drinks and meals. It was all clean, bright and happy. For a kid from the northern suburbs of Sydney, Disneyland was a magical kingdom.

As for the food – holy cow. In fact, it usually involved the whole damn cow. Everything was BIG. I remember ordering a banana split; at least that sounded healthy, Mum said. It was the biggest thing she'd ever seen. She welcomed its arrival with a loud announcement – 'You can't eat that! It's far too big!' – and instructed my father to take half of it away. He did, with pleasure. Welcome to America.

My expectations of America were big too, but still everything exceeded them. In Los Angeles I kept expecting an LAPD patrol car to whoosh down the street (*Adam-12*) in pursuit of a bad guy with a beard in a beat-up Cadillac. LA felt like a movie set, and Hollywood was amazing, although I was a little disappointed that the studios used a lot of tricks to make television look the way it did. My fantasy of American television was revealed as just that.

San Francisco was different, and disappointing in another way. The gorgeous streets and cable cars couldn't mask the tragedy of homelessness. We almost stepped over people sleeping on the streets. My parents never addressed the issue, nor had I ever seen it in the movies or on *The Streets of San Francisco*. It was very confronting for a naive Sydney boy.

It would be some years before I returned to America.

* * *

I was lucky enough to attend a great Jesuit school, St. Aloysius' College, on Sydney's Lower North Shore. After that, I was the first member of my family, including both Mum's and Dad's sides, to go on to university. I view much of what I received in education as a gift of the Australian middle class. The reward for all my parents' hard work came in the form of better lifetime opportunities for me. I've felt all my life that I had to repay that debt to Australia.

Perhaps this was why, upon leaving school, I was intent on enrolling in the Royal Military College, Duntroon. I wanted to serve my nation, and the Army seemed the best way to do so. I loved my time as a military cadet at school. As I saw it, military life seemed safe (ironic, I know), predictable and fun. But when I graduated from school in 1983, much to my adolescent disappointment, there were no wars. There was nothing much at all for Australia to be involved in, and the Defence Force's budget was being ripped apart by successive governments. People were joking that the Australian Army had more guns than bullets. Morale (and confidence in the military) was falling.

Not only that, but back then the Royal Military College required you to sign up for a minimum of nine years. So I was faced with the distinctly unexciting prospect of spending nine years training for a battle that I would never fight. Nine years is a big ask at that age, and I wondered: *What if I go through my career doing nothing?*

University seemed like a better alternative, and for me it was. Importantly, it laid the foundations of my political career.

Life events are what form your character, and we are all the creative genius of our own experiences. At university I learnt about life. Sure, studying Arts (history, politics and economics) and Law (torts, contracts and alcohol) left me with a legal career, but it was campus life that set me upon my journey. It was at the University of Sydney that I discovered politics, policy, principles and partying. The salacious stuff is for another day, but it did transform me from an innocent North Shore schoolboy into a more worldly, ambitious adult.

I was just twenty-eight when I was preselected for the seat of North Sydney, and then elected to parliament in John Howard's 'class of 1996' landslide. While many would describe my preselection as lucky, they're underestimating what had prepared me to take that chance. Sure, I had a bit of luck, but I also had to seize the opportunity when it presented itself, and use everything at my disposal to make the most of it. These were the same skills I would rely on throughout my political, diplomatic and now business career.

Successful politicians know how to read people. From John Howard to Bill Clinton to Angela Merkel, great politicians listen and empathise. They win trust by sharing the journey of someone they are trying to win over. They earn respect, and never assume that it comes with the job title. Most importantly, they are self-aware. They know their limitations and seek to have others around them who are smart and capable. They are not threatened by the success of others.

Dad once wisely advised me that life, especially in politics, is influenced by exhilaration and pain. 'The exhilaration should be shared,' he said. But when it comes to pain, 'you can either observe pain or feel pain – it's up to you to either listen or learn'.

When selling real estate, Dad convinced every buyer that he was their agent, even though of course he was paid by the seller. 'Today's purchaser is tomorrow's vendor,' he would say. When I first started the arduous task of door-knocking my electorate of some 60,000 homes, I was struck by how many people not only knew my father, but adored him. He made them feel like they were the most important person in the world.

Bill Clinton is the same type of character. I spent seven hours playing eighteen holes of golf with him once, and we didn't stop musing about everything in the world. I felt like I was the only focus of his attention during that round of golf. We talked, hit balls, talked and chewed cigars. He is worldly, charming and, when it comes to golf, very particular about getting every shot right – the ball needs to be very close to the hole! Most significantly, he asked me a lot of questions, about my family, friends, education and life experiences. There were no unseemly interruptions. He didn't look at his phone or get frustrated or bored. That helped me avoid both anger and frustration with his golfing proclivities.

Donald Trump also asked a lot of questions; he does have a very curious mind. Barack Obama and George W. Bush were different again. The very best politicians are those who don't assume they have all the answers. They make you feel like you are part of the answer. That's the gift.

Studying law and history taught me to ask lots of questions. Unlike in maths or the sciences, there is generally no black-and-white answer when it comes to the humanities. So, too, in human engagement. Every person has a different character.

My capacity to read people comes from my desire to understand and learn from them. Combined with hard work and an ability to take chances when necessary – a cliché, but a true one – it has helped me be successful in my journey.

* * *

In later life, I had the chance to lead my party and perhaps my nation. It was a crucial moment. A culmination of all those lessons of politics. I tried but I failed.

It was 2009 and I was poised to become the leader of the Liberal Party, which would give me a shot at contesting for the prime ministership. Malcolm Turnbull's first stint as Liberal leader was turning into a disaster. The federal Liberal Party was tearing itself apart over its response to the proposed carbon emissions trading scheme of the Labor government of Kevin Rudd. A series of self-inflicted wounds had also severely damaged Turnbull. Tony Abbott had already attempted to run against Turnbull for the leadership and was poised to do so again.

I concluded that should Turnbull fall and the role was vacant, I would stand for the leadership. A Newspoll in late November had me ahead of both Turnbull and Abbott as the most popular choice for Liberal leader. I was a supporter of Malcolm's position on the emissions trading scheme, but in the event of his leadership bid falling short, I felt an obligation to stand for Party Leader. I felt I was up to the job of unifying the Liberal Party.

Abbott had initially said that he wouldn't run if I was a candidate. He later changed his mind publicly when he disagreed with my position to allow Liberals a conscience vote on the emissions trading scheme.

Meanwhile, Turnbull told me and others that he would not run if the Party Room voted to oust him from his leadership position. As it turned out, there was a leadership spill when Turnbull lost a no confidence vote. But Turnbull changed his mind at the last minute and decided to run, notwithstanding that the Party had just fired him from the top job.

History would show that Turnbull's decision on 1 December 2009 to recontest the leadership split my vote, costing me my chance to become Liberal leader. I was eliminated from the three-cornered contest, and in the second round Turnbull lost to Abbott by a single vote. And of course Abbott, after narrowly losing the 2010 federal election to Labor under Julia Gillard, would go on to win the prime ministership in 2013.

After the 2009 leadership ballot I was angry. Really angry. I was convinced that I was the best candidate and I had no doubt I would have been a good prime minister. But I had been defeated, and after being consoled by disillusioned supporters, I decided to soldier on. Tony Abbott showed humility and grace, and pleaded with me to remain in the most senior position on his team as Treasury spokesman.

I'd known Abbott since we were at the University of Sydney together. We'd had many disagreements over the years – including a well-documented fistfight on the rugby training field. But I've always had the view that if you do your job properly, the rewards will come – and that attitude has served me well throughout my life. If life gives you lemons, I told myself, make lemonade.

Tony Abbott and others were telling me that I'd had a blessed rise in politics. That meant they thought my star was rising too fast. In truth, I'd earned every promotion. And even when I was moved sideways or had a loss, I made it look like I was getting on with the job. If you survive in politics, you are usually a raging success.

At thirty, I'd been elected to a safe and iconic Liberal seat in the federal parliament. At thirty-three, in 1998, I became the Minister for Financial Services and Regulation, the first in Australia. I was in charge of the entire financial system, from banking to stock markets, competition policy to consumer affairs. It was a big job with lots of challenges – the biggest of which was the jealousy of my parliamentary colleagues.

Then, three years later, I was made Minister for Small Business and Tourism. I saw it as a demotion, but John Howard taught me a good life lesson about humility along the way.

Members of parliament really sweat the phone call from the prime minister after an election. That call will make or break your career. You rush to the phone for every call, and whether it's a friend, family member or supporter, you hurry the conversation in case the prime minister can't get through. You visualise the conversation: 'Yes, Prime Minister, it would be an honour to serve as Minister for Finance …' You wonder where you'll be when the call comes, and who you will call afterwards.

But when my call came, I felt that the prime minister was dudding me. I'd made huge sacrifices for the team, and I felt his offer would be seen by the media and others as a demotion. I would be slipping down the ladder. And Howard could tell I was angry and disappointed. I am hopeless at hiding my emotions – a legacy of my Armenian Palestinian genes.

'Why are you doing this to me?' I said to the newly re-elected prime minister.

'Are you saying you don't want to be in my team?' asked the PM, becoming increasingly angry himself.

'You're punishing me, and I deserve better,' I said. I was probably overstepping the mark at this point.

'I'm giving you twenty minutes to think about it,' Howard said. 'Or you can cool your heels on the back bench. There are plenty of others who will want this job.' And with that he hung up.

It's at moments like these that you turn to the people you really trust. Of course, my first call was to my wife, Melissa, but she was caught in a meeting and I couldn't get through. I then called Sandy Weill, the global CEO of Citigroup, who had previously offered me the job of a lifetime in New York. The offer still stood.

Finally I called Warwick Smith, a wise and urbane former Howard government minister; he told me that if you knock back an offer from a prime minister, you'll never get another.

Peter Costello, the treasurer and deputy leader of the party, then rang and urged me to accept. He had clearly been speaking to the prime minister, and I took this as an olive branch from John Howard. He wanted me to be a part of his team.

Melissa rang back, and immediately she could sense my anger. I love her for her wisdom, among many other attributes. 'We haven't come this far to give up now,' she told me. It was the 'we' that woke me from my self-pity. I entered politics for others, not for myself or my ego.

I rang the prime minister, expressed my gratitude and accepted the offer.

'Joe, I know you're disappointed,' he said calmly, 'but you will recover and you will go on to a very high office. I am glad you are part of my team.'

Howard was under no obligation to be so gracious. His own humility and grace had helped make him a great leader in the eyes of many. He was at his very best at this moment, and it had a huge impact on me. I was never one of Howard's protégés, but he must have had a regard for me because he kept me in his ministry and kept promoting me for the rest of his term in office.

In 2004, I became Australia's first Minister for Human Services, in charge of all health and welfare delivery by the federal government. Then in 2007, I was promoted to Minister for Employment and Workplace Relations. In that role I was tasked with trying to save WorkChoices, the most radical industrial relations laws in Australian history. That didn't go so well.

In opposition from 2007, I had become shadow treasurer. Now, having failed to take the Liberal Party leadership in late 2009, I swallowed my disappointment and agreed to continue as Treasury spokesman under Tony Abbott's leadership. I threw myself into the role and gave it my very best.

When we were elected to government in September 2013, I pledged to Abbott that there wouldn't be a cigarette paper of difference between us on policy. We both believed that we needed to repair the budget, strengthen the economy and deliver on our promises. We set about doing that, trusting that our colleagues would be part of that journey in the same way we had been back in 1996, when John Howard was elected.

Regrettably, the worst arrows came from behind us. Several colleagues tried to pull me down in order to pull Abbott down. The internal party machinations at that time were very difficult. There was a disease that afflicted Australian politics where people were more interested in being popular than they were in being effective. Selfishness replaced selflessness. The net result was that when Tony Abbott was felled in September 2015, so was I. By then I was so disgusted with some of my colleagues, and so distrustful of everyone around me in politics, that I no longer had any desire to lead my party or my country. I was almost relieved to get out.

I suspect the new prime minister, Malcolm Turnbull, would have been happy to get rid of me. Over time he could have seen me as a potential threat; I'd seen this happen before in politics, when a rival remained on the front bench, and it could lead to instability.

It was on a Monday night that Abbott lost his leadership to Turnbull, and the next day I spoke to the new prime minister. I was considering whether to leave my role as treasurer immediately, but he wanted me to stay on for a few more days to get through the parliamentary week. Even though I was inclined to walk, I felt a duty to do my job and then leave with some dignity.

Over the course of that week, I had a number of conversations with Turnbull.

'What do you want to do?' he asked me.

And I bluntly replied, 'I want to stay treasurer,' although I knew full well that was not going to happen.

Turnbull said he couldn't do that. He'd done a deal with Scott Morrison, he told me: Morrison had agreed to back him in the leadership challenge, and in return Morrison would become treasurer. It was clear I wouldn't be returning.

'Well, what about Defence?' Turnbull asked. We had an honest conversation about that. I was of the view that the Department of Defence was largely run by the uniforms. And in my experience the job also tended to be the last one you'd have before your retirement from politics.

Frankly, I had also formed the view that if you've already served as treasurer, there's only one other job you should do afterwards – and that's the prime ministership. Clearly, that wasn't going to be happening.

On the Friday of that week, Turnbull contacted me again. 'You can have any job you want,' he told me, 'in Australia or outside.'

As it turned out, the selection of the next Australian ambassador to the United States was still pending, because Tony Abbott had chosen to extend former Labor leader Kim Beazley's time in Washington, DC. Kim was doing a really good job. He loved the role, and Abbott hadn't wanted to be rushed into a decision on his replacement. I had heard that Peter Costello wanted the gig, along with many others. But Tony had been waiting until he found the right person. Now the decision was in Malcolm Turnbull's hands.

'What about Washington?' he asked me.

I said I would have to talk to Melissa about it, and would get back to him in twenty-four hours.

She and I discussed the Washington proposal, and agreed that it would provide us with a wonderful opportunity to get away from Australian politics. We'd had enough of the ugliness of Canberra and were keen to start afresh. It would be the break we needed from the life we were living. I also felt it would be good to have something new to look forward to, rather than just brood over what had happened to my political career. There's nothing worse than an angry politician hanging around parliament and throwing stones.

I got back to the prime minister the next day. 'Alright, Malcolm, that sounds pretty good. I'd like it in writing,' I told him.

The prime minister agreed, and that's how it was decided that Joe Hockey was going to Washington.

It was important for me that I was in control of my departure from politics. That Sunday I announced that I was resigning from public office. I wanted to make sure that I gave a thoughtful valedictory speech on the floor of the House. I loved the Australian Parliament, and adored the House of Representatives. The vast chamber had borne witness to all my emotions – laughter, anger, embarrassment and, yes, lots of tears. It was the right place for me to say farewell.

'Most people leave this Parliament as a result of defeat, death, disillusionment or disgrace,' I said. 'We all have to work harder to leave with dignity.'

I was leaving on my own terms, and with dignity. That mattered so much to me.

My family were on the floor of the House as I gave my valedictory speech. In particular, I wanted to thank the people of my electorate, my Liberal Party colleagues and everyone else who had made my political career possible. That was the day I gave thanks for the opportunity to serve.

It meant an awful lot to me that the House was full as I said farewell. At the end, I received a standing ovation from both sides of the chamber. The farewell speeches from all were generous and heartfelt. The words of Bill Shorten, the leader of the Labor Party, were particularly moving to me, given that we'd engaged in some tough political battles. The tribute of a foe is the most honest tribute of all.

CHAPTER 3

GOODBYE, CANBERRA

**What I miss about parliament, politics at
its worst and why I bled for the G20**

I wanted to be prime minister, and I hope for the right reasons. I'd
never believed that only Joe Hockey could save the nation. Some
prime ministers seem to think that they're smarter and more capable
than everyone else. It's just not in my DNA to think that way.

It wasn't in Tony Abbott's, either. He and I engaged in great
combat over many years, and despite all that I ended up as his
trusted treasurer.

The Jesuit edict to be 'a man for others' is something I take
seriously. That's why it was so hard for me to resign as the member
for North Sydney after almost twenty years in parliament. That's
why I sat at my desk for ten minutes, holding the pen above my
resignation letter. I felt I was walking away from the electorate,
and from a lifetime of ambition. From the time I was just fourteen,
people had told me I'd one day be prime minister – and now that
dream was gone.

So I took comfort in the fact that I was doing everything for
the right reasons. When I was drafting my valedictory speech,
I reassured myself that despite the last few weeks, my political
career had been a success. I had accomplished some great things
for my community and my country.

Most of what you achieve in life is forgotten over time. But
some decisions endure. The COVID-19 pandemic would have

been far harder for Australia to manage without some initiatives I took in 2014, such as setting up the $20 billion Medical Research Future Fund, and putting $8.8 billion of extra funding into the Reserve Bank. Both initiatives were heavily criticised at the time. Similarly, when I forced the banks in 2015 to hold additional capital, many bank CEOs were so angry they tried to get me sacked. But in 2020–21 that additional capital helped prevent the pandemic recession from being far worse.

Moving the federal budget towards surplus, making it a bipartisan initiative to repair the budget, and then starting to get the debt under control are achievements of which I am unashamedly proud. The 2014 budget was absolutely right. Budget repair will never be popular. It was well received by the people who understood what we were trying to do, but there were various ministers who weren't prepared to defend the decisions in their portfolios.

The media became obsessed with the trivial. Images of Mathias Cormann and me smoking cigars still run on social media. (They never hammered Bob Hawke or Kim Beazley for smoking cigars ...) My wife was criticised for wearing a Carla Zampatti dress to my budget speech. My nine-year-old son was criticised for the music he listened to in my office that day.

Within our government, there were too many who were more focused on polls than on policy. The sickness of populism afflicts the weak. That didn't stop them from engaging in duplicity and deceit. I know of some ministers who were actually lobbying the independent senators *against* their own government's budget policies. Too few were prepared to defend, protect and promote core values of the government and the Liberal Party. Despite all this, we persevered because we believed in delivering good policy. By the time the Abbott government was brought down, we had won the policy debate but lost the politics. You need to win both battles.

I made mistakes in my political career, but I don't have any regrets. A wise man once said to me that there are three things in life that you can never recover: the spoken word, the spent arrow and the lost opportunity. I lost the opportunity to be prime minister. I fired some arrows in the parliament or against political opponents that I wish I hadn't fired. And yes, I said some things I wish I hadn't said. But I can't recover them. I can only try to make myself a better person and do better things.

Despite the rancour that (sadly) is ever-present in politics, I did become close to some Labor MPs. I was often credited with aiding the rise of Kevin Rudd due to our appearances together on Channel Seven's *Sunrise* program. For ten years we appeared together every week on morning television. We became mates, but obviously our relationship was more difficult when he became prime minister.

I have always been close to the current Labor opposition leader, Anthony Albanese. We were both members of the parliamentary class of 1996, when I was elected to North Sydney and he took the seat of Grayndler, in Sydney's inner west. The issue that brought Albo and me together was oppressive aircraft noise over our electorates. In 1996, John Howard put me in charge of the redesign of all the flight paths over our city. I built a coalition with Albanese that relieved the noise burden over both of our electorates, and shared the burden more fairly across the Sydney community. It has never been a problem since those days.

Throughout our entire twenty years in parliament together, Albo and I worked together on that issue. Such was our cooperation that when I was treasurer, I got Tony Abbott over the line to build Sydney's new Badgerys Creek airport. I put the money for it in the 2014 budget. Albo then delivered the Labor Party's support for the laws that will give Sydney a second international airport. That was a totemic achievement that could not have happened without both sides of politics working together.

Albo and I became particularly close in 1998, when we both went on a parliamentary delegation to Palestine and Israel. I took my dad with me, and it was a very special moment for him to revisit his homeland with his son, a member of the Australian parliament. Like my dad, Albo had grown up never knowing his father, and the two of them formed a real bond. In 2015, when Dad passed away, Albo was there at the funeral. He's a very decent human being, Anthony Albanese.

Most Australians look at politics and see only the slings and arrows. In fact, Question Time gives a poor sense of what actually goes on in parliament each day. Even so, I loved Question Time. The witty asides and the sharp banter I enjoyed immensely. It kept you on your toes. I was never a fan of nastiness, but I loved the opportunity to fiercely defend or attack the policies of the moment. I enjoyed finding ways to cut through with a message that would win the hearts and minds of your colleagues and the community.

It could be really tough too, of course. I played Rugby Union for twenty-five years, and if I didn't get butterflies in the belly before each game, then I didn't play my best. It was the same in parliament. Every Question Time for twenty years – well, at least for the seventeen years that I was either a minister or shadow minister – I always felt an adrenaline rush. Question Time, like sport, doesn't make character – it reveals character.

* * *

One of my significant achievements in politics was successfully hosting meetings of the G20 finance ministers and Central Bank governors in Australia and Washington. In retrospect, that role gave me the perfect preparation for a diplomatic career. Herding senior politicians and officials from various countries and trying to find creative ways to get your point across is what diplomacy is all about.

It should be said that my first experiences at the G20 were underwhelming. I had gone to Washington for the first time as treasurer not long after we were elected, in late 2014. The International Monetary Fund's annual meeting was taking place as well, and there were G20 meetings on the sidelines. All these finance ministers and their advisers from around the world were seated around an enormous hollow square table. We must have looked like Bond villains, but the script was nowhere near as interesting. Each representative got up and gave a presentation on the state of the global economy. These presentations weren't only dull and long, they were repetitive. After all, we all had access to the same information – we really didn't need to travel halfway across the world to hear this.

Keep in mind that organisations such as the G20 are inherently conservative and risk-averse. Things are done more or less in the same way they've always been done – and that's what's expected for the future, too.

I got back from the marathon dinner meeting and asked the head of G20 operations in Treasury, Mary Balzary, one of my staffers, how we could improve things. It struck me that the point of these meetings was to have person-to-person contact, rather than subject each other to a series of dull presentations. I resolved that when Australia hosted the G20 in 2014, we would do things differently.

First, I decided to introduce some practical measures. So people couldn't drone on, four-minute clocks were introduced. It seems incredible, but before Australia hosted the finance ministers' meetings, the only way you could stop one of these interminable presentations was to stage a leader's intervention. We made sure the meetings ran on schedule and kept to the agenda so we didn't waste precious time sitting around the table when we didn't need to.

Second, we reduced the size of the ridiculous communiques that came out of the meetings. Such was the length of these documents that they were largely devoid of meaning. I wanted to get them down to a couple of pages at most. I also wanted to refine the drafting process. The previous year, in Russia, there had apparently been about twenty hours spent on a single line.

Ultimately, however, what my team and I really wanted to do was create an environment where these global leaders could communicate and get to know each other. Everything was done in order to facilitate better personal relationships. I've always had the view that if people know each other, they're more likely to find consensus. When we ran the meetings in Australia, we tried to include business people and the broader political class – from both sides of politics – at various forums.

So that dour three-hour meeting in Washington was really what forced us to change things for the better in the G20. And the changes we made for the Sydney meetings in February 2014 were successful. Australia was recognised for running a particularly good show, and it was largely the result of our different view on how things should be done.

One of the big challenges of hosting the G20 meetings in Australia was the fabled 'tyranny of distance'. To get these world leaders to the other side of the globe for the meetings was no small feat. I worked with the secretary of the Treasury, Martin Parkinson, to do things differently. I emphasised that we had to make the gathering a special experience, because the world's leaders would not travel for days on end simply to endure these tedious meetings. We tried to emphasise our national characteristics of fun and natural beauty, and to move away from staid ceremony wherever possible.

The finance ministers' meeting in Sydney turned out perfectly. We posed for photos in front of the Opera House on a glorious day, and the meetings were held in the New South Wales governor's residence overlooking Sydney Harbour. We set out a bold agenda and mixed it with a harbour cruise, great food and much time for one-on-one interactions. It just couldn't have gone any better, really. At one point I found myself watching the finance ministers of China and Japan in deep discussion over a cup of tea. The significance of that moment wasn't lost on me.

It was also an opportunity to meet new global players. At that meeting I established a good connection with the new chair of the US Federal Reserve, Janet Yellen, and our relationship has grown over the years. She is now the Treasury secretary under President Joe Biden.

At that G20 meeting in Sydney, Janet was under enormous pressure. It was her first international meeting, and at that time developing world economies were being smashed by an appreciating US dollar. Developing world nations borrow money in US dollars, and during the global financial crisis the US dollar surged in value. As a result, the developing countries' currencies collapsed and their debt-servicing costs exploded.

Before the first meeting, I met Janet and she sought my advice on how she should handle things. I said I thought it was really important to address the most critical issues up front. Straight talk from a New Yorker would be appreciated. I also helped her out with some insight on the personalities in the room. Choosing who speaks before and after her intervention could shape the mood of the meeting, and that was at my discretion.

The United States is naturally a key player in all these forums. One of my main challenges in 2014 was making sure that the US Treasury secretary, Jack Lew, would attend the finance ministers' meeting that took place in Cairns in September. Lew was not only the Treasury secretary but also a former chief of staff to President Obama. Needless to say, if he hadn't turned up, it would have been a very bad look. Cairns is remote and somewhat difficult to fly to. Unlike the leaders, finance ministers could never be seen in a government jet, and commercial travel was time-consuming and exhausting.

In our early discussions about the meeting, Jack said to me, 'If I come to Cairns, will you let me snorkel on the Great Barrier Reef?'

'For sure,' I said. 'I promise I'll organise that.'

I was a former tourism minister, so I figured this would be easy to arrange. But it turned out there's a whole lot more hubbub if you're trying to get the US Treasury secretary out to the Great Barrier Reef.

First, Lew didn't want to be seen going snorkelling, as it would look like he was in Australia on a junket. So we had to discreetly, at the end of the meeting, organise boats to get him out there. The security involved was a nightmare. I was prepared to scuba dive with him, as I'm a licensed scuba diver, but then we discovered that he was only allowed to snorkel. So we took a boat out to the reef, joined by the Secret Service members, who had a small flotilla of boats out there with us. Sitting among all this, in a wetsuit and with thick prescription goggles because he's as blind as bat, was the tall, skinny figure of Jack Lew.

We then had to transfer into Zodiac rubber boats, which had metal handrails. While jumping in, I slammed my kneecap on the side of the boat. I cut my knee open and was in quite a lot of pain. But being the pseudo-tough Aussie I am, I played it down. 'She'll be right,' I said.

Lew's security detail took one look at me and my bleeding knee, and then formed a semicircle around their boss.

'Mr Treasurer, sir,' one large agent said to me, 'you cannot go in the water with the Treasury secretary.'

'Why not?' I implored, grimacing but trying to hide the pain I was in.

'Well, two things,' he replied officiously. 'One, you're bleeding very badly and you should get it treated. The second thing is that you're now very attractive to sharks, and that's a security risk to the Treasury secretary.'

'What do you want me to do?' I pleaded rather pathetically.

'If you insist on entering the water, please go and snorkel over there,' he replied, pointing to an area of water about 100 metres from where we were.

So, trying not to take it personally, I paddled around the reef by myself, trailing blood everywhere and doing my best not to pass out. I was like a floating smorgasbord for sharks. A hundred metres away, the US Treasury secretary was snorkelling with about ten guys around him. The things we do for our country.

I got out of the water, and now decided I needed to attend to the gash on my knee. Our security entourage called ahead, alerting the AFP to a kind of 'medical emergency' on board our boat, which set off a minor panic among the various security details back on land. We eventually got back to Cairns and waved goodbye to Jack Lew, who soon jetted back to America. At least he'd had a good day out. For me, the whole thing, as well as being painful, was rather embarrassing.

When I got back to the hotel, Mary Balzary nearly died with fright when she saw the cut. She called a doctor, who put four stitches in my knee. To this day, I think of it as my Jack Lew scar from the G20.

* * *

Three weeks later, in October 2014, I was in Washington, DC for the G20 finance ministers and Central Bank governors meeting. I was due to have my stitches out from the Great Barrier Reef misadventure, and I wasn't in a good mood.

That day I was insanely busy, trying to conduct sideline meetings with the Turkish finance minister, while that evening I was hosting a gala dinner at the Library of Congress. Rupert Murdoch was our guest speaker, but I was yet to see a copy of his speech. His PA had promised to send it through a day before the event.

Once my meeting with the Turkish minister was concluded, Treasury Secretary Martin Parkinson came to see me in my makeshift office at the World Bank headquarters. He walked in rather sheepishly.

'Treasurer, we have a problem,' he said, mimicking that great line from *Apollo 13*.

'Okay, what's the problem?' I replied.

'Well,' he began slowly, 'we gave Rupert Murdoch the wrong date for the dinner, and he thinks it's next week.'

'Oh, no …' The situation felt every bit like a scene from *Yes Minister*.

'And' – Martin was yet to deliver the coup de grace – 'he is currently in Los Angeles.'

'Oh, no,' I said. 'This is bad, very bad. You have to fix it!'

'Well, I'm not sure how I can fix it,' Martin replied.

'I don't care if you have to hire him a jet,' I snapped. 'You've got eight hours to get him here for our 6 p.m. dinner.'

When I'd first suggested to Martin that Murdoch should speak at the G20 dinner, he and the other officials didn't like the idea. They'd never had an outside speaker before at the G20. But I thought it would be great to get Rupert along to talk about the challenges of business. He was, after all, Australia's greatest ever businessperson.

I really like Rupert Murdoch. In fact, I really like and admire the whole Murdoch family. They are good people, honest and tough. But they are also very humble. Importantly for me and the G20, Rupert was an exemplary business figure. He understood the interface between government and enterprise better than anyone else. He also understood most, if not all, of the G20 economies, having done business in the majority of them. Perhaps he was too right-wing for the G20 – but so what? I was over trying to pander to the left-wing technocratic class.

The Treasury team, too, thought it was a very bad idea to have Rupert speak. Perhaps they were showing a bit of bias, but I didn't care and I was determined to proceed.

The lead-up to the G20 dinner would also play a role for George Osborne, the UK chancellor of the exchequer, to make his case to Rupert Murdoch on the dangers of potential Scottish secession from the UK. In the months prior to the 2014 Scottish independence referendum, scheduled for September, George had become increasingly concerned about the position of Murdoch's newspaper in Scotland, *The Scottish Sun*. In his opinion, the paper was running a pro-independence line, and Murdoch himself had made tweets indicating some personal preference towards Scottish independence and admiration for Yes vote leader Alex Salmond. In George's view, Scottish succession would be a disaster.

In the months before the G20 dinner, George had asked me to organise contact with Murdoch to give some friendly advice on the speech's economic themes. Being owed a favour from the UK chancellor of the exchequer was an opportunity I did not pass up.

When he spoke with Murdoch about the G20 speech, Osborne also took the opportunity to make clear why he thought Scottish independence was a terrible idea for the UK, England and Scotland itself. *The Scottish Sun* ended up editorialising a neutral stance on the referendum, merely imploring voters to 'make the right choice'.

Whether or not Osborne's conversation with Murdoch had any impact is unclear, but in the chancellor's view it certainly didn't hurt and he was very appreciative.

It was so important to the G20 that we got Murdoch to Washington to give the speech that night. Mary Balzary got on the phone with Rupert's PA, stressing the seriousness of our predicament. She was informed that Mr Murdoch had only just flown in from New York the night before, and it would be near impossible to get him over from Los Angeles. Anyway, we were told, there wasn't a pilot available. As Rupert's pilot had just flown overnight, he wouldn't be allowed to fly again today.

My stitches were itching me, so I trudged over to the medical centre. Mary joined me – she was as white as a ghost. She explained to me how we'd managed to give Rupert the wrong date. As it turned out, it wasn't some Machiavellian attempt by Treasury staff to sabotage Rupert's appearance. In all our correspondence with the Murdochs and News Corp about the engagement, nobody had realised the date on the invitation was wrong.

Sitting in the medical centre, I pondered what on earth we could do. Rupert's no-show would be an utter disaster for me, and for George Osborne. Following the No vote outcome on the referendum for Scottish secession in September, we planned to seat George near Rupert at the G20 dinner so the chancellor could continue to make his case against any future Scottish independence vote.

As the stitches were being removed, Mary's phone buzzed with a new message. 'Rupert has told his PA to make it happen!' she burst out, the relief written all over her face.

To Rupert's great credit, and after some miracle-working by his staff, he got his private jet fired up and was flying to Washington. As we paced anxiously at the Library of Congress, he landed at Dulles Airport about an hour before the dinner. We organised a police escort from the private jet terminal at Dulles to the Library of Congress to get him there in forty minutes. I nearly kissed him as he got out of the car!

Despite the drama, the whole evening went incredibly well. As is often the case with Rupert Murdoch, he dispelled the myths about him through personal engagement. He is often painted by critics as a zealot or an ogre. In fact, he is quietly spoken, thoughtful and has a terrific sense of humour. This was totally disarming for many of the ministers and central bankers in the room. He gave a fantastic speech that went over very well – even with Martin Parkinson.

Things also went to plan with Rupert and George. The pair were deep in conversation at their table for most of the night. The next day, I had a quiet word with George. 'How'd it go?' I asked.

'I owe you,' he replied.

It didn't take me long to call in that debt from George Osborne, either. My pet project as chair of the G20 was to establish the Global Infrastructure Hub. I've always been an advocate for public–private partnerships in infrastructure. Ever since my first days in public service back in 1992, I've advocated for enterprise over bigger government. Smart infrastructure investment would drive productivity and improve the quality of life for billions of people around the world. The G20 could help drive that.

We needed to set up a G20 agency that would facilitate the world's best practice in infrastructure. In funding, design, construction and benchmarking, we would help make the next generation of infrastructure in road, rail, broadband, energy, water supply and so on the best it could be. But the Global Infrastructure

Hub needed funding. It would be based in Sydney, and Australia would put in seed funding, but without other countries making a financial commitment, it would fall over. And asking finance ministers to fund a multinational agency is like asking a mother bear to give away one of her cubs.

The first finance minister I 'shirtfronted' at the G20 meeting was the chancellor of the exchequer. 'I need £4 million from you, George,' I said, sounding every bit the man calling in a loan.

'What the hell for?' he replied.

'For the Global Infrastructure Hub. Remember?'

At this point George started to vacillate. It was almost like he didn't know what I was talking about. 'Well, um, you see, Joe, I don't know if I can.'

I stopped him at this point. Raising one finger in the air, I smiled and quietly said, in my best William Wallace accent, 'Scotland.'

A look of recognition spread across his face. 'I'll see what I can do.'

The United Kingdom led the way, and five other countries followed soon after.

* * *

The G20 leaders' summit in Brisbane in November 2014 was a career highlight for me and for Prime Minister Tony Abbott. It was a great challenge to get all the world leaders to travel across the globe for another summit, notwithstanding the very positive agenda. The logistics and security cost Australia around $1 billion, and we made sure that the money left Brisbane with the security infrastructure worthy of a global city. Hosting the G20 successfully unquestionably helped build domestic and global confidence that Brisbane could host the Olympic Games and other massive events.

Of course, when you host global leaders, you also have a constellation of egos to manage. Every leader had an entourage wanting different things. The Russians wanted to bring their own army of goons with machine guns, swinging out the back of trucks behind Vladimir Putin's armoured presidential vehicle. There were arguments between some countries about how many vehicles should be in their motorcades. It got to the absurd point that one leader's motorcade was longer than the one block he had travel to get from his hotel to the G20 meeting. It was a logistical nightmare, but Tony Abbott and his office were very engaged in the details.

Putin had almost not come at all. November 2014 was not long after the atrocity of the shooting down of the passenger jet MH17 above Ukraine, which killed 298 innocent people, including twenty-seven Australians. There was no doubt in the minds of the Australian government that Russia was to blame, and there was support within to ban the Russian leader altogether. But, as with boycotting an Olympic Games, I saw no benefit in not permitting the Russians to attend. Other nations might have joined them because of their domestic political situation. I was not alone in this view. The legendary German finance minister Wolfgang Schäuble addressed me with stern Teutonic words: 'The Bear needs to be in the room, Joseph.'

I had formed a warm friendship with Sergei Storchak, the deputy finance minister of Russia. While I had a good working relationship with Anton Siluanov, the long-standing Russian finance minister, his limited English – not to mention my lack of Russian – prohibited any warm engagement. Sergei was charming and smart, and his life had seen many twists and turns. Born in Ukraine, Sergei had risen through the ranks to become deputy finance minister – until he was arrested for alleged corruption in 2007. Obviously, prison had an impact on him, but he was released by President Putin in 2009 and reinstated to his role. Before too long, the charges against him were dropped. He was obviously the victim of a power struggle in the Kremlin, but had survived.

Sergei knew that, despite all our differences, if we stopped talking, the risks for peace and good order in the world would multiply. I treated him like a mate and asked for his help in getting President Putin to Brisbane. He nodded his support – and he delivered.

As it turned out, Angela Merkel used the opportunity of Putin's presence in Brisbane to have a bilateral meeting with him until 3 a.m. They were resolving deep differences over an issue I didn't fully appreciate. Given the history of the relationship between Russia and Germany, this is where jaw-jaw is better than ... well, the gruesome alternative.

It's funny the things that stand out in your mind about the people at these events. I recall a fascinating discussion with Prime Minister Narendra Modi of India about issues totally unrelated to high-level politics. We did, however, have a subsequent discussion about India's energy needs that reflected the enormous challenge a leader faces when he has 1.5 billion citizens and a booming middle class with an insatiable demand for electricity.

Another thing I will never forget is Vladimir Putin's eyes. He is a diminutive figure (many leaders are not very tall!), but his eyes were piercing. They didn't so much look at you but scoped you for intention and outcome. He was reading you like a hacker reads a computer screen.

Following the Brisbane G20, Angela Merkel began a short state visit to Sydney. We organised a small dinner at Government House, and even though Merkel had been up all through the night trying to negotiate a better outcome on Ukraine with Putin, she was energetic, curious and engaging. At one stage Tony Abbott asked her when it was that she thought Germany really reunited after World War II. Merkel, a former East German engineer, said she didn't think it was until the football World Cup in 2006 that Germans really wore their colours with pride. Regardless of which province they were from, for the first time since the end of World War II they could all be proud to say they were German.

The November meeting was also the venue for one of the most entertaining incidents (intentionally or otherwise) during my time at the helm of the G20. Traditionally, the finance ministers have taken a secondary role at the G20 leaders' summit. We were due to have a big dinner, and I wanted our whole Cabinet there.

It was important to me that we reflect Australian culture. In my experience, the finance ministers had seen the very best artistic performances in their own countries. We were in the pleasant surroundings of the Brisbane Contemporary Art Museum but it wasn't exactly La Scala. So I thought we'd get something more Australian. Something slightly more self-deprecating. I decided to get the Singing Waiters.

Now, if you've never seen the Singing Waiters, it's necessary to set the scene. At first they pretend to work as waiters, actually serving food to the guests. By the time the first course has been served, one of them loudly drops a plate. Another then loudly berates their clumsy colleague from across the room in Italian. Another yells in French, then another in English. It eventually becomes clear they're not part of the real wait staff when they break into operatic arias. They close with a stunning rendition of 'Nessun Dorma' from *Turandot*. It's an entertaining dinner performance, but also playful and self-deprecating in an Aussie way.

The ministers and Central Bank governors were standing up on their tables, cheering and filming the performance. The finance ministers were all loving it – and none more so than China's Lou Jiwei, who was holding up his phone camera and yelling like it was the best thing he'd ever seen. By the end of the performance, guests were slapping me on the back and saying, 'How much fun was that? That's the best dinner we've ever had!'

One attendee, however, who was not a fan of the Singing Waiters was our then attorney-general, Senator George Brandis. Now, George was also our arts minister, and a Queensland senator, so he'd brought along a table of Brisbane's best and brightest from the arts and culture scene. They were sitting right up the front, near the stage, and included (apparently) some world-renowned opera singers.

George came up to me after the dinner, saying he'd never been so embarrassed. He was furious with me. He thought it was awful. He just didn't get it.

A week later, George still hadn't forgotten about it as he brought it up in a Cabinet meeting.

I love George, I have to say. He would go on to have his own diplomatic career as the Australian High Commissioner in London. It was, safe to say, a Singing Waiters–free zone.

For me, I think you need creativity in diplomacy. You also need to be true to your national character, and, as Australians, having a sense of humour is important – it's the way others see us. International relations are full of intense stand-offs and ceremony, so engaging in a bit of self-deprecating humour can release the pressure valve and produce good outcomes.

* * *

When it was decided that I was going to Washington as Australia's next US ambassador, I rang Kim Beazley to let him know. It would still be a while before I moved to DC. I needed to clear my head after resigning from parliament so I decided to backpack in Europe for a few weeks. In October I flew off to the Rugby World Cup in England, and I also ended up going to Paris, Italy and Spain. I was relieved that I was never recognised. It felt like real freedom for the first time in many, many years. At one point I was literally skipping around in a European airport, I was so excited to be away from politics. Until then I hadn't appreciated how much I needed a change in career.

Before we moved to Washington, DC, the Department of Foreign Affairs and Trade (DFAT) put me through 'Diplomatic School'. It was meant to go for six weeks, but I insisted on a truncated program. I was impressed by the quality of the public servants who briefed me during that period. In particular, the

briefings from the intelligence agencies were illuminating. The
security test I had to go through was extraordinary. It struck me as
rather funny, though, that I hadn't needed to sit one in order to be
a member of the National Security Committee.

Melissa was doing the heavy lifting in organising our house
move and getting our children into schools in Washington, a
difficult and time-consuming process. My new job meant big life
changes for us all.

Another thing that was proving difficult to arrange was my
commencement date. It was beginning to feel like Kim Beazley would
need to be removed from the embassy in Washington with a crane.
He loved the job and was good at it, but I was told several times that
he had delayed his departure. I heard from one public servant that a
former Australian ambassador had to be physically evicted from his
residence after refusing to leave at the end of his term. Thankfully,
that wasn't necessary in this case! Kim and his amazing wife, Susie
Annus, were gracious and helpful in our family transition.

During the months before we left Australia, I had time to
reflect on the opportunities ahead. I had previously said to myself
that there was no way I'd become an ambassador. Frankly, I was
never interested. The constant small talk of the diplomatic cocktail
circuit was anathema to me. I am a straight talker, and nuance
wasn't a language I was familiar with. Besides, having to report to
the senior public servants who previously had (indirectly) reported
to me was unappealing. I couldn't stand the thought of going to
a railway station, airport or port to meet and greet an incoming
minister – especially the ones I just didn't like.

It was really the idea of change that kept me going. More than
anything, I was keen to get out of politics and leave Australia for
a while. As I said in my valedictory speech, if I'd stayed I would
have become bitter, even vengeful. I would have hated watching
my successors dismantle everything I'd worked for.

In corporate life, senior people who leave or are sacked get paid
large sums of money to keep quiet. Silence makes your successor's

job easier, and it's in the best interests of all stakeholders not to have an unseemly brawl. Moreover, in the private sector you can join a rival and start again. In politics, a loss leaves you nowhere to hide. You certainly can't switch sides for a better job.

Like any politician, I have a bit of an ego; some might say more than a bit. Arguably, it's necessary for success in politics to have a strong sense of self in order to survive the constant slings and arrows. But I've never been carried away with myself – at least I hope not. My thinking was that the country didn't need me as much as I needed it. Therefore, I was going to put aside that selfishness for the sake of helping my family and giving everyone a break.

We are all a little cynical when people say they are retiring 'to spend more time with the family'. But Melissa had made many sacrifices for my career and our three young children, so that sense did weigh on me.

I thought back to a Saturday morning during one of my toughest periods. I was about to leave home to take my son Xavier to his soccer match. Delta Goodrem, who was a neighbour of ours, tipped me off that there was a media pack out the front of our home. I ran out the back with Xavier and we ended up climbing over the back fence and going through another neighbour's yard to avoid the press. It's difficult explaining to a ten-year-old why he has to jump over the neighbour's fence in order to get to his football match. The tragedy is that that's one of his enduring memories of my political career.

Coming to America was a chance for all of us to look forward. To move on. I would still be serving my country, which I wanted to do, but without all the grief of politics. As an ambassador, you're an observer rather than a participant – or so I thought.

But I was under no illusions about the role I was taking on. Turnbull, Abbott and other leaders all said it was the most important appointment, aside from the governor-general, a prime minister had to make. That's because our relationship with the

United States is the most important to Australia, on almost every level. While China might be our biggest trading customer, the United States is by far our most significant economic and strategic partner. And the ambassador is the custodian of that relationship.

Ambassadors also have a significant degree of freedom, which was very appealing to me. Having been treasurer, I also had influence within Australia that would give me more independence than any other public servant. Malcom Turnbull and I would talk very regularly about many issues – and not just US politics. That made my job much easier.

So there I was, a former politician who always thought he'd be prime minister about to become an ambassador, a job he swore he'd never do. It was January 2016 when we arrived in Washington, and President Obama was beginning his final year in office. The primary season to determine the parties' nominees for the presidential election was about to begin. Bernie Sanders was already giving Hillary Clinton a contest for the Democrats, while the Republican field was wide open. Political gurus were predicting that it would be a ho-hum contest ending with a presidential race between Clinton and former Florida governor Jeb Bush.

I soon learnt that, much like my political life in Australia, nothing in America is predictable either.

CHAPTER 4

TRUMPAGEDDON

Arriving in Washington, the 2016 campaign
and Donald Trump's miracle win

Call it an omen. We arrived in Washington, DC during one of the largest and most destructive blizzards the city had seen in decades. It went by several names: Winter Storm Jonas, Snowzilla and (my personal favourite) Snowmageddon. In retrospect, I can't help but think of it as a portent of the drama that would envelop the United States in 2016.

One of the bizarre blessings of travel from Australia to the West Coast of the US is that, at certain times of the year, one can arrive in LA before you've even left. The Babbage-Hockey family arrived in Los Angeles on 20 January 2016, having left Sydney 'later' the same day. We were met at the airport by the Australian government's consul-general in Los Angeles, Chelsey Martin, a long-time US resident. This was no easy task, as I was carrying the proverbial kitchen sink. We had twenty-four checked-in bags, four bikes and ten pieces of hand-luggage. It appeared that the Babbage-Hockeys were hitting America with enough luggage for a ten-year posting.

We took the kids, Xavier, Ignatius and Adelaide, down to Santa Monica Pier to try to allay their anxieties about coming to live in a new country. We were in a hurry to get to Washington, DC, though, ahead of the expected blizzard that was set to dump over a metre of snow on the city. We were told that DC didn't cope well with snow, and it was sure to bring the capital to a standstill for some days.

By some miracle, a flight got us into Washington, DC by 9 p.m. the next day. Our plane was able to land, amid thousands that were being cancelled that week across the US northeast. Thankfully, the embassy team were well prepared for our arrival, with a convoy of trucks ready to accommodate all our luggage. It was like a Rolling Stones tour.

A further challenge was that the Beazleys had been unable to get removalists to assist with their exit from the ambassador's residence. Again, the pending storm had complicated things. The Australian government owns an entire block in Washington, DC, comprising five homes for senior embassy officials, including White Oaks. By chance, a senior embassy officer, the consul-general, was heading back to Australia and their home was being made available to us.

The whole time was one of great stress. On our way to our temporary home, Melissa insisted on stopping by the supermarket for some supplies for the kids. Of course, there were huge queues in the shops as Washingtonians bought enough groceries to see them through a month of impassable roads. It was not the last time I would witness empty shelves at the local Safeway.

The next day, the storm hit, and it didn't disappoint. It brought the city to a standstill. The District of Columbia train, metro and bus services would be suspended for the longest period in their history. Washington, DC's mayor, Muriel Bowser, declared a state of emergency after tens of thousands lost power in the region. Five people died in Washington alone as a result of the storm.

Amid all of this, we were trying to line up my first meeting with President Barack Obama. The 'Presentation of Credentials' by a new ambassador to the head of state is essential prior to any senior engagement with the US government. The Americans are very strict about such protocols, and will prohibit an 'uncredentialed' ambassador from engaging with the administration until the ceremony has been completed. The timing of these events is at the discretion of the president, and it can be weeks or even months between ceremonies. If you miss a window of opportunity, you are a lame duck ambassador.

A ceremony was scheduled to be held on 26 January, and so we were doing everything we could to get to Washington by then. Thankfully, the White House and the State Department were hugely helpful in making sure we could attend. So, that morning – which, I was pleased to note, was Australia Day – a motorcade was waiting for us outside the Australian ambassador's residence, ready to take the Babbage-Hockey family to meet President Obama.

I had made it clear that I wanted to take my whole family along, so our kids would have the opportunity to meet the US president. The Babbage-Hockeys piled into the black limousines, with Xavier riding in one car with me, and Melissa in the other car with Ignatius and Adelaide. We were all excited by the prospect of being driven through the city with a police escort. Washington was covered by a thick blanket of snow, and with almost no cars on the road it was an eerily beautiful journey to the White House.

The motorcade moved at pace down the empty boulevards of post-blizzard Washington, DC, passing the Kennedy Center as we looked down towards the Washington Monument and the Lincoln Memorial. Finally we arrived at the motorcade entry for the White House, located just behind the magnificent US Treasury building. For a moment I reflected on my own Treasury career.

The White House itself was almost camouflaged amid the Washington snow. At that moment, I had, perhaps for the first time, a true realisation of the incredible privilege I had been given, and the adventure I was embarking upon.

We joined a long line of black limousines that were waiting to drop off their new ambassadors. The order was based on the timing of your arrival in the United States, and so I was near the end of the queue. However, it gave me another moment to pause as I recognised the flags on the two limousines immediately beside ours. To the left was the new ambassador from Armenia, the homeland of my paternal grandfather. To my right was the ambassador representing New Zealand, the birthplace of my maternal grandmother.

We drove up the long and winding driveway to the southern entrance of the White House. Lined along the route were guards of the US Army, Navy, Marines and Air Force. The military ensemble played as we alighted, to be greeted by the Chief of Protocol, a presidential appointment much sought after in each administration.

Our children were beaming as we walked through the grand halls of the White House. Our escort generously allowed us to deviate from the official route so we could see the Cabinet Room, where the president meets his team. Xavier even tried out President Obama's high-backed chair.

It meant the world to me that our children were there. It was unusual for young kids to escort their parents to a Presentation of Credentials, but mine had endured the worst of politics, and I was never going to leave them behind that day.

The night before, Melissa and I had conducted our own family briefing on meeting President Obama.

'Okay, kids, you're going to meet the president of the United States tomorrow,' I announced. 'What are you going to say to him?'

'I'm nervous about guns,' Xavier replied. 'So I'm going to ask him what he's going to do about getting rid of guns in America.'

'Good question,' I replied. 'The president will be interested in that. And what are you going to ask, Adelaide?'

My eight-year-old daughter looked serious for a moment, then replied: 'I'm worried about terrorism, so I'm going to ask him how we can keep safe.'

'That's good too. And, Iggy, what are you going to ask?'

'I'm going to ask how I can be Black!' our six-year-old son chirped, seemingly excited at the prospect of humiliating his parents on the world stage.

Melissa and I were hyperventilating with embarrassment. 'You can't ask that,' I told him sternly. 'And why would you ask the president of the United States that anyway?'

'Because I want to play basketball and jump as high as Michael Jordan. I saw that the president plays basketball too,' he replied innocently.

Even though I'm sure President Obama would have seen the humour in Iggy's question, we agreed on an alternative that was a little more diplomatic.

The children's behaviour that day wasn't helped by their own presidential gift: red, white and blue M&M's. These M&M's are a limited edition that you can only get from the president, and they were in plentiful supply in the Roosevelt Room that served as the ambassadorial waiting room, immediately next to the Oval Office.

And so I feel there is at least some shared responsibility for the events that followed. We had three children ten and under, and we were almost last in a long line of ambassadors waiting to meet the president. As the queue progressed, so did the children's hyperactive behaviour, helped along by all the free M&M's, chocolate cake and soft drinks.

Hopped up on sugar, Iggy was spinning around and at one point knocked over the fireplace tools, which sent an enormous bang resounding throughout the White House. We attracted a displeased glare from the Secret Service agents. This was bettered by Adelaide, who, upon seeing the new Saudi Arabian ambassador in his ceremonial keffiyeh, screamed: 'There's ISIL in the building!'

We were fast becoming unpopular with all the White House staff, and by now I was praying our turn would come before things fell apart completely. Then the White House Chief of Protocol appeared and we knew our audience with the president was approaching. We were officiously informed that there were strict rules. We should enter the Oval Office in a particular formation; the president would be standing in front of the Resolute Desk. We had three minutes for a photo and small talk, then we were to progress out the other door and down the famous colonnade to the exit. There would be only official photos, and no autographs.

Fortunately, I'd met President Obama at the G20 and on a couple of other occasions. So when the door was flung open, all protocol went out the window.

'Great to see you, Joe,' Obama said, gliding across the Oval Office carpet with his hand outstretched. 'Welcome to Washington.'

He was warm and engaging with Melissa, and great with the kids. We even had time for an extended chat about the future of the Trans-Pacific Partnership (even though we weren't supposed to be discussing official business at that point). The whole experience was a real high, and a wonderful way to start my time as Australia's ambassador.

For our children, too, it was a special thing to be part of, even if they didn't fully realise it at first. The following day, Xavier was in his new classroom at St. Albans School. He'd only been at the school for three days, so he was a bit embarrassed when his teacher asked him to stand up.

'Xavier, can you explain to your classmates what you did yesterday?'

'I went to the White House,' he replied.

The other children were getting excited.

'And what did you do at the White House?' the teacher asked.

'Um, we went to the Oval Office.'

'And who did you meet?' The teacher was becoming increasingly frustrated.

'President Obama,' he finally told the class.

A gasp went around the room, and soon Xavier found himself fielding questions from classmates impressed by this new Aussie's political contacts. Connections in DC are everything – even among fifth graders.

'Xavier, that's such an exciting experience,' the teacher said.

'Doesn't the president meet everyone that comes to America?' he asked.

* * *

Within a few days of presenting my credentials and settling the family in at the ambassador's residence, the traditional travel itch of a former politician kicked in. In order to understand the country, I knew I needed to get out of the capital. Duty called, and my first outing would be to California for the larger-than-life global sporting extravaganza that is the Super Bowl. Little did I suspect that this trip would almost end my diplomatic career before it had begun.

There is no better introduction to the United States than the Super Bowl. Nor was this any old Super Bowl: this was (in my best American sports broadcaster's voice) Super Bowl 50! The fiftieth anniversary of the NFL game that had come to represent the all-singing, all-dancing, sensory explosion of American sport and entertainment. Taking place on 7 February 2016 at Levi's Stadium in Santa Clara, in the San Francisco Bay Area, it would be the fancied Carolina Panthers up against the experienced Denver Broncos, led by superstar quarterback Peyton Manning.

I was invited as a guest of the Greater Western Sydney Giants AFL team, and I would have been mad to turn them down. Two long-time friends, Joseph Carrozzi and Tony Shepherd, had secured incredible front-row tickets for key Giants sponsors, and they wanted the Australian ambassador there too. I was happy to oblige.

Unfortunately, not everything went to plan. The game itself was incredible. Our proximity to the action gave us an insight into the pure physicality of the game. When you get a good look at these guys up close, you appreciate why they're considered the fastest, largest and most physical athletes in the world. At one point I met Eli Manning, Peyton's brother, from the New York Giants. He told me about the impact of hitting another human at 30 miles (50 kilometres) an hour, time after time, for three hours a game. Across a season, it's like your body (and brain) are in a car accident every weekend.

The national anthem was sung by Lady Gaga, while the halftime show was a concert by Beyoncé, Coldplay and Bruno

Mars. The entertainment was a blur of music, lights and megastars. So the noise, colour and movement of the Super Bowl was nonstop. There never seems to be a break in the action, even though the football only takes up twenty per cent of the day. In the end, the Broncos beat the Panthers 24–10, and Peyton Manning retired as a two-time Super Bowl winner. By the time it was all over, if not for the confetti in my hair I'd have sworn the whole experience was a fabulous dream.

Given all the excitement, it was little wonder we were in the mood to party. We made our way back into downtown San Francisco and went in search of a drinking establishment. The problem, as any post-football group of revellers can attest to, is getting into a bar. Following a great Australian tradition, none of us had organised anywhere to go afterwards, and so we just staggered around downtown like a lost tribe of confused Aussies. Everywhere we went, security demanded ID (which I didn't have) or they looked at us unsympathetically and just shrugged: 'It's Super Bowl Sunday – we're full, whatcha expect?'

Then we hit upon the Hotel Fairmont, where, thanks to one of my fast-talking mates, we were allowed in. The Fairmont has one of the oldest and most elaborate tiki bars in all of the United States. The Tonga Room & Hurricane Bar features an artificial lagoon in the middle restaurant, complete with tiki-style huts for exclusive tables, and a band playing on a pontoon in the middle. It felt like I'd died and gone to Elvis Presley movie heaven. The ten of us managed to score a table in one of the bar's finest huts, and we ordered a round of drinks to celebrate.

Pretty soon a group of big guys in suits started staring and pointing at us from across the room. I ignored them for a while, but when I got up to go to the toilet and one of them followed me to the door of the gents, it became a little weird. At one point he began speaking into a lapel microphone. Narcissistically, I thought for a moment that this must have been an additional layer of protection for me. I was, after all, the new Australian ambassador – perhaps our American friends had secretly provided additional security.

When I left the bathroom, the tall figure was still waiting for me, and had been joined by two San Francisco police officers. The group surrounded me and I froze. What the hell was going on?

The man with the earpiece revealed himself as the head of hotel security. 'Sir, can I please see some ID?' he asked in the classic tone of US officialdom.

Thinking that perhaps my crime had been entering a bar without ID, I shrugged. 'Sorry, I've just arrived in the country and I don't have a drivers licence yet. But,' I said, rummaging around in my wallet, 'you can have one of these.'

To the Australian embassy's great credit, they had already printed business cards for me. Handing over a card emblazoned with the Australian coat of arms and the words 'Joe Hockey – Australian Ambassador', I looked around the little group, smiled and awaited an apology.

'Sir, you are not the Australian ambassador,' announced the official. 'I'm going to have to ask you to leave the hotel.'

My face dropped. 'What are you talking about? You're throwing me out?'

'Yes ... now leave.'

'Why?'

'You are impersonating the ambassador, sir. Please leave.'

Utterly confused, I looked at the police officers, who were similarly perplexed. 'Do you understand the implications of what you're doing?' I asked the suit. 'What about my group?'

'They're all being asked to leave as well.'

With horror, I looked over at our table and saw security and police officers rounding up my friends and telling them to leave. As we were walking to the door, I had a police escort of San Francisco's finest removing me from the Tonga Room. Needless to say, this wasn't the way I had envisaged my first diplomatic road trip ending.

Now, rewind a moment back to when we were trying to get into the Fairmont. As it turned out, a quick-talking member of our party was dropping my name – or should I say my new title – as a means of entry: 'We have the Australian ambassador here, you know, and he really needs a drink ...' You get the idea. And after letting us in, the meticulous security guard in the suit and earpiece had done a Google search to double-check that I was who I said I was. The problem was, he wasn't *that* meticulous. Because back at the beginning of 2016, of course, when you googled 'Australian ambassador to the United States', your result was a photo of Kim Beazley grinning affably back at you.

Given that I bear no resemblance to Kim Beazley – I am, of course, darker, younger and less handsome – our security guard had concluded that I was out on some kind of identity-stealing bar crawl with my mates. I suppose he imagined some ruse whereby we'd print out a few fake business cards and get into San Francisco bars after passing me off as the Australian ambassador. And, to be fair, Australian sports fans have probably done stranger things.

Meanwhile, here I was, the actual Australian ambassador, and at the centre of what seemed likely to become a full-blown 'diplomatic incident'. While being frogmarched out by the cops, I started to think about the awful implications. What if I get arrested? Who can bail out an ambassador? Do I have to call the prime minister? What if it gets in the paper?

I started to imagine the coverage: 'Touch Down: New Ambassador Hockey in Post–Super Bowl Bar Brawl'. It's done. I'm done. 'Sacked: Hockey Gone in Super Bowl Bar Bust Up'.

I got a hold of myself and began to think more clearly. 'Hang on,' I said, 'if you don't think that card is real, then check this one out.' I produced another business card, this one stating in bold type: 'Joe Hockey – Treasurer to the Commonwealth of Australia'.

The three of them peered at the card curiously and looked at me again.

'And take these too,' I said, handing over keycards and anything else with my name on it.

At this point, one of the genuinely more meticulous police officers began his own Google search. 'Umm, this guy does look like this Hockey guy. And it says he's a politician. It also says he's the new Australian ambassador to the United States.'

The frogmarch out of the hotel stopped in its tracks, and the security guard's face paled.

'Yes!' I told them. 'As I've been saying, I'm the real Joe Hockey.'

The police, at this point, excused themselves and apologised. The security and concierge began the excruciating task of backtracking. 'Sir, we're terribly sorry. Can we offer you and your party free drinks?'

I'd had enough. 'No, thanks, that won't be necessary,' I said. 'We're leaving.'

For months afterwards I was inundated with offers of free drinks, dinners and accommodation the next time I was in San Francisco, 'to make up for the unfortunate misunderstanding'. I never took them up on the offer.

That night, as I got out onto the sidewalk in front of the hotel and breathed in the cold, sobering air, I just thought, *Holy cow ...* Imagine if the first thing Australia found out about my posting was that I'd been thrown out of a hotel after the Super Bowl. That would've been the end of my second career. Nobody back home would be finding out about this in a hurry, I decided. And at least – unlike our former Prime Minister Malcolm Fraser – I still had my trousers on.

* * *

In early 2016, my office was struggling to make meaningful contact with the Obama administration. It was not that the relationship was poor. Far from it. Malcolm Turnbull had made a successful visit not long before I came, and Kim Beazley had done an outstanding job as ambassador. Among other things, Beazley had a deep affection and understanding for the US military, which is, of course, a central facet to the alliance. Indeed, I used to joke with him that he knew the serial number of every tank in the US Army.

The problem was partly complacency within the White House. Because there was nothing wrong with the relationship with Australia, there didn't seem to be any urgency in engaging with me and the team. The sole exception to this was the Trans-Pacific Partnership (TPP). The two leading presidential candidates in 2016 had come out opposing the TPP, which caused great concern to the Turnbull government. And so the TPP would be the subject of our most critical dealings with the Obama administration. But aside from that, such was the complacency towards the Australian relationship that it was almost six months before Obama's national security adviser, Susan Rice, made herself available to see me.

When I walked in the door to her office, she said, 'Oh, I'm so sorry for taking so long to see you. The problem with this town is it's the squeaky door that gets the oil.' As I tried my best to be understanding, she told me that the Obama administration had no issues with Australia, and was probably guilty of putting off a meeting that had no particular purpose other than for the two of us to meet.

Compounding this was that it was an administration that was very bureaucratic. Some secretaries and deputy secretaries even refused to meet with ambassadors, outsourcing the job to lower-level staff. As a former federal treasurer and chair of the G20, I just wouldn't cop that. This was one stark difference between me and career diplomats. If you aim low in your engagement, everyone below your rank will also have their level of access to high-ranking officials compromised. If you aim high, then everyone seeks higher access in the administration. And I wanted face-to-face meetings with cabinet secretaries when it mattered.

Another key factor was that the Obama administration was exhausted. They'd been at the summit of US politics for almost eight years and knew the clock was counting down to the end.

They were all lining up jobs in the private sector or planning a well-deserved break. They'd done their best for their country and now they were ready to leave. Having been exhausted by politics myself, I understood what was going on, but it wasn't the best environment for a new ambassador to be entering.

Everyone I spoke to in Washington was utterly dismissive of the notion that Donald Trump could become president of the United States. They basically viewed their final months in office as a preordained handover to the incoming administration of Hillary Clinton.

Yet Trump won three out of the first four Republican primaries in February, and the polls were showing him as a popular choice among Republicans. After finishing second in Iowa, he took the strategically important New Hampshire and then the electorally significant South Carolina and Nevada primaries, carrying seventy-five delegates between them. I was perplexed as to how Democrats could be so dismissive of his chances in a two-horse race with Hillary or Bernie Sanders.

During an election campaign, it is the instinct of any politician to get out and about. I'm not sure it's the instinct of every diplomat. But having been a candidate or involved in elections all my adult life, I felt the need to get on the road during the primaries. I wanted to get a feel for what was really going on in the USA beyond New York, Washington and the other major cities on the east and west coasts. As it turned out, Clinton won the counties incorporating the thirty largest cities in the United States, but lost the election. That means anyone who was in those cities throughout the campaign would have found it difficult to get a feel for what was happening across the nation.

The Australian embassy has a congressional liaison team of about six people. They form a unit based in Washington, DC, and are primarily tasked with finding out what's going on in politics. Their initial reports on the Republican primaries were extraordinary in many ways. They reported that, based on their analysis of the media and what the other campaigns were saying, Trump had no ground campaign and no backup support. There was nobody out there supporting this guy with campaign machinery, and as a result he would be toast when things got serious.

Instinctively, I didn't believe this. I wanted them to get beyond the cities and find out what was happening in rural America. 'Hit the road,' I told them. 'I need to know what's happening in the Midwest and beyond.' They returned shell-shocked. Every little town they went to had Trump signs everywhere. Trump/Pence banners were littered throughout front yards and on every street corner. There was massive enthusiasm for this guy who supposedly had no 'ground game'.

But it was more than that. The Trump campaign had a very sophisticated social media campaign. Later, we found out about the unethical role of Cambridge Analytica and Facebook in collecting identity data, but the Republican digital engagement team was sharper and more strategic than that of the Democrats, who were still riding high on the successful Obama social media campaigns. That old sporting cliché applies: you are only as good as your next game.

Donald Trump was always a polarising figure. For many blue-collar white Americans, he was the anti-Washington hero. They were proud to fly his flag and wear his 'Make America Great Again' hats, and they evangelised his policies. But as you moved up the wealth ranks, overt support for Trump dissipated. Middle-class Americans were less overt in their support. Very few of the wealthy in cities like New York, San Francisco or Los Angeles would ever want to be associated with Trump. He was the antichrist for those 'establishment' Republicans. But that didn't mean they wouldn't vote for him.

Because of Trump's personal behaviour, there were many Americans who wouldn't be open in their support. As a friend of mine in Dallas, Texas, said, 'I live in one of the richest neighbourhoods in America. There is no way anyone would put a Trump sign out the front of their home here. Our gardens may end up getting trashed! But let me tell you, 90 per cent of the neighbourhood will vote for Trump.'

This combination of social media and ground-level support was a winning formula. Our team started to see what was happening in key states like Pennsylvania and Wisconsin. They did a road trip to Michigan, and when they got outside the major cities, they met Trump supporters everywhere. Meanwhile, I went down to Florida and North Carolina and then across to Arizona, where I was seeing a lot of the same thing.

In the end, Trump won North Carolina by just under 4 percentage points, Florida by just over 1 point, and each of Michigan, Wisconsin and Pennsylvania by less than 1 point. The closeness of the margins illustrated the difference between what was happening in the cities on the one hand, and in the smaller towns and rural areas on the other. But this was all lost to the media experts in Washington, DC. During the primaries and the campaign, they had no awareness at all of how Trump's social media campaign was targeting key demographics in key states.

I returned to Florida for the Republican primary debate in March. Not long before the debate, Jeb Bush, the former governor of Florida, had dropped out of the race. A few months earlier he'd been the hot favourite. I have a great deal of respect for the Bushes, including Jeb. He's a smart, humble and highly intelligent guy. Like all the Bush family members I've met, he is very down to earth and has a great sense of humour.

The Bush family is the most successful political family in US history. The Kennedys get significant airtime, but they can't match the record of the Bushes, who had served as president or vice president for two decades, and had two other members who served as governors of Texas and Florida, respectively. George W. Bush is one of the funniest guys I've ever met – he's mischievous and totally at peace with himself. I'd also met his brother Marvin at a golf club I was a member of, and always found him very easy to get along with.

Although Jeb had been forced to pull out of the race, he retained his sense of humour. 'Mr Ambassador,' he told me, 'some would say that in order to be a good ambassador you have to visit every state in the United States. Well, let me tell you something, whatever you do, don't go to North Dakota!'

Although he remained jovial, there was an air of sadness about Jeb's failure in the campaign. He had in many ways been bullied out of the race by the brand of politics that Trump represented. Trump was the antithesis of the gentlemanly, institutional Republicanism that the Bush family practised. And, fair or not, Jeb was the perfect target for Trump's arguments against rule by elites in the United States. Trump made the Republican primary contest a bar-room battle, and Jeb just couldn't get down and dirty like The Donald.

When I arrived at the University of Miami arena for the debate on 10 March, I noticed that only the British ambassador and I were present from the diplomatic corps. The lack of interest from other senior diplomats in Washington struck me as odd, given only four contenders remained in the race at that point: Trump, Marco Rubio, Ted Cruz and John Kasich. 'Super Tuesday' on 15 March would feature winner-takes-all contests in Ohio, Kasich's home state, and Florida, Rubio's home state. While it was clear that Kasich wasn't going to go the distance, Rubio, on home turf, was expected to shine.

Before the debate, I'd wandered into the enormous media hall. It was double the size of an Australian budget lock-up. I met several key Florida political figures, including Governor Rick Scott, who would later serve as a senator alongside Rubio. CNN anchor Jake Tapper was on stage with other journalists from his network, and the energy in the room reminded me of the lead-up to a big football match.

The 2000 party faithful were definitely on the side of Rubio, the local boy and son of a Cuban émigré bartender. There was great hope in Florida that he would break through in this debate and become a real contender against Trump.

When things got going, Rubio did land some blows. Trump had the previous evening asserted that 'Islam hates us', and claimed that Rubio was being 'politically correct' after he defended the record of American Muslims. 'I'm not interested in being politically correct,' Rubio now told the crowd. 'I'm interested in being correct.' There was great applause. Even so, it was not a cut-through performance, and like other, more fancied candidates before him, Rubio was ultimately muscled out of the contest.

Trump's attitude towards foreign affairs and trade was, at times, not popular with the crowd. I could hear booing coming from segments of the audience when he said he would 'negotiate' on deals from Israel and Palestine to Iran and China. It was classic Trump messaging: 'I am the great negotiator – I will fix the mess.' Donald Trump did not have a deep grasp of policy detail, so his default response was always to 'negotiate a better deal'. For his followers, this was an adequate response. Trump was rich and successful. He'd even 'written' a book called *The Art of the Deal*. And, of course, Trump was really, really rich because he was really, really smart.

It intrigued me that the critics who did not consider Trump to be really rich mostly didn't have their own golf courses, planes, boats or multitude of homes. But the fact is that for many Americans, wealth is a scorecard, and they could see Donald Trump had a lot more points than most.

Texas Senator Ted Cruz seemed to be the only person who could beat Trump. He could win the conservative base on traditional values, and had a proven voting record on guns, God and taxes. But Cruz was not a street fighter. At one point he began to brag about the victories he'd had over Trump in the primaries. His primary line of attack was that 'if we nominate Donald Trump, Hillary wins'.

Trump retorted, finishing off with an ominous warning for Clinton: 'I have about 1.6 million votes during this primary season, more votes than Ted. The other thing is, I beat Hillary, and I will give you the list, I beat Hillary in many of the polls that have been taken. And each week, I get better and better. And believe me, I haven't even started on her yet.'

After the debate, I approached Jake Tapper and introduced myself. 'Did you hear all that booing of Trump during his answers on foreign policy and trade?' I asked.

'No, we didn't hear anything,' he said. 'We had our earpieces in the entire time and couldn't hear the crowd.'

After the debate, the media and the candidates meet in an adjoining building in what is called the 'Spin Room'. That's where candidates and their representatives do short media interviews and lobby for their teams. It was hard to get into the Spin Room, but I came across a fellow Aussie working in the media, who offered to give me their pass. Deal done. I was now an ambassador pretending to be a journalist.

There were at least three hundred people in the room, perhaps thirty camera crews, fifty radio correspondents and a heap of print journalists. And the only candidate to turn up in person was Donald Trump. And he brought members of his family along, including Melania and several of his children. The media were all around him like he was a Kardashian, jostling for his attention.

I asked a few more journalists, 'Did you hear the crowd booing?'

None of them had – they all thought he'd done well.

In politics, your own team often causes you more damage than your official opponents. A room full of Republicans booing Donald Trump should have been the end of his campaign. But through unlikely circumstances and the bravado that he had sold to millions around the world, Donald Trump had escaped that fate. He had the teflon coating that every politician wants.

At one point in the melee, I turned around and found Donald Trump himself standing next to me. Trump looked at me suspiciously and eyed my press pass, which identified me as a representative of Google Media. 'You guys never give me a fair go,' he said. 'Why don't you give me a break?' This was a mere preview of his long-running battles with the tech giants. Bizarrely, it was almost the same way he greeted me as president when I met him on the golf course.

Leaving the debate that night, I couldn't help but think everybody – including me – had underestimated Donald Trump.

On that same trip to Florida, I attended one of the final Democratic Party debates between Hillary Clinton and Bernie Sanders. Given that it was a two-horse race, the dynamic here was very different. Frankly, I found it all a little predictable. The vocal support from Sanders' supporters during the event was revealing. I thought, 'Even the Democrats are cheering for an anti-establishment candidate.'

Many Democrats couldn't bear a re-run of the Clintons. In the same way that not all Republicans were enamoured with Trump, Sanders was getting a cheer from many Democrats who may not have liked everything about him, but loved the fact that he was an anti-establishment candidate. The one consistent theme out of both debates was that people were sick of Washington.

When I arrived back in DC, I compared my own experiences in Florida to what our diplomatic intel was saying. It was at this point that I formed the view that Donald Trump really could win the US presidency.

* * *

The Hillary Clinton campaign operated like a kind of shadow administration. It was built on vast networks of contacts within politics and business that dated all the way back to the days when her husband was elected governor of Arkansas. It was structured much like an actual government bureaucracy, and was characterised by rings within rings of power. At the centre of this structure was Hillary – and, to a lesser but still important degree, Bill. They weren't easy to contact personally unless you went through the circle.

Despite the residual anger some still felt at Obama, who had beaten Hillary to the Democratic nomination in 2008, the campaign's proximity to the White House made it effectively an administration in waiting. They stood ready to move in, once given the inevitable green light by the American people.

The Trump campaign couldn't have been more different: you could reach out to any of them. It was operated by a hodgepodge of characters, ranging from senior Republican office holders (New Jersey Governor Chris Christie) to possibly brilliant but enigmatic oddballs (Steve Bannon and Roger Stone). If you could make contact with one of these people, all of a sudden you had contact with the inner circles of the Trump campaign (depending, of course, where your contact was in the pecking order on that day).

Not long after the March primary debates, we managed to make contact with two of these players, Dr Sam Clovis and Stephen Miller.

Clovis was a former fighter pilot and US Air Force colonel. After leaving the Air Force, he moved between academia, lobbying and a media career, and eventually ended up as a leading Republican in Iowa, running for the Senate and state treasurer. He missed out both times but had become a respected player in Republican circles. Eventually he was brought in to head up Rick Perry's 2016 presidential campaign. Not long after, he jumped ship to Trump's campaign. When we met, his title was 'co-chair of the Trump campaign'. Sam Clovis was also (and I say this with the greatest respect for large men) a *very* big unit – he was twice the size of me.

Stephen Miller would become one of the Trump presidency's great survivors. Back then, though, he was just a campaign adviser. As the world would soon learn, and as I would surmise from my own dealings with him, he was also a man obsessed by the issue of immigration.

The pair came to the ambassador's residence on a Friday afternoon, and we sat down in a wood-panelled room from the

1930s. The residence had once been the home of General George S. Patton, a famed World War II commander, who rented the mansion largely thanks to the wealth of his wife. I could just imagine Patton sitting around with global military and political figures while smoking cigars and drinking brandy in what you could only describe as a real gentlemen's den.

Legend has it that Patton's daughter escorted a suitor to morning tea in downtown Washington in the early 1930s. On their return, they found Patton sitting in a chair with his dog just inside the entrance of the home. It seems Patton disliked the man escorting his daughter, because he discharged a shotgun into the architrave just above the front door. Apparently, the shotgun pellets are still there. (Needless to say, the suitor never returned.)

So there I was, sitting across from the enormous Sam Clovis and the very thin Stephen Miller. They made for an odd duo, rather like a political equivalent of Laurel and Hardy. I had in the room with me my head of congressional liaison, Peter Heyward, a former Australian ambassador to Pakistan.

My opening words to Clovis and Miller were: 'I think you guys can win.' They looked at each other in what seemed like shock, but the fact was that I believed it. That was why I was meeting with them. I quickly moved to what was the most important trade and foreign policy issue for Australia of the day: the future of the Trans-Pacific Partnership.

'I really want to try and convince you that Candidate Trump should support the Trans-Pacific Partnership,' I told the pair.

'Well, that's not going to happen,' Miller snapped back immediately.

Clovis put up his hand to Miller, as if to say, *Hang on a moment.* 'Okay, Ambassador, let's hear why we should support the TPP,' he said.

I launched into my spiel about the importance of the partnership for Australia and the United States. I spoke about regional prosperity and stability, and how the deal was consistent with the values not only of the Republican Party but of Donald Trump himself.

Clovis was enjoying the cookies we'd laid out, so we got some more in and I continued making my case. When I finished, he looked at me, smiled and said. 'Ambassador, that is the most convincing case I have ever heard for the TPP. Unfortunately, there is no way Candidate Trump will endorse the policy.'

Miller was intense on that point too, so I thought it best to leave the TPP for the time being and move on to the Australian–US military relationship. 'We'd also want Candidate Trump to remain committed to the Indo-Pacific strategy,' I said.

The pair of them looked at me in a particularly unenthusiastic manner and said a few things like, 'Well, we don't know, we'll have to see about that.' Clovis started talking about his own military career, apparently in a bid to demonstrate his *bona fides* with Australia, but without committing to anything.

It wasn't until we got to the issue of immigration that Miller's eyes lit up and he started asking questions. He wanted to know all about our immigration policies. We agreed to send some details to him about Australia's tough immigration laws. Of course, Miller would go on to become responsible for some of the most controversial aspects of President Trump's immigration policy, including the southern border wall and his ban on arrivals from a number of majority-Muslim nations.

When the meeting concluded, Peter and I went back to my office, and I asked him to send the information we had promised Miller and Clovis on immigration. In good faith, Peter also sent Canberra a note, telling them we'd had a meeting with the Trump campaign and we were supplying them with some publicly available information on Australia's immigration policies.

Well, Canberra went nuts. The email trail was bizarre. There were twenty-five people from five different departments all giving an opinion on whether we should be engaging with the Trump campaign or not. It got to the point where a deputy secretary wrote, in an email to over twenty people, that if I wasn't smart enough to work out that it was bad for Australia to engage with the Trump campaign, perhaps I shouldn't even be in Washington.

I was aghast. It was utterly unprofessional and reflected the deep-seated bias of many senior public servants. More alarmingly for me, most were 'armchair experts' on politics; none of them had run for elected office in their lives. They were posing as experts on US politics from 16,000 kilometres away in Canberra. I was furious.

Exacerbating the public servants' concerns was the fact that Malcolm Turnbull and Julie Bishop were also anxious about the outreach. They preferred me to remain at arm's length. I took the autonomy of the office of the ambassador seriously. Even if the prime minister was now my boss, I was a former treasurer of Australia, and I wasn't prepared to write off Donald Trump's chances. Whether Trump's politics were favoured by DFAT, the foreign minister or me was irrelevant. I had formed the view that Donald Trump could win, and as I saw it that created a duty for me, as the senior representative of Australia in the United States, to pursue contact with his campaign.

Nonetheless, after this incident I remained more covert than overt in my engagement with the Trump campaign, and I certainly avoided reporting it all back. I even decided not to tell my own embassy team what I was up to, lest they feel the need to report it back to Canberra.

It remains quite the conundrum for any ambassador. Do you reveal all that happens or hold things back? Canberra always wants to know everything, and the Washington mission, with representatives from all major departments and agencies in the federal government, is under constant pressure to provide inside information back to the respective head offices.

I had the seniority to withhold information when it was in Australia's best interest, but I withheld nothing from the prime minister. I knew this posting would be the end of my public service career and I was not reliant on anyone in Canberra for my next job, so I wouldn't be held hostage by the demands of a few public servants back in Australia. Moreover, I was uneasy about the information and where it would end up if I did report it back through the usual channels.

Of course, we also engaged with the Clinton campaign. We went to New York to visit Hillary's campaign headquarters at 1 Pierrepont Plaza, in Brooklyn. Her campaign operation was an amazing machine that occupied a number of floors of the building. But although they appeared open to contact, none of the senior Clinton campaign operators engaged much with foreign diplomats – or not with Australia's, at least. Once again, it suggested that they were taking our friendship for granted. You had to take a position in the queue with the Obama administration, and now also with the Clinton campaign.

What was worse was that whenever we engaged with middle-tier operators from the Clinton campaign, we got a lecture on what we should be doing more in the Indo-Pacific region. Not only that, Clinton's campaign wouldn't commit either way on the Trans-Pacific Partnership. We were told it was Obama's TPP to manage and that was that.

* * *

My next major engagement with the Trump campaign was with New Jersey Governor Chris Christie, who had dropped out of the race for the Republican nomination in February and was now a senior Trump campaign official.

Christie had been a Republican frontrunner, but he was politically damaged by a scandal in which his office was accused of intentionally causing traffic jams on the George Washington Bridge between New Jersey and New York. So his presidential campaign was stillborn, but he did land a massive blow on Marco Rubio before he quit. He destroyed his Republican rival in the New Hampshire debate at a time when the Floridian senator was building momentum in his campaign. Trump thus owed Christie a very large favour, and Christie had sealed this by giving Trump a ringing endorsement. Although he'd clashed with Trump as a candidate, Christie quickly slotted into a role as one of Trump's senior campaign advisers.

Later on, Christie half-jokingly filled me in on the history of the two men's relationship. They had been friends for many years. When both had entered the race for the GOP nomination, they struck a deal to swap votes and support should the other fall out of the race. Christie expected Trump wouldn't last as a candidate, but even so, he was obliged to stick to the deal. His endorsement of Trump was unexpected but highly influential.

Then when Trump was deciding on his running mate, Christie was at the top of his list. In fact, it was widely expected that he would be selected. However, Jared Kushner, Trump's son-in-law, had other ideas. Jared blamed Christie for the jailing of his father, Charles Kushner, over eighteen counts of illegal campaign contributions, tax evasion and witness tampering back when Christie was attorney general of New Jersey in 2005. Although Charles Kushner pled guilty to the charges (and was later pardoned by Trump in the final weeks of his presidency), the son never forgot, and certainly never forgave. Jared changed Trump's mind, and as a result Christie was frozen out of the vice presidency, and later from the Trump administration altogether. Revenge is a dish best served cold – or so they say.

Before these events unfolded, Peter Heyward and I caught the train up to New Jersey to see Christie. The governor and I hit it off immediately: I considered him one of the smartest and most engaging political figures I'd ever met. And he was fun to be around. In addition to his predictable New Jersey forthright manner and toughness, he could be irreverent, honest and self-deprecating.

Christie was interested in my role as an ambassador with a background as a senior politician. With this in mind, he asked me a question: 'With your experience in politics, what does Donald Trump have to do to win over the working class?'

Stopping to think for a moment, I replied: 'Well, the biggest driver of economic growth in the United States and Australia is growth in household consumption. It's the consumer. It's two-thirds of our economic growth. If Donald Trump commits to increase the minimum wage to, say, $15 an hour, I think that'll win the hearts and minds of the working class. The big benefit of the wage rise is that anyone on that sort of money would spend most of it. Which would then stimulate economic growth. It would become a virtuous circle.'

Christie looked at me ponderously. 'In New Jersey, about 4 per cent of the workers are on the minimum wage,' he replied. 'We have to compete with Tennessee and Oklahoma. It would be very hard to introduce a $15 minimum in New Jersey because we're trying to keep manufacturing in our state.'

'But in DC, how can you justify someone working in a restaurant getting $5 an hour plus tips?' I asked.

'Yeah, but "plus tips" is key. They can do well out of tips.'

We had a really good debate on the subject. I talked about Australia having the highest minimum wage in the world, and explained how less than 1 per cent of Australians are on the minimum wage, and half of them are on it for less than twelve months.

By the end of our conversation, Christie seemed open to the idea. 'Look, let me have a chat with Donald Trump about it and see what he thinks.'

Peter and I came back on the train that afternoon. We talked about the meeting and the prospect of him investigating the tax cut and a higher wage offset, but we didn't think much more about it.

Less than a week after my meeting with Christie, Peter came rushing into my office. 'Oh my God. Donald Trump has just been on Fox,' he burst out. 'He rang up in the middle of the day and floated the idea of a $15 minimum wage rise!' Peter was half-laughing, half-concerned. 'We have to stop talking to these guys.'

'What do you mean?' I said. 'That's fantastic!'

After the Fox interview, the idea of a mandated minimum wage of $15 per hour took off for about half a day. Trump at first said he thought it was a good idea – and then some advisers got in his ear, and a few hours later he started to wind it back.

The whole experience gave me a salutary lesson in how Trump worked throughout his campaign and into his presidency. It was clear that Trump and his team didn't have a playbook. Trump's only real plan was to define and destroy Hillary. Then, on the campaign trail, he just developed a few policies that got big cheers at rallies. Trump's lack of a sophisticated campaign strategy was extraordinary in an age when hundreds of millions of dollars are spent by candidates on political consultancies, focus groups and polling. Trump had all that stuff too, he just wasn't listening to what they were telling him. His strategy of road-testing policies at rallies was unpredictable but highly effective. When a thought bubble got a loud response, he would take note and then run with it – hard. These policies were often picked up randomly from advisers or others. Of course, all politicians do this to a degree, but with Trump it was almost his whole strategy.

A great example of this came from *The New York Times* columnist Tom Friedman. Tom is a good friend of mine, and a great golfer. He shared with me the story of his own appearance on MSNBC's *Morning Joe* early in the campaign. Friedman had known Trump for years, and would disagree with him about almost everything, but one thing they agreed on was the need to control the US borders. So on *Morning Joe,* Friedman suggested that the United States build a wall on the border with Mexico to block unauthorised entrants. He did, however, qualify his call with the condition that the wall had to have a 'big door' to permit regulated traffic between the two countries.

Trump was a big consumer of morning television, and he rang Friedman straight after the program went to air. 'Tom, that was fantastic,' he enthused. 'It was great. I love the idea of the wall, and having a wall with Mexico.'

'Hang on,' said Tom. 'You've got to have the door, because you've got to have the people you want to come and go.'

'Yeah, yeah, yeah, the door too, but can I use the wall line?'

Tom obliged, saying Trump could use it, and reminding him to mention the door as well. Trump then hit the airwaves. In his first couple of interviews, he talked about a wall with a little, little door. Then, progressively, the little door just disappeared, and soon enough Trump never mentioned a door again.

I heard stories like that everywhere. Trump was just grabbing ideas from all over the place.

To be fair, most of Trump's policies were informed by his own beliefs. For example, Trump had never really liked America's long military engagements in the Middle East and Afghanistan. He might have initially supported them, but he was consistently opposed to open-ended military commitments. Other core policies that reflected Trump's public positions over the years included lower taxes, less regulation, protectionism and opposition to trade agreements, and an aversion to 'borrow and spend' government. Some, such as Trump's refusal to reduce welfare expenditure, were at odds with the Republican Party's own policy platform.

The more research we did, the more we began to understand what a Trump presidency might look like. The key thing about Trump is that there's nothing terribly complicated about him. This is especially the case if you understand where he's coming from and where he wants to go. Most Americans didn't want to do much research on him, because they'd already formed an opinion of him. They were all too familiar with the Trump story. There was no mystery.

Around the world, there wasn't much understanding of Trump. He was a known but little understood US personality. As a result, the Australian government and public service dismissed him as a serious candidate. In some cases, people took it upon themselves to publicly express their disbelief that America would ever elect someone like Donald Trump.

The public service in Australia is a really impressive institution, and overwhelmingly people in the public service I dealt with were incredibly professional, sharp and hardworking. However, I often found myself in a battle with them because of their own political views. They read and studied so much stuff in the media or academia that many felt they were experts in politics. After spending my adult life in politics, I can emphatically say that nobody is an expert in politics. The best politicians are the ones who listen, and the same largely goes for the public service. Public servants often thought politicians were predictable, and that their job was to predict outcomes. Some were already operating on the basis of the scenarios they predicted. And maybe six times out of ten they'd be right. Maybe even seven times out of ten. But when they were wrong, it would come at great cost.

The advantage I had was that I was on the ground in the US. That meant I was experiencing things first-hand, which gave me a greater understanding of events and meant my views of individuals were more nuanced. I realised that the internet and global media had diminished the value of the diplomatic cable: there was a temptation among some in Australia to believe they could get more from the internet – where most media ran an anti-Trump narrative – than from Australia's own diplomats. As ambassador, I was identifying things they couldn't see, and appreciating things to which others had closed their minds – such as the possibility of a Trump victory.

I didn't hold a consistent view throughout the campaign that Trump would win. At times I almost wrote him off. In contrast, Hillary Clinton was disciplined and predictable. However, in a two-horse race you'd be crazy to write off one of the contenders.

Some of my critics conflated my opinion that Trump could win with an endorsement of Trump. I was aghast at some of the things he said and did. But my job was to be professional – to apply my knowledge and instincts to the environment I was in – and, ultimately, to provide the Australian government with my considered opinion.

Donald Trump was one of the most authentic political candidates I had ever seen. For many, he was confronting, rude and naive. For others, he was a breath of fresh air. He was all too often forgiven for his outrageous behaviour and statements. How he survived the emergence of the *Access Hollywood* tape – in which he was caught on a hot mic some years earlier bragging about grabbing women 'by the pussy' – was extraordinary. He was gone, surely, everyone thought. Any other candidate for public office would have been finished. But he survived. Those who voted for him dismissed his comments as rude and sexist, but they knew he was authentic. And they were sick of polished political candidates.

This became his key selling point. Trump was what he was. The more he talked about 'fake news', the more he highlighted his own authenticity. Authenticity is the defining quality of politics in the twenty-first century. Donald Trump had it, whether you liked it or not. People didn't think Hillary Clinton seemed true to herself.

Trump also had the other great quality necessary in modern politics: character. That is not to say he was of *good* character, in the classic sense. But he was *a character*. To quote Mr Wolf from *Pulp Fiction*: 'Just because you are a character doesn't mean you have character.' Trump's authentic character really resonated with many in the electorate. He wasn't a Capitol Hill cardboard cut-out.

The stereotypical politician with a nice family and three kids has all too often been exposed as having massive character flaws. People have been so burnt by the hypocrisy of individual politicians that when a candidate says something that's authentic, even if it's something they get criticised for by the media, a lot of people think: 'This person is real. I'd rather watch someone real than someone that's fake.' More and more, people around the world are resigned to having the politicians they've been given, rather than the political leaders they really hope for. Character frailty is almost a virtue now, and ugly honesty is lauded.

The problem with Trump was that his comments and actions would regularly cross the line, demonstrating not just poor character but particularly offensive views towards women. The incidents were almost too numerous to mention. Apart from the *Access Hollywood* tapes, there were sexist and disgusting comments about the Fox News host Megyn Kelly, and about the *Morning Joe* host Mika Brzezinski. The latter were an absolute disgrace, and enough to disqualify him from elected office, in my view. I was appalled at the things he would tweet or say; I sometimes found myself screaming at the television: 'Don't say that!' But because Trump defined himself as anti-establishment and was 'authentic', he continued to get away with it. Not for the media or his opponents, of course, but in the eyes of many voters – including many women.

To this day, it still stuns me that in the 2016 presidential election, Trump won more votes from white women than Hillary Clinton. In fact, among non-college-educated white women Trump's final margin of support over Clinton was 23 per cent. Despite Black women and college-educated white women voting overwhelmingly for Clinton (by margins of 98 per cent and 26 per cent, respectively), the clear preference for Trump among middle-American women meant that a majority of all American women were willing to not only forgive him, but to vote for him.

Amid the madness of the campaign, and revelation after revelation about Trump's past, I would still get men and women whispering to me in Washington, DC that they were actually going to vote for Trump. This is a town that regularly votes around 94 per cent Democrat, so it reinforced my view that the election would be a lot closer than anyone was expecting.

* * *

Former UK chancellor of the exchequer George Osborne was in Washington on the night of 9 October 2016, when the second debate between Hillary Clinton and Donald Trump was held. George had recently lost his job following the resignation of Prime Minister David Cameron. Like so many others, George was a casualty of the Brexit vote.

Given my own recent experience of losing my job as treasurer, the pair of us formed an informal 'failed finance ministers' club'. I asked George to come around to White Oaks that night, where we'd crack open a bottle of Penfolds or two and watch the debate.

We were both initially sceptical about Trump's performance. He seemed nervous, and clearly wasn't going to match Hillary in debating skills. He was also coming across as physically intimidating towards her, which played into every poor perception of him. It was not a good start. That was until his reply to a question about whether he could be a US president for all people.

'What do you have to lose?' Trump told viewers.

George and I looked at each other. 'Oh my God,' I said, 'that's the cut-through line.'

Trump had put this line to African American voters at his rallies, and now he was using it on the entire electorate. 'I would be a president for all of the people, African Americans, the inner cities,' Trump told CNN's Anderson Cooper that night. 'Devastating what's happening to our inner cities. She's been talking about it for years. As usual, she talks about it, nothing happens. She doesn't get it done. Same with the Latino Americans, the Hispanic Americans. The same exact thing. They talk, they don't get it done. You go into the inner cities, and you see it's 45 per cent poverty. African Americans know.

'The education is a disaster. Jobs are essentially non-existent. I've been saying big speeches where I have 20,000 and 30,000 people. What do you have to lose? It can't get any worse. She's been talking about the inner cities for twenty-five years. Nothing's going to ever happen. Let me tell you. If she's president of the United States, nothing's going to happen.'

Trump was holding a mirror up to America so it could see its own failings. It was a country that many believed was heading in the wrong direction. Trump was clear that, with Hillary in charge, it would be more of the same. The alternative Trump offered was riskier – but Americans were at rock bottom, he argued, so why not give him a go?

Between George and me, we'd been members of parliament for a combined forty years. We'd been in election campaigns for our entire adult lives, and both of us had been through the egg beater. We instinctively knew that this was the cut-through line of the Trump campaign.

This was a pattern with Trump. For all the rubbish he churned out, every so often he would land with something that was really sharp and stuck with you. He may have stolen his best lines from others. Much like his policies, he would lift one-liners from here, there and everywhere. He didn't come up with 'Make America Great Again', for instance – Ronald Reagan used that in his 1980 campaign, Bill Clinton used it again in 1992, and, somewhat ironically, Bill even used it in a commercial for Hillary's 2008 Senate campaign in New York State. It didn't matter, though: Trump liked the line, and he knew how to sell it.

The 'MAGA' message – that America was in a ruinous decline – was not a fair reflection of what I saw in the country from day to day. It was overly negative about the nation's incredibly hardworking people and their potential. As I saw it, all the doom and gloom about America was simply not justified.

* * *

As an ambassador, I avoided the media, but in August 2016 I was asked to speak at a breakfast organised by the hugely influential Ohio Republican caucus during the Republican Convention.

This was quite an honour, because the convention to nominate the Republican candidate was being held in Cleveland, the state's largest city. The governor, John Kasich, after losing to Trump in the primary, refused to attend the nomination event being held in his own state, so all eyes were on his delegation.

That morning I shared the speaker's podium with influential Arkansas Senator Tom Cotton, Ohio Treasurer Josh Mandel, and none other than former Cleveland Browns quarterback Bernie Kosar. I had no doubt that the breakfast crowd would be more interested in what the former football star would be saying than the Australian ambassador, but I wanted to make it clear that I thought America was still great and could be an inspiration to the rest of the world, in particular to close allies like Australia.

'The relationship between Australia and the United States is deep, and it's enduring,' I told the breakfast. 'Australia is the only country on earth to have fought with the United States in every major battle since July 4, 1918. The one thing I want to say to you as an outsider looking in is America was great, America is great. You're the greatest economy on earth, the greatest democracy on earth, you've got the greatest military on earth – as of today, America is still great. That's why people want to come here. I want you to believe in yourselves as much as I and the rest of the world believe in you … Your democracy is vibrant, it's strong and it's a model because it does, at the end of the day, work.'

The only Australian media outlet that reported the speech was SBS, which headlined the story 'Donald Trump and Joe Hockey don't see eye to eye on America's greatness'. 'Mr Hockey, the former Australian treasurer and current ambassador to the US, shot down Mr Trump's most prominent election slogan in a room full of Republicans in Cleveland on Monday,' they reported.

In a sign of things to come, I also attacked Trump's anti-trade rhetoric, particularly given the importance of the TPP to Australia's trade agenda. I warned that the rest of the world would stop looking to the United States as a leader if it turned its back on these tenets of free trade and democracy.

'If you start to doubt whether freedom is right, or democracy is right, or enterprise is right, or free trade is right, or if you start to doubt that immigration is right, all of the sudden you will see the gravitational pull of the world turn elsewhere. And we don't want that – because your values and our values are not just shared in joint words, they are shared in spilt blood.'

The speech went down exceedingly well: I received a standing ovation from the four hundred people in the room. I was pleased it had gotten a good reception, as the tone and tenor of earlier speakers had been decidedly negative about America's future and place in the world – a fact that saddened me a little.

Allen County Ohio Republican Party chairman Keith Cheney told *The Delaware Gazette* (who did cover the talk): '[Hockey's] message to Americans was that we have a country with freedom. I think that resonated with the crowd without exception: "We love America just like you love America, and we're here to stand with you." That was great to hear from the ambassador.'

The *Columbus Dispatch* observed: 'One thing nobody mentioned: presumptive Republican nominee Donald Trump, who will accept his party's nomination on Thursday ... Australian Ambassador to the USA Joe Hockey and former Cleveland Brown Bernie Kosar, also, never mentioned Trump by name, talking broadly instead about the values of the United States.'

It was true that neither I nor any other speaker had mentioned Trump by name. There were a couple of reasons. One was that Ohio was John Kasich territory. Many delegates were Kasich loyalists, and all of Ohio's sixty-six votes would be going to the former congressman and Ohio governor after he had carried the state in the primary.

The other, more obvious reason I didn't go after Trump by name was that I was a diplomat. Given I had formed the view that Trump could win the coming election, it would have been particularly unwise to directly attack him – he might be the US president in a few months' time. Anyway, as I would find out, I would have plenty of chances to annoy Donald Trump and his team in the coming years.

* * *

Washington during the last weeks of the presidential election campaign was decidedly dull. Everyone was out of town campaigning. And if you believed the media and experienced strategists, it was simply a case of Hillary by how much.

Then came the bombshell: just eleven days out from the presidential election, FBI director James Comey notified Congress that he was reopening the investigation into Hillary Clinton's emails. The controversy concerned Clinton's use of a private email server while she was conducting government business as US secretary of state.

My experience told me you could not spend the crucial last week of a close election campaign defending yourself. In the final days before the ballot, you wanted to be fighting on the issues that could win you votes, not issues that might lose them. And Hillary Clinton was forced to spend the last week talking about her emails and the FBI – a sure sign for me that her campaign was in trouble.

The controversy also gave the appearance of truth to the horrible epithet Trump had given Hillary: that she was 'crooked'. When the FBI reopened its investigation just a few days out from the election, I felt the result was sealed: Trump would win the presidency.

To the incredulity of officials back in Canberra, I began preparing for the likelihood of a Trump victory. While many in business, politics and the media have since claimed they called a Trump win, I publicly stated my beliefs. What I said at the time was that all the fundamentals for an outsider victory were there.

Just six days out from the election, on 2 November 2016, I was asked to give a speech for the United States Studies Centre at my alma mater, the University of Sydney. I gave my speech the title 'The US–Australia Relationship Beyond November 8'. While I spoke about the chances of both candidates, I made the point that the concern Americans felt about their nation's future often served as the catalyst for a dramatic shift in leadership.

'Americans are engaged because they are very concerned about the direction of their country,' I said. 'Consistently, polling shows that at least 70 per cent of the American people think the United States is heading in the wrong direction. This is normally a game changer in politics. As we all hear regularly, politicians look to convert that concern, anger and fear into votes. In America it is even more complicated because getting people to vote is a complicated process. It is also comparatively hard to be involved in the process. So it is particularly useful to have a cause to stimulate participation at all levels. The Trump campaign has been exceedingly successful so far in galvanising participation without relying on a sophisticated team.'

The impact and importance of anti-establishment candidates in the election was also a point I highlighted. I was amazed that a candidate like Bernie Sanders, who had up to 30,000 people at his rallies, had been the runner-up in the Democratic race. 'With less than a week to go before election day in the US, it is increasingly apparent that there is no absolute certainty about the result,' I acknowledged. 'What is certain is that the anti-establishment fury that secured the Republican nomination for Trump – and catapulted him past sixteen other challengers – will not disappear after November 8. That same anti-establishment fury gave Bernie Sanders such a powerful voice during the Democratic primary.'

While repeating my message from the Republican convention speech that I didn't think the level of pessimism in the United States was justified, I made it clear that I thought Americans were out to punish the political establishment:

'Americans drawn from across the country; from Democrat-leaning states and Republican-leaning states; from predominantly rural areas; and highly urbanised cities ... All [are] united by the feeling that those in charge have betrayed them ... and they must be punished at all costs. This is the real fact of the 2016 election, and the context that Australia must absorb as a close and enduring ally of the United States.'

As *Guardian Australia* reported at the time, I told the audience that the election was 'too close to call'. I did make a veiled reference to DFAT's dissatisfaction with my positive engagement with the Trump campaign: 'The greatest fear of the Department of Foreign Affairs was that I wouldn't be diplomatic.'

* * *

On 8 November, the Australian embassy in Washington held its traditional election-night party. Before the polls had even closed there was a great deal of bonhomie among Democrats, who were ready to party. Given that this was a Democratic town, there was genuine excitement in the air at the prospect of a Clinton win.

A Clinton presidency would welcome a great era of Democratic control of the White House, which some supporters assumed would also bring control of both the House of Representatives and the Senate. Many around Washington (and many Americans generally) were also excited by the historic prospect of the first female president of the United States.

We'd cleared out the downstairs space and put in chairs, streamers and the obligatory large televisions, with all the cable channels represented – plus plenty of good Australian wine and beer. There was even a smattering of Australian celebrities (and good mates), including Eddie McGuire and Mick Molloy. As the night wore on, however, the celebratory tone went decidedly downhill. Much to the shock and horror of the vast majority of attendants, Donald Trump was winning. Faces were becoming sullen and pale with the realisation of what was happening.

As swing states like Florida were called for Trump, a distinct chill swept across the room. When 'blue wall' states like Michigan and Pennsylvania fell, most guests made for the exit. Only a small cohort of Trump supporters, Aussie neutrals or those too drunk to care remained.

Meanwhile, I was transfixed as to what was going on in the share market back home in Australia. I was confused as to why the ASX was plummeting on the increasing likelihood of a Trump win. Hadn't they read his policies? Tax cuts and less regulation weren't going to be bad for business. Futures trading in New York was also plummeting, and many people got badly burnt the next day and beyond as the share market surged to record highs.

I received a call from Prime Minister Turnbull that night. He was shocked. He thought there was still some doubt, as Hillary had not yet conceded, but I told him it was all over. During our regular phone calls in the preceding months, Malcolm had been interested in my view on Trump's chances. Although nervous about engagement, he was not entirely dismissive of my thoughts. The same could not be said for others.

As the night of 8 November went on, I felt justified. The final results filtered through in the early hours of the morning, and stunned broadcasters threw to Trump's victory speech. In recent weeks I had been fearful that my stint as federal treasurer and the events of my first year as ambassador might have affected my political antennae. Had I misread the situation we were dealing with in America? I'd been told I was ridiculous for even considering Trump as a viable candidate, but now my political instincts had proven correct and my actions had been justified.

I felt, for the first time since losing my career in politics, that I was back on track.

CHAPTER 5

DEALING WITH THE TRUMP ADMINISTRATION

Who's who in the zoo, 100 Years of Mateship and playing Trump at Trump

Most political leaders are narcissists. They not only need to be the centre of attention, they often think they are the smartest people in the room. They also have fantastic egos. They believe they can charm the leg off a billiard table with their quick wit and nice smile.

Enter Donald Trump. He caught everyone by surprise (including his own family) by winning the presidency. Suddenly the most powerful leader in the world was a mystery to all other political leaders. So what do they all decide to do? Get on a plane and show Donald Trump how smart and important they are.

What followed in the aftermath of Donald Trump's election win I can only describe as an unseemly scramble to be first in line to see the new president.

Politicians, business leaders and, of course, diplomats made a beeline for Trump and his team even before he was sworn in as president. Trump, who paid no attention to protocol, was happy to be courted by friends and enemies alike. When it came to foreign leaders, he felt that the fawning visits and phone calls legitimised him. The property developer from Queens whom everyone had scoffed at was now the big boss. It was his admission into the Establishment, against which he had railed all his life.

Domestically, a conga line of sycophants was lining up to seek Trump's favour – and an appointment to the new administration. Some, genuinely, wanted to serve their nation. Others were cravenly opportunistic. In the end, many were utterly humiliated. And Donald Trump made sure the media knew when they came to visit him at Trump Tower. Trump was happy to dangle a golden carrot in front of them, largely if not solely for the satisfaction it brought him to see them prostrate themselves before him. This was particularly obvious in the case of Mitt Romney.

Romney, a fellow Republican presidential candidate, and multimillionaire, was basically the 'anti-Trump' voice in the Republican Party. A Mormon, an institutional Republican, a former governor of Massachusetts and a renowned decent individual, Romney had previously described Trump as a 'fraud' and 'phony', with 'promises as worthless as a degree from Trump University'.

Having been told that Trump was considering him for the role of secretary of state, Romney would now be forced to kiss the ring (in a Catholic papal sense). And so he showed up at Jean-Georges restaurant in New York – only to find press photographers at the table, who had been permitted to take pictures of Trump and Romney at dinner. Trump's gleaming face and Romney's obvious embarrassment symbolised the almost medieval humiliations of the post-election period. Of course, Romney didn't get the job. Trump was never going to give it to him.

In diplomacy, the scramble was made doubly complicated by the protocols around engaging with a president-elect. The White House had strict rules about the level of contact countries could make with a president-elect while there was another president in the White House. But, as ever with Trump, you had to be thinking outside the box.

Much like with other protocols and conventions around elections, Trump didn't like the whole concept of a 'transition', because it seemed to be putting the cart before the horse. Plus,

he had little regard for his transition team, despite it being led
by his friend Chris Christie (who, immediately after the election,
was sacked from the role and replaced by Vice President–elect
Mike Pence).

It was important for me to broker a meeting between Trump
and Prime Minister Turnbull, but how was I to do that? All I
needed was the direct line of Trump's office in Trump Tower in
New York. So I went through my Rolodex calling in favours, and
there under 'G' – for 'Golf Mate' – was Greg Norman.

Greg is a mate of mine, and a patriot. Although he's lived in
the United States for many years now, he is still very much an
Australian first. I knew he was a friend of Trump's, too, so I called
him up and he was happy to give me Trump's cell phone number.
'This may work, mate,' he told me.

'If it does, you'll get a knighthood out of this,' I replied with
a laugh. On hanging up, I reflected that a knighthood would
probably have been more likely under Abbott than Turnbull.

I held the piece of paper with Trump's number up in front of
me with some trepidation. 'How many people in the world want
this number right now?' I mused. I wasn't certain it would still be
current, but I sent it on to Malcolm anyway.

Much to our mutual surprise, it worked. Straight through,
apparently. I felt like a national hero. That first conversation
between the pair was, in fact, one of the first the president-elect
had with any foreign leader. It was a warm and engaging phone
call in which they spoke about common interests, including their
life experiences with Kerry Packer. Trump also mentioned that he
wanted to visit Australia soon.

That first conversation between Trump and Turnbull also
got my mate Kim Darroch, the British ambassador to the United
States, in a degree of trouble. Only one other world leader had
reached out to Trump at that point, and it wasn't the UK's prime
minister, despite the supposedly 'special relationship' between the
two nations. The British Foreign Office was flabbergasted as to

how the Australian prime minister had secured a phone call with Trump ahead of their leader. Kim had to explain to Whitehall that it was a golfer who had facilitated the connection.

'You're being a pain in the arse to me, you know, Joe,' he told me in that particularly British way, simultaneously insulting and endearing.

* * *

There'd been no playbook for the Trump campaign, and nothing looked like changing now that he had won. All the normal transition procedures and traditions were thrown out the window. The men and women of his transition team were soon overwhelmed. Given that almost none of them had any experience in government, they were all learning on the go as a tidal wave of demands hit them.

In the weeks that followed Trump's election, there was an unexpected visit to Trump Tower in New York by Japanese Prime Minister Shinzo Abe, who clearly had a good sense of how the president-elect wanted to operate. Under diplomatic conventions, a meeting between the Japanese prime minister and the US president-elect was a major misstep. But Abe understood that when dealing with Trump, you needed to throw out the rule book.

Following the Abe meeting, Malcolm Turnbull told me he wanted to come and visit Trump as well. I said no – for two reasons. First, I didn't think the prime minister of Australia should appear to fawn over Donald Trump. Malcolm and I had spent considerable time discussing Trump's personality, and we agreed that he was the sort of person who would have little respect for sycophantic banter or fawning new friends. Second, the Obama administration was very upset about people going to visit Trump, and we were still working on a number of sensitive issues with them.

Moreover, after the Abe visit, the White House made it very clear that they would know if someone was planning to visit Trump: the manifest of the visiting leader's plane and their flight plan into US airspace would now be more closely monitored.

Ultimately, we agreed a better strategy was to make contact with Trump after his inauguration, when things had settled down a bit. We'd already arranged a call between Trump and Turnbull, so it wasn't necessary for us to elbow our way in the queue to meet the president-elect personally.

But that's not to say those crucial ten weeks between the election and the presidential inauguration were a quiet time at the Australian embassy. On the contrary, I would have several extraordinary encounters.

One was with the retired General Michael Flynn, who was being touted as Trump's pick for national security adviser. Despite strong advice from the Pentagon that Flynn was not an appropriate candidate for the role, it was clear that Trump was intent on appointing him. Flynn was a former US Army lieutenant-general and a former director of the Defense Intelligence Agency. In many ways he was well qualified. However, his connections to foreign powers, particularly Turkey and Russia, were of real concern. And if Australia knew about them, the whole of Washington probably did as well.

In 2014, Flynn had set up a consultancy called the Flynn Intel Group, and at the very time Trump was running for the presidency, Flynn was working for a Turkish company and a Turkish/Dutch businessman named Kamil Ekim Alptekin. It was all very close to Turkish President Recep Tayyip Erdoğan. Unbeknown to us, the work had netted Flynn over US$500,000, and he was eventually forced to register as a foreign agent.

All this was complicated by the fact that President Erdoğan had been involved in the opening of Trump Towers Istanbul a few years earlier. In December 2015, by which time his relationship with Erdoğan had deteriorated, Trump acknowledged that he had an issue in dealing with Turkey: 'I have a little conflict of interest, because I have a major, major building in Istanbul ... It's called Trump Towers. Two towers, instead of one. Not the usual one, it's two. And I've gotten to know Turkey very well.'

Four days out from the inauguration, I was invited to a breakfast Michael Flynn was hosting in Washington for about twenty people. It was clear by then that Flynn would be Trump's pick as national security adviser, so from my point of view it was a good opportunity to meet him. It had been made clear to us by the White House that no foreign ministers were welcome in the United States prior to the inauguration. Despite this, at the Flynn breakfast I was seated next to none other than the Turkish foreign minister, Mevlüt Çavuşoğlu.

Shocked, I turned around to the British ambassador. 'This is really inappropriate,' I whispered.

'Apparently, Flynn has some "special relationship" with the Turks,' replied Kim Darroch.

'It's really inappropriate,' I reiterated.

'Get used to it,' Kim said.

Flynn would be forced to resign just twenty-two days into the job, after the FBI found he had lied to Vice President Mike Pence about his contact with the Russians while working as a consultant. There were still three years and eleven months to go of the Trump presidency.

Amid the circus, I was getting requests from all over the place about access to Trump and tickets to the inauguration. Foreign Minister Julie Bishop wanted to attend, and I had to repeat that foreign ministers (along with heads of state, for that matter) weren't allowed to come. By tradition, only ambassadors could attend the inauguration.

Meanwhile, I was trying my best to make contact with Trump's picks for Cabinet secretaries, while still respecting the protocols prior to their Senate confirmation hearings. We had to make sure Australia wasn't left behind in key areas like defence and trade. And as luck would have it, I secured the first diplomatic contact by any nation with the incoming secretary of the Department of Defense, Jim Mattis.

I had flown over to San Francisco, to the Hoover Institution at Stanford University, to chat with George Schultz. He was one of these giants of politics and culture, part of an extraordinary generation of Americans. Schultz was ninety-seven years old at the time, but still incredibly sharp and full of intellectual curiosity. We had a robust conversation about a number of things, including climate change, and at the end of our talk he asked me: 'Have you met Jim Mattis?'

'No, never,' I replied.

'Well, he's in the office next door to me – why don't you come over and meet him?'

He didn't have to ask twice, and I followed the shuffling Schultz over to meet his neighbour.

Mattis was surprised and a little embarrassed, but polite and generous all the same. 'You know, people can't get to me until the inauguration, but you did!' He smiled.

'Here I am,' I replied with a grin and a shrug.

We had a nice conversation, and Mattis had plenty of good things to say about Australia. When I returned to Washington, I got on to Canberra and told them I'd had a good meeting with the incoming defense secretary.

'How'd you get to Mattis?' one puzzled senior bureaucrat asked.

Those in Canberra seemed confused by my unorthodox methods of engagement. But in the new Washington, DC, every angle needed to be played. US society is no more complicated than any other: it's about who you know and how you build and use your network.

* * *

After a British coronation (which apparently only occurs every seven decades!), a US presidential inauguration is perhaps the grandest global political event. And I had a (nearly) front-row seat.

Ahead of 20 January, a huge amphitheatre was constructed at the top of the Mall, in front of the Capitol Building. The swearing-in ceremony has taken place here since 1829. For security reasons, we were told to arrive four hours before the event. Meeting at the State Department early that morning, the world's diplomatic elite looked like arrivals for a school camp. We were issued with ponchos to protect us from the freezing rain and sleet that was falling that day, and then bussed over to the venue. Our spouses were whisked away from us; I later learnt that Melissa and other partners had seats immediately in front of the inauguration stage. After the presidential family and then members of Congress, foreign ambassadors have the next priority seating at the inauguration. It was very respectful.

Even with the meticulous planning, I had no idea how long we would be waiting outside. And in the middle of a Washington, DC winter, I can assure you we felt every one of those minutes in the freezing cold. Our tickets gave us no idea where we would be seated, although we did know it would be in order of precedence. Everything in formal Washington diplomacy happens in order of precedence – that is, according to how long you've been on the scene. It didn't matter if you were from France, Japan or indeed Australia, you had to line up in order of your seniority within the diplomatic corps of DC.

A fellow by the name of Hersey Kyota was the ambassador of the Republic of Palau, a tiny nation with a population of 18,000 – making it about the same size as Broken Hill. Hersey had held his position as his nation's ambassador in Washington since the second term of the Clinton administration. Having served in DC for several decades, Hersey Kyota of Palau was always first in line at any major function. He even had the formal title of Dean of the Diplomatic Corps for being the longest-serving ambassador in Washington. To my knowledge he's still in Washington; he'll soon qualify for his own DC monument.

As one of the newest ambassadors, I was down at the end of the queue with my friends from New Zealand and the United Kingdom. We were shown to our seats, which, consistent with our station in life, were right up the back. This actually turned out to be a blessing in disguise, as they afforded us an incredible view. We were seated in the top row of the amphitheatre, right next to where the president would be sworn in. We could look right down the Mall at the massive crowds.

We watched the dignitaries arrive in order too, most receiving raucous applause from the growing crowd: the new president, his family, leaders of the Senate and the House of Representatives, members of Congress, the Supreme Court judges and past presidents. I looked right down on George W. Bush and the stony-faced Clintons.

Another benefit of being at the back was that I could stand up through the entire ceremony to take it all in, as I knew it was a once-in-a-lifetime opportunity. First Mike Pence took his oath of office as vice president, and then Chief Justice John Roberts administered the oath to Donald Trump. Looking on, I was feeling almost overwhelmed by the atmosphere and emotion of the occasion – but then Trump began to address the crowd.

His speech was an absolute shocker. It was not the speech you'd ever give for a presidential inauguration. Inauguration addresses are special. The occasion has been the venue for so many great presidential speeches, with the eyes of the whole world upon them. For many, their lasting memory of President John F. Kennedy, for instance, was his 'ask not what your country can do for you' speech, made at his inauguration. Meanwhile, Trump began his presidency with a fearful and aggressive diatribe, which will likely be remembered as the 'American Carnage' address.

'Mothers and children trapped in poverty in our inner cities, rusted-out factories, scattered like tombstones across the landscape of our nation, an education system flush with cash, but which leaves our young and beautiful students deprived of all knowledge, and the crime, and the gangs, and the drugs that have stolen too many lives and robbed our country of so much unrealised potential. This

American carnage stops right here and stops right now,' Trump bellowed across the Mall that morning.

The speech undermined the goodwill of the moment and diminished the inauguration itself. While Trump was aiming to make legitimate points about US troubles, it was a speech that painted an almost entirely negative picture of American society.

'We've made other countries rich while the wealth, strength and confidence of our country has dissipated over the horizon. One by one, the factories shuddered and left our shores, with not even a thought about the millions and millions of American workers that were left behind. The wealth of our middle class has been ripped from their homes and then redistributed all across the world,' he said.

The speech gave very little hope for the nation, despite its claims to do so, and seemed to be fighting wars that Trump had already won. It was largely a continuation of a campaign address, rather than a speech from the new president. It was also big on 'borders' as a byword for the threats posed by illegal immigration. Reportedly it was co-written by Stephen Miller, the adviser I had met with during the election campaign.

I looked down at Hillary Clinton, who had sat graciously throughout the ceremony. She was beside George W. Bush, who at the end of the speech famously whispered in her ear: 'Well, that was some weird shit.'

Not for the first time, I had to agree with George W.

* * *

In the days leading up to the inauguration, Washington society had entered another stage of grief. The realisation that Donald Trump was about to be sworn in as president was beginning to hit home in a city that had voted overwhelmingly for Clinton.

After the election in November, I'd seen people in tears, even days later. Some just went into a form of hibernation, disbelieving what had happened. Ahead of the inauguration, I'd started to see real anger out on the streets. One morning, while out on my morning bike ride past the Trump International Hotel on Pennsylvania Avenue, I saw a fully grown man, in respectable attire, giving the finger to the hotel from the sidewalk. It was a gesture of anger and defiance. What possessed a seemingly sane individual to act like that? President Donald Trump, apparently.

While Trump's inauguration speech showed no grace or goodwill, I couldn't help but feel that the Washington establishment was acting in a similar way. There was very little self-examination or awareness as to what the recent election had revealed about America. Much like the man giving a building the finger, there was just a lot of anger, and seemingly a desire to make life as difficult as possible for the new administration. A combination of Trump's behaviour and Washington's resentment made the days around the inauguration very tense, and there was genuine concern about riots breaking out.

Ahead of their inauguration, there's a tradition that the incoming president stays at Blair House, a grand property located directly across the road from the White House. It's a big, old and rather rambling series of terraces with a rich history and very attentive staff. Trump, of course, wanted to break this tradition. He wanted to stay in his own hotel, a few blocks away. The Trump International Hotel was newly renovated (it used to serve as the main post office in DC). In the end, he gave in to tradition but was notoriously grumpy about the quality of the stay at Blair House on inauguration eve.

In fact, it was Lend Lease, the legendary Australian developer, that had been responsible for the massive renovation. Traditionally, of course, they have their own signs all over a building site, but as the Trump campaign gained momentum, the Lend Lease signage got smaller and smaller. Still, they met their deadline and did a great job: the hotel opened just a few weeks before the election.

Another tradition is that the president walks down Pennsylvania Avenue to the White House after the inauguration ceremony. As the years have progressed, the security risk has made this a nightmare for the Secret Service. On Inauguration Day, Trump predictably stopped the presidential motorcade outside his hotel and got out: he wanted to go the rest of the way on foot along Pennsylvania Avenue to his new home.

The symbolism seemed rich: Trump was walking past his own hotel as Trump the businessman and checking into the White House as President Trump. The entire world knew that Donald Trump was going to do things his own way.

* * *

Later that night, Melissa and I were lucky enough to attend several of the presidential balls that were taking place in DC. Although I use the term 'lucky' pretty generously, because these balls were not exactly the great occasions they're cracked up to be. They essentially serve as fundraisers, and while everyone is dressed up beautifully, the venues and huge crowds make them rather pedestrian events.

There were six or seven of these balls around town, and we were invited to two. The first was the diplomatic one, and the second one was a more chaotic affair at the Convention Center. There were so many people there you could hardly move. There wasn't much food and there wasn't much to drink. You were just shoved together cheek by jowl, in the hope of getting a glimpse of the new president.

The balls are run by party committees, and are a means either of raising money or of rewarding donors. It was close to midnight by the time Donald and Melania Trump turned up. Melania, of course, looked incredible, and she and Donald danced on stage for a short time, but that was it. The famous Inauguration Ball was a disappointment all round.

Some of the anger being expressed in the streets of the capital was understandable, given that what Trump called 'the Washington swamp' had been a focal point of his campaign, but at the end of the day, he was now the president of the United States. And Washington, DC, of all places, didn't seem to feel it had to accept that fact. Washington's revenge would come through leaks (although Trump's own people were pretty good at that too), but also through petty acts that aimed to demonstrate the city's disdain for Trump.

As one of my first ambassadorial functions following the election, I hosted the National Cathedral Choir fundraising committee to support the outstanding work of the National Cathedral. I was told that members of the choir were refusing to sing at the inauguration because Trump had won the election. The choir did end up performing, but for the first time ever some choristers were absent.

I was appalled. I found myself launching into a monologue with friends and family that the American people had spoken. Whether it was a majority or not, he had won under the US electoral system. While President Obama and Hillary Clinton promptly acknowledged Trump's victory, some Democrats in Congress tried to argue against Trump's legitimacy as president from day one. The highly respected civil rights activist Representative John Lewis, a Democrat from Georgia, said he did not regard Trump as a legitimate president, citing Russian interference in the campaign. A group of half-a-dozen Democrats in the House attempted to officially reject Trump's electoral college win during the joint sitting called to validate the presidential vote. Ironically, it was the then vice president, Joe Biden, who had to tell the group that their pursuit of Trump was futile: 'It is over,' he said during the joint sitting. And despite acknowledging Trump's win in January, Nancy Pelosi, the Democrat minority leader (today the Speaker of the House of Representatives), tweeted in May 2017: 'Our election was highjacked. There is no question. Congress has a duty to #protectourdemocracy and #followthefacts.'

Claims like these gave confidence to Clinton supporters who would never accept Trump as a legitimate president. Following the election, Clinton supporters in Democratic cities like Portland and Chicago were out on the streets chanting, 'Not my president!' and 'We reject the president-elect', while #notmypresident went viral on Twitter.

Other candidates before Trump had claimed the presidency when they hadn't won a majority of the popular vote. Clinton supporters might not have agreed with him, but he had been duly elected – and one day, it struck me, they might need to rely on the quality of their democratic institutions to remove him from office. Four years later, it came as no real surprise to me that Trump used false and more extreme claims to undermine the legitimacy of Joe Biden's election as president: it was both payback and a dangerous new tool he could wield against his opponents.

The day after Trump's inauguration, I witnessed another example of the deep divisions between the Washington establishment and Trump's administration. Once again it involved the National Cathedral.

The Episcopalian cathedral at the top of Mount Saint Alban is one of the great secrets of Washington, DC, and one of my favourite places in the city. Its construction began in the early twentieth century, but it wasn't really finished until after World War I. It relies entirely upon private funding, because under the US Constitution the state cannot give money to religious institutions. This was particularly problematic when the cathedral was damaged in an earthquake in 2011. It didn't have earthquake insurance because Washington is so rarely hit by them, but the Virginia earthquake that year was so powerful it damaged the spires and caused some of the Neo-Gothic gargoyles to fall off.

It has been a recent tradition for presidents to attend a mass at the National Cathedral the day after their inauguration. Although nominally an Episcopalian church, the Presidential Prayer Service it holds is an ecumenical one. Joe Biden, a Catholic, attended virtually the day after his inauguration in 2021, but the only other Catholic president, John F. Kennedy, had not. Both Kennedy and

Biden attended mass at St. Matthew's Cathedral the day after they were sworn in. I suppose Biden did two services after his inauguration in case God didn't notice that he had taken over the White House.

Although Donald Trump had worked hard to win the Christian vote, I only ever knew him to attend the National Cathedral twice in his four years in office. The first time was the day after his inauguration, and the second was for the funeral of George H.W. Bush in late 2018.

Almost every detail of the inauguration is controlled by the staff of the incoming president, and the National Cathedral's service is no different. But because of the deep distrust between the Washington institutions (including the Republican 'Never Trumpers') and the incoming Trump administration, there was basically nobody in the new team who had any experience in running large government events. Paranoia was running high, and Trump's staff feared that a bunch of Democratic Trump haters would turn up to the cathedral and disrupt the service.

With such dysfunction in the organising committee, the result was a disaster. Half the cathedral was empty. People who wanted to go couldn't get in because there was no system for distributing tickets. It was a terrible look. At the last moment, people out on the street were shuffled inside to fill some of the pews, but it was all too late. The Secret Service went nuts because people were being invited in off the street to boost numbers, and were a horrible distraction for the rest of the congregation. It was an early indication of what the days ahead would be like, and the media didn't miss the message.

One of the more absurd debates that sucked up valuable air from the sails of the new administration was the debate about the size of the crowd at the inauguration. The obsessive Washington media took Trump's bait and tried to make it a fact-checking template. Looking down the Mall on the morning of the inauguration, I saw a lot of people. There's no doubt there were plenty more people in attendance at Obama's inauguration – but focusing the debate in this way missed the point.

The main catchment for Obama's inauguration included the 6.25 million people living in the greater Washington, DC area, more than nine in ten of whom always vote Democrat. Add in the populations of nearby Baltimore, Philadelphia and New York City, and toss in some Obama magic, and you rightly have massive crowds to welcome America's first Black president to office. Trump's electoral support came from different areas of the United States, all of them further away. For his inauguration, families travelled massive distances to be there. In and around Washington, DC you could see number plates from Ohio, Iowa, Arkansas and as far away as Montana and Louisiana.

So it was a very different America that attended Trump's inauguration, but this reflected the brilliance of democracy: the people had freedom to travel, and freedom to support without fear of retribution or humiliation. Whatever the respective sizes, the crowd at each inauguration viewed the event as a moment of hope for a better America.

Trump should have buried his ego and made this point. His voters had stood up against the establishment, they had stood up against sanctimonious lectures about how they should live their lives from presidents and journalists to late-night talk-show hosts. Trump's voters had been shouted at for years about their plight in life and their religious values. They were belittled if they were against gay marriage or abortion. They were humiliated if they worked in a coalmine in Virginia or in another industry not considered fashionable in climate change politics. They felt like irrelevant spectators in their own community.

When Trump was elected, all that came to the fore. These were the people who had quietly voted for Trump, and they saw this as the moment when they would reclaim their destiny.

Trump let that point get away from him. He made the debate about the inauguration crowd an issue about him, rather than a considered reflection on what the differences between the crowds said about America. Washington was never going to come out to support Trump.

Making matters worse for Trump, a Women's March took place the day after the inauguration, and then it really did feel like there were a million women in the Mall, if not more. They were essentially anti-Trump, and all of Washington sure turned out to signal their protest against the new president.

* * *

If my first major task following the swearing-in of Trump was to line up another phone call with Prime Minister Turnbull, my second was to repair the damage of that disastrous call after it leaked to *The Washington Post* and was published on 2 February, just thirteen days after the inauguration.

To our benefit, *The New York Times* published the results of a poll the following day that had asked over 7000 Americans, a huge sample, which nation they viewed as the closest ally of the United States. Democrat voters had ranked Australia as number four, beaten by Britain, Canada and France. But among Republican voters Australia was number one. Never waste a good poll, I say.

Considering both the data from the poll and the deep-seated anger about the phone call, I could see a compelling case for the re-establishment of a congressional grouping known as the Friends of Australia Caucus. The idea had been germinating in my head for a while. The original caucus had been created by an earlier Australian ambassador, Michael Thawley, back in the early 2000s to support the passage of the Australia–United States Free Trade Agreement through Congress. Regrettably, the caucus had since been disbanded – and I felt that now was the time to bring it back.

With the presidential campaign complete, and concern about where the Australia–United States alliance was heading, we decided to put 'Operation Aussie Caucus' into action. We invited members of the House and the Senate from both parties to join. The caucus was headed by a Republican and a Democrat from both houses. In the Senate, there was the Democrat Dick Durbin from Chicago and the Republican Roy Blunt from Missouri, and in the House Joe Courtney, a Democrat, and Mike Gallagher, a Republican.

While the leadership was a blokey line-up, it was much easier to get people involved who'd had some links with Australia over the years. Usually, military veterans who had fought alongside Australians were the first to respond, but the caucus also included members of congress who had visited our country or who had Aussie relatives or friends.

The Friends of Australia Congressional Caucus turned out to be a massive success. Americans have a great phrase: 'I've got your back.' As it has turned out, in the stormy weather of Washington, DC, congressmen and congresswomen and senators in the caucus have had our back. The benefit is mutual, and the partnership is meaningful. For example, during a trip by Foreign Affairs Minister Marise Payne and Defence Minister Linda Reynolds to Washington, DC in 2020, at the height of the COVID-19 pandemic, only one event was held: that was on Capitol Hill and it was with the Friends of Australia Congressional Caucus.

The American Australian Association was another crucial body of support around this time, and showed the importance of having a representative body for the Australian diaspora. It was founded by Sir Keith Murdoch in New York in 1948. The AAA had initiated commemorations for the seventy-fifth anniversary of the Battle of the Coral Sea, to be held aboard the retired aircraft carrier USS *Intrepid*, which had been turned into a fantastic museum on New York's Hudson River.

John Berry, the chief executive of the AAA, was a highly regarded ambassador to Australia under the Obama administration (succeeding the equally impressive Jeffrey Bleich). On Berry's return to America, the AAA wisely snapped him up, and he'd given the organisation a large dose of new energy. Berry asked me whether I thought I could get both President Trump and Prime

Minister Turnbull to New York for the Battle of the Coral Sea commemoration on 5 May 2017. I was aghast. I've never been afraid to be bold and ambitious, but I also wanted to be realistic. But after reflecting on the suggestion for a few days, I hatched an unlikely plan that would bring them together in New York.

To be honest, I had serious doubts that Turnbull would risk coming if there was any chance he would once again be embarrassed by Trump. He would be anxious about it right up until they met and shook hands. I also didn't like our chances of convincing Trump's team to do it. Trump was running a big and bold agenda. He was all in on Washington politics, and while he would go to Mar-a-Lago, I wasn't sure he would come to the heavily Democratic New York City for the first time as president to meet a world leader with whom he'd had an ugly and public fight over the phone. And I knew that New Yorkers hate presidents coming into Manhattan, even at the best of times. The city goes into gridlock as roads are shut down for the presidential motorcade.

Despite all the issues, I had nothing else, so I had to give John Berry's idea a go.

First I called Reince Preibus, the president's chief of staff. I put it to him that this would be the perfect way for us to rebuild the relationship, making every argument I could think of. 'It'll be two leaders coming together to commemorate a major event that profoundly affected both our countries,' I said. 'Reince, it'll be broadcast live on Fox News. I'll get every billionaire I can find to laud the president's economic agenda. There'll be so much military brass in the room, every brass monkey in America will be jealous.' And so on.

'Let me think about it,' Reince said. 'But I have to warn you, it doesn't look good. For starters, the president hasn't gone back to New York since the inauguration. Also, the president doesn't wear dinner suits, and this is a black-tie event. Not to mention getting him in there is a logistical nightmare. And to top it all off, we're negotiating the end of Obamacare in the House that week.'

I hung up the phone feeling rather deflated, but I remained determined to make it happen. As I'd learnt while climbing both Mount Kilimanjaro (which stands almost 6000 metres high) and crossing the Kokoda Trail in Papua New Guinea (almost 100 kilometres through dense jungle), the only way to start is by putting one foot in front of the other. And my first step here was dealing with the predictable anxiety coming from Canberra about the prime minister visiting New York.

Malcolm Turnbull was understandably nervous about being set up and stood up. As a result, we had regular conversations – daily conversations, at one point – about the logistics and politics of the trip. I kept reassuring him it would be a good idea, but it was proving harder to get him to come to New York than to convince the president himself.

A week had passed, and time was running out. I was starting to give up hope. Then a surprise call came through from Priebus. 'The president's coming!' he said.

'I have your word?' I replied, ever cautious.

'Absolutely,' he replied.

I rang John Berry, who was so excited that I could almost hear him crying with joy. What I didn't tell him was that I still had not locked in Malcolm Turnbull.

When I called the prime minister, he was pumped, but clearly I was on the hook. 'Trump won't embarrass me, will he?' he asked.

'No, Prime Minister,' I assured him.

'Is that a guarantee?'

'Sure,' I said. 'I give you that guarantee.' In truth, I was writing a cheque without knowing if I had the money in the bank, but I was uneasy and didn't want to be the fall guy if things went wrong.

After many assurances, it was, finally, game on.

The USS *Intrepid* event needed to be a full audio and video educational experience for the president of the United States. Trump learns in a visual manner, so AV material was a genuinely important tool for him. We were not assuming any knowledge about Australia or the United States–Australia relationship. I contacted the Murdochs and asked if Rupert would speak. Fortunately, he accepted the invitation – we made sure we had the right date this time – while Fox News agreed to broadcast the speeches.

It turned out to be an extraordinary night. Greg Norman, the man who had given me Trump's number the day after he was elected, and probably Trump's favourite Australian, again played a crucial role, delivering a great speech. Admiral Harry Harris, the outstanding commander of the US military for all the Pacific, gave a tribute to fallen soldiers. He subsequently gave what was the speech of the night, in which he spoke with great emotion and won a spontaneous standing ovation.

One of Australia's most successful businessmen, Anthony Pratt of Visy and Pratt Industries in the United States, stood up and offered to build a new factory in the United States. Pratt was a big Donald Trump fan, having immediately understood what the president's low-taxation, high-growth and deregulation agenda offered a company like his.

What the rest of the world didn't know was that right up until late that afternoon, the president almost didn't make it aboard, as he was still grappling with the House of Representatives over the repeal of Obamacare. The anxiety in the Turnbull camp was almost intolerable. Following the disaster of the leaked phone call, I didn't want to start imagining the implications of a Trump no-show.

That afternoon Turnbull and I, with a large entourage, visited the headquarters of the New York Police Department. The police commissioner was giving us a briefing about the new technology they were using to catch bad guys around the world, and Malcolm was asking me what seemed like every ten minutes whether we had heard from the White House.

When Trump did finally arrive and met Turnbull aboard USS *Intrepid*, it was like the two men were the best of friends.

We were only a few kilometres from Broadway and I was immensely proud of my two lead actors. The meeting delivered the rapprochement we had all hoped for – and the media loved it. The reporting was positive, not just in the Aussie media and on Fox News, but also in *The New York Times*, whose story that night bore the headline 'Despite Earlier Spat, Smooth Sailing Aboard *Intrepid* for Trump and Turnbull'.

'President Trump and Prime Minister Malcolm Turnbull of Australia on Thursday played down the testy phone exchange that began their working relationship as they met face to face aboard the aircraft carrier *Intrepid* in Manhattan,' it read. '"We get along great. We have a fantastic relationship, I love Australia, I always have," Mr. Trump told reporters who witnessed a portion of the meeting between the two wealthy, iconoclastic, deal-making politicians in a room near the ship's main dining area.'

Turnbull also loved the fact that parallels were being drawn between the two men in terms of their individual wealth (although Trump, as ever, knew he was winning). It was, frankly, a big benefit for Turnbull that he, too, was a wealthy man as, rightly or wrongly, Trump respected him for it.

It was obvious the president himself was anxious about the event. He knew it really mattered. That poll in *The New York Times* had had an impact on him, because it showed him that those in his base loved Australia. There's no doubt that the angry response of John McCain and other Republicans to the leaked Turnbull phone call had had an impact on him as well.

People in the inner circle of the administration, like Secretary of Defense Jim Mattis and Treasury Secretary Steven Mnuchin, were aware of the massive outpouring of good feeling towards Australia from grassroots Americans.

The TV host and former Republican congressman Joe Scarborough put it well on his influential MSNBC morning show, *Morning Joe*: 'Of all the countries to pick a fight with, why would you pick one with Australia? You know, of all the countries to have an argument with … Australia?'

I think Trump was stunned by this reaction, and he saw the meeting with Turnbull on USS *Intrepid* as an opportunity to start over. Trump is a proud man (to say the very least), but he's also pragmatic. He'll muscle up on you, but then he has the capacity to be your best friend. He's a trader. Malcolm Turnbull is a trader as well. In some ways they're similar characters – but only in some ways.

The USS *Intrepid* event was the first great success of my time as ambassador. From a furious phone call to a rapprochement aboard a World War II aircraft carrier, it was quite a ride. I was able to hope we had secured peace in our time.

* * *

The role of a diplomat in an uncertain world is to provide clarity for your host nation about your country's values and policies. But it's also invaluable if you can use your platform to hold up a mirror to your own country about how we are perceived around the world.

I looked at the British and their constant reference to the 'special relationship' between the United States and the United Kingdom. The Brits always referred to it – in press releases, at joint press conferences, whenever there was a significant bilateral engagement with the United States. The 'special relationship' set the Brits apart. They can thank Winston Churchill for the definition (who was, it's often forgotten, half-American himself). I also reflected on how Barack Obama had said on numerous occasions that 'we have no greater friend than country X'. I'm sure he meant it at the time, but he did use the phrase many times with a lot of different countries. It became an ongoing joke among humourless diplomats.

To be heard in Washington – particularly with Donald Trump – I knew we needed a cut-through narrative. What we came up with was a celebration of Australia's and the United States' shared military history, a campaign we called '100 Years of Mateship'.

When I arrived in the United States as ambassador, I studied the shared military history of our nations. It was not only interesting, but particularly relevant in the context of the diplomatic relationship, as about half the staff at our embassy were military personnel or attachés.

Australia and the United States first fought together in the Battle of Hamel, on the Western Front in France, on 4 July 1918. The fact that the battle occurred on the United States' Independence Day was a good story in itself. But as I dug deeper, it got better.

By 1918, Australia was exhausted from the Great War. Our casualty rates were high and the Western Front was more of a bloodbath for us than the more familiar Dardanelles disaster. Lieutenant General John Monash was leading an exhausted bunch, and in May 1918 was ordered to launch another push against the Germans – this time at the small town in northern France called Le Hamel. Monash pointed out that his troops were already stretched as a result of the recent German reinforcements coming back from the Russian front line, after an armistice was signed between the newly-formed Soviet government and the Austro-Hungarian Empire in December 1917. That had freed up a million German troops to come to the Western Front. Monash needed more soldiers.

Enter Uncle Sam and his 'doughboys', supposedly named after the Revolutionary War Continental Army soldiers, who had a clay stripe in their uniforms. When it rained, their clothes got soggy like dough. (Go figure!) So twenty companies of US troops started training with their Aussie brothers for the Monash-led assault on Le Hamel. They were going to deploy a combination of air support and infantry, with tactics devised by Monash. In particular, for this battle they chose to attack Hamel with the tanks in front of the troops, leading the charge, rather than having infantry soldiers take the first line of fire to protect the tanks. (This seems bloody obvious, but you can imagine the arguments Monash had with British High Command.)

The Americans and Aussies formed a real bond over that short training period. They became mates and buddies. They had a shared history as new migrant nations. The troops were also united in their disgust at the British; the Germans came next.

When the formidable US General John Pershing heard that his troops were about to go into their first major battle in World War I under a foreign commander, he fumed. 'Americans only fight under American commanders,' he reportedly said, before ordering the withdrawal of his soldiers. The US troops, many from Illinois, rebelled. They offered to swap their uniforms for Aussie infantry gear. They were not going to abandon their newfound 'mates' at the eleventh hour. Pershing relented, and allowed ten companies to stay. Out of respect for the US contribution, Monash delayed the attack until 4 July.

The battle lasted ninety-three minutes, just three minutes longer than Monash had predicted. Around 1400 of the 7000-strong attacking force were killed or injured. But their victory was instrumental in turning the war, and the tactics Monash deployed led to further wins, and ultimately to victory a few months later. American soldiers were recognised with British awards for their courage under fire. It was mateship at work.

From that day forth, Australia is the only country in the world to fight side by side with the United States in every major conflict. (The United Kingdom took a leave pass for Vietnam, and the Kiwis avoided direct conflict in Iraq, serving only in non-combat roles.) Americans value loyalty and sacrifice. It is the glue that binds their country together. One flag, defending freedom and protecting democracy. These are the things that make the nation tick.

This story was the key for my decoding of America. It was the narrative that Australia needed to explain our relationship. In America, everyone has a story. American culture is built on stories, whether fact or fiction, from Broadway to Hollywood and everywhere in between and beyond.

Donald Trump, of course, had little regard for national history. If it didn't involve him, then it almost didn't exist. All that counted was: 'What have you done for me lately?' Even with long-term allies like Canada, Trump would invoke the incorrect suggestion that the Canadians had burnt down the White House. (It was actually the Brits, and it happened during the War of 1812.) He viewed Germany and Japan as nations America had to defeat in World War II, and then had to spend billions of dollars on after the war.

Trump liked strong and powerful leaders. Recep Tayyip Erdoğan (Turkey), Vladimir Putin (Russia), Jair Bolsonaro (Brazil) and Rodrigo Duterte (Philippines) were favourites. Kim Jong-un of North Korea won a special mention. Even President Xi Jinping of China was immune to direct criticism. Trump liked the way he'd made himself president for life. Trump had little knowledge of Australian politicians, but he knew Rupert Murdoch ('I love Rupert') and Greg Norman ('one of the greats'). He also knew Kerry Packer ('big gambler') and Anthony Pratt ('he is really rich'). After that it tapered off. Later, our greatest female golfer, Jan Stephenson, told me that a then single Donald Trump chased her from tournament to tournament in an attempt to win her heart. The president never mentioned that Aussie link.

But there was no new narrative around Australia that excited Donald Trump at the time he won the presidency, and this was a problem. Compounding this was that the first thing we were asking of the new president was to stick to a controversial refugee deal agreed by his predecessor. That not only ran counter to his election promises, it was also something he just didn't want to do. He'd just become the most powerful person in the world and now he was being asked to swallow a bitter pill. So we had to find a way to justify to Trump why he should do something unpleasant.

Trump is a very visual person. His language always focuses on size, scale and appearance. Something big is 'huge' or 'great'.

'Beautiful' is one of his most favoured adjectives. He often references someone's 'good looks' (perhaps a throwback to his beauty pageant days). So too the worst things he could say about someone: think of 'little' Marco Rubio, or the way he dismissed allegations that he assaulted certain women by referring to their looks.

So I decided to do everything I could to communicate with Trump through imagery. The '100 Years of Mateship' campaign focused on America's image of itself. Patriotism has always been a powerful unifying tool in the United States, and even more so since the horrors of 9/11. My own early experiences confirmed this. I felt it when Lady Gaga was singing the National Anthem at Super Bowl 50. At every Washington Capitals ice hockey game, the only standing ovation comes when a veteran is recognised in the crowd and thanked for their service. In almost every corner of American life, it's considered honourable to serve.

As I saw it, we could use the imagery of diggers and doughboys sharing a smoke in the trenches of World War I to convey the message that Australia had America's back. If we did this, I felt Trump and much of America would see Australia in a new light. We would move beyond being simply 'great people' and a safe place to visit; we would become family.

The '100 Years of Mateship' campaign was integrated across all our public and media relations, the embassy's branding and figured in almost every official event that year – and indeed after. It worked as a strong basis for much of the contact with the Trump administration as well as Congress, and it was effective across the political divide.

Leaning on the narrative of 'mateship' may sound hokey to some, but it struck a chord in Washington. And it was not just about appealing to the Trump administration. It was an important foundation for the formation of the bilateral Friends of Australia Caucus. In fact, the '100 Years of Mateship' campaign became the most successful touchstone for the US–Australian relationship in years.

* * *

In those first few months following the inauguration, I had begun to understand how the White House really operated. It wasn't pretty.

The first time I walked into Donald Trump's West Wing, it seemed like conservative politics' version of the bar scene from *Star Wars*. Everyone with a political grievance seemed to have a key to the door. I saw police officers from Illinois, a sheriff from the Deep South, pastors, businesspeople, nurses and sportspeople. They were standing in corridors and leaning against doors – the place was like an open community forum. There was no discipline, little security and certainly no formality.

Was that a good thing? Not in a White House that lacked leadership and was leaking like a sieve. Trump ran the West Wing like it was the set of *The Apprentice*, where everyone around him was competing for his attention and approval.

Seemingly everyone had the title of 'senior adviser to the president', but it was impossible to tell who actually had the ear of the president that particular week. It was also virtually impossible to rely on somebody being in a senior role for more than six months. If you hadn't established a relationship with that person prior to their being appointed, chances were that once they arrived in the White House, they wouldn't be in the job long enough for you to do so.

The Trump administration was also unusual in that some of the people you dealt with weren't those with the biggest titles. While grandiose titles were ubiquitous, some people who at first glance were not very senior would suddenly become influential because Trump took a liking to them. There was a range of individuals who weren't widely known as being at the apex of Trump's White House, but who were nonetheless influential – and particularly helpful to Australia.

Robert O'Brien was an early contact. He is a really fine person. Robert was a Californian lawyer who had one of the more interesting titles in the White House: Special Presidential Envoy for Hostage Affairs. He worked hard to help get Australians out of captivity around the world. The relationship with O'Brien continued to prove fruitful when he was appointed national security adviser in 2019, after Trump sacked John Bolton.

We had also established a good relationship with O'Brien's new deputy, Matthew Pottinger. Matt was very influential as the Asia director of the National Security Council, and was one of the few who weren't self-promoters. He was a genuine asset to the office, and to Australia.

One of the other more memorable influencers in Trump's solar system with whom we built a relationship was Cliff Sims. He is an interesting guy. He had appeared on the Trump campaign's radar through his Alabama-based conservative news website, *Yellowhammer News*. He'd made his name bringing down the god-fearing Republican Alabama governor Robert Bentley after Sims got hold of a leaked audio recording of a conversation between the governor and his long-time lover.

His title was something like Special Assistant to the President for Strategic Communication, but I don't think he was even in the White House communications team. Trump loved him because he was a bit of a hustler. But his fate was similar to all others who were close to Trump (apart from his family, of course). Cliff was sacked and then wrote a hilarious, and somewhat disturbing, insider's book about the White House, *Team of Vipers*.

Trump was furious and went out on Twitter attacking Cliff. 'A low level staffer that I hardly knew named Cliff Sims wrote yet another boring book based on made up stories and fiction,' the president tweeted in January 2019. 'He pretended to be an insider when in fact he was nothing more than a gofer. He signed a non-disclosure agreement. He is a mess!'

Cliff hit back, filing a lawsuit against Trump, claiming he never signed a non-disclosure agreement, and one couldn't be enforced even if he had. Hilariously, Trump went on to read the book, realised it painted him in a pretty good light, all lawsuits were dropped and Sims ended up working in the administration again! His last job was senior adviser to the director of national intelligence. And this guy had no experience in national security. It was a great example of how you could have nine lives in the Trump administration.

Cliff introduced me to a friend named Andrew Surabian. The two operated like a kind of tag team. Surabian's title was 'Adviser and Spokesman for Donald Trump Jnr'. Setting aside the oddity of a child of the president having a designated adviser, Surabian had some useful insights into how the president and those around him operated. As far as I know, Surabian is still working for Donald Trump Junior, helping him with his own political ambitions.

Another interesting personality was Marc Short, who served as director of legislative affairs in the White House but left in 2018. He went on to work in public relations, but by the time we met up for lunch he was back in favour as Vice President Pence's chief of staff. This was the world we were living in.

Of course, we also had regular dealings with the more recognisable figures of the Trump administration. After my first meeting with Stephen Miller, I would never have guessed that he would go on to become one of the great influencers and survivors of the administration. Miller may have been an unnerving character for many, and he certainly was obsessed with immigration, but he does have a good intellect. I always worked well with him despite our differences.

I met Reince Priebus early in my time in Washington. We met at a Google party associated with the White House Correspondents' Dinner. Reince was then the Republican National Committee's chairman, and of course became Trump's first chief of staff. But he lasted only six months in the job. It was a classic example of the way Trump burnt through these senior and often very talented individuals.

The first time I met Steve Bannon was, as I've related, the day I went to the White House after the Turnbull/Trump call was leaked. Bannon was unswerving in his hatred of the immigration deal we'd struck with Obama, but from then on I found him charming and engaging. Steve Bannon was good company. The best term I can think of to describe him is 'rascal'. He had very strong fixed views, which have been well documented, but he possessed a quirky charm, which I think helped him prosecute his ideas successfully. Well, at least for the seven months he survived in the White House.

Bannon was very smart, had convictions about issues and knew how to push them. There was not a lot of ambiguity about where he stood on anything. But he was also a real pragmatist: he knew when he was going to lose on an issue, and knew how to accept it. He was represented as an ogre at times, the epitome of far-right politics, but in my dealings with this scraggly-haired ex-sailor who made millions from investing in *Seinfeld*, I could never quite buy the 'Prince of Darkness' routine, which he seemed to perpetuate as much as anyone. I'm not entirely sure he believed everything that he said, either. I suppose only he can ever know.

Someone I made contact with early on in my time in Washington, and who I still regard as a really close mate, is another of Trump's former chiefs of staff, Mick Mulvaney. He had previously been a Republican congressman, and one of the founders of the Tea Party. When he was appointed as the director of the Office of Management and Budget in the White House, I went to see him, and I brought a copy of my speech 'The End of the Age of Entitlement'. In effect, Mick was the president's minister for finance, controlling and influencing where money was spent.

Despite the fact he was the second longest–serving of any of Trump's chiefs of staff (one year and eighty-nine days), Mick was only ever 'acting' in the role. His longevity was a testament to the job he did. Trump's appointment of four chiefs of staff during his term was another example of the way he treated people in his

White House (although it should be noted that Barack Obama also burnt through four chiefs of staff in his first term).

Mick is a really good guy. He has strong views around faith, loyalty and service, but he also has that Irish mischievousness and love of a chat that endears him to others. And it was through Mick that I first played golf with Donald Trump.

* * *

One of the benefits of working for the Trump White House was that Mick Mulvaney could play golf at Trump National in Potomac Falls, Virginia – or indeed at any Trump golf course. I was playing a fair bit of golf by this time, even if my game was ... let's say 'inconsistent'. Others might go so far as to call it 'erratic'. Despite my less than stellar golf skills, Mick rang me one week in early April 2018 and invited me to join him that Sunday for a round of golf. 'I'll ask Bret Baier from Fox News, and we'll play at Trump,' he said.

Bret was also a good mate, and I readily accepted. I suspected something interesting was happening, but I couldn't put my finger on it. To this day, Mick says it was just a coincidence, but I had a feeling we would have a special guest as our fourth.

I texted Malcolm Turnbull: 'I think I might be playing golf with Donald Trump on Sunday.'

'Do you think that's a good idea?' he wrote back.

'Well, I am,' I texted, and left it at that.

Mick picked me up in his bulletproof Secret Service black SUV (they are actually very uncomfortable). On our way there, the phone rang.

It was the president. He was apparently just calling around looking for a game. 'Mick, I'm playing with you – see you up there,' President Trump told Mulvaney.

'Okay, see you then, Mr President.'

The prospect of playing with President Trump at Trump National was more than enough to make me the most nervous I'd been on a golf course for a while.

'Mick, you know I play off twenty-four, don't you?' I said, mindful that, in golf, the higher your handicap, the more forgiving the other players might be.

'I know, you're a hopeless golfer, Joe,' replied Mick. 'Don't tell the president, and let's get to the practice range as soon as we can.'

Not long after we started warming up, Trump arrived, accompanied by forty or fifty security staff in golf carts. I was told there were even snipers stationed around the course. This remarkable display of force did nothing to soothe my nerves.

We arrived at the first tee, and there was the president.

'So, Joe, what do you play off?' President Trump asked me.

'These days twenty-eight, Mr President,' I said, exaggerating my handicap now, in the hope I wouldn't be viewed as too hopeless.

'Well, I'm only giving you eighteen,' Trump snapped.

'It's not a negotiation, Mr President, I really do play off twenty-eight,' I said. I was trying my best to not get pushed around early, to avoid making a complete fool of myself.

'It's my course, and I'm giving you a handicap of eighteen,' he replied sternly. 'Oh, and you team up with Mick. I will team up with Bret.'

Negotiation over.

Trump National sits on the banks of the famous Potomac River. It's what is known as a links course: it has no trees and lots of bunkers, and on a very cold, windy, wet Sunday in April it was as intimidating as hell.

As has been well chronicled, Trump is both an enthusiastic and genuinely good golfer, with a handicap of twelve or thirteen. I've golfed with him a few times and he always played in the spirit of the game, albeit fiercely competitively.

It's very stressful playing golf with the president of the United States. When he got going, Trump really flew along the course, and of course all the other carts with the Secret Service members would flock after him. That doesn't give you a lot of fairway to play with.

At one point I was playing my second shot, hitting to the green, but I looked up to see that Trump had already parked his cart on the manicured putting green – unusual behaviour in itself – and he was lining up his ball to putt.

'Oi! You know I have to hit my ball?' I yelled to the president at the top of my voice.

'Hit it here. C'mon, Joe, hit it here!' Trump yelled back, waving me on from the green.

I stood there and pondered my situation. Could I really hit my ball right at the president of the United States? I wasn't sure if he was serious. How many people in the world would want to be in my position right now, I wondered.

'Hit it, Joe, hit it!' he continued, gesticulating on the green.

So I pulled out my eight iron to play the shot, which I judged was around 150 metres.

All of a sudden, my thoughts were interrupted by a deep voice behind me: 'Do not hit the president of the United States, sir.'

I looked around to see a Secret Service agent in a suit and sunglasses standing behind me with a club in his hand.

'But he's on the green – he's waving me on,' I said. Meanwhile, Trump was still yelling in the background.

'You can hit it to the right, you can hit to the left, you can hit it over his head. But you're not hitting it at the president of the United States.'

The agent handed me a five iron, and I hit the ball way over Trump's head. The president watched the ball flying over the green, then waved his hand dismissively and moved on.

When he wasn't charging ahead, Trump asked me a lot of questions. Indeed, throughout my dealings with him as ambassador, Trump was constantly asking questions. He displayed a lot of genuine curiosity about people and events, and in pretty much everything going on around him. And one of his first questions was: 'What do you think of Malcolm Turnbull?'

Now, Malcolm was not only my boss, he was Australia's prime minister. The last thing I wanted to do was kick off another feud between the pair by saying the wrong thing.

Much to my relief, before I could say anything Trump answered his own question. 'I like him now,' he said.

Apparently, their meeting on USS *Intrepid* had had the intended effect.

Trump knew Kerry Packer from the 1980s and '90s. Referring to Malcolm being Packer's one-time barrister, 'He [Malcolm] must be pretty smart because he kept Kerry Packer out of jail,' Trump said nonchalantly.

I wanted to explain that Kerry was not guilty of anything and wasn't even charged in that case, and that he was one of Australia's most revered businessmen. Before I could, Trump started going through his Cabinet, asking my opinion of his people. He'd obviously done his homework, because he knew I'd met General Mattis. ('They call him Mad Dog, you know?') I was highly complimentary of Mattis, and especially of his attitude towards the Indo-Pacific and the US–Australian relationship.

But the person he really wanted to ask me about – indeed, I suspect this was the reason he came along to play golf with us that day – was Alexander Downer (or 'Downing', as he always referred to him). In May 2016, Australia's former foreign minister was our High Commissioner in London, where one day he met with George Papadopoulos, a Trump campaign adviser. It was Downer's report about this meeting that led the FBI to open a counterintelligence investigation into the efforts of the Russian government to disrupt the 2016 US presidential election. Trump thus consistently blamed Downer for sparking the investigation led by Special Counsel Robert Mueller, which caused him so much grief between 2017 and 2019.

We decided to head back to the clubhouse after just thirteen holes because the weather was awful. It was a windy, rainy and very cold afternoon. Mick and I were playing as partners against

Bret and President Trump. According to the scorecard at the end of the twelfth hole, each team had won six holes. It was all square. I had to sink a twelve-metre putt on the last green to win.

It was a horrendously difficult putt – the ball basically had to do a cartwheel to get into the hole. As I lined it up, my heart was racing. I was thinking about the implications of missing – and the implications of landing it. Would the president of the United States take offence if I beat him? Would a victory place a new strain on US–Australian relations? Regardless, I was going for the win.

I hit my putt, and the eyes of the president, Mulvaney, Baier, the caddy and about forty support staff and Secret Service agents followed the little white ball along the green. To the amazement of us all, it went into the hole. Fortunately, there was a photographer there who took a great photo: Baier and Mulvaney are jumping up in triumph, and the president is standing there with a grin on his face.

In golf, you only need one good shot to bring you back. I'd just beaten the president of the United States on the golf course!

After the game, we headed back to the clubhouse for lunch.

'That was amazing, Hockey,' Mick said to me as we walked. 'Where did you pull that from?' Before I could respond, he continued: 'He'll respect you more for doing that. The last thing the president wants is for someone to throw the game.'

Oh yea, as if, I thought. *I could sink those all day!*

The clubhouse at Trump National reflects its proprietor's oversized personality. It has high ceilings and breathtaking views of the fairways. In the dining room, all the TVs were set to Fox News. As we ordered lunch, Trump insisted that we all try the clam chowder, saying it was fantastic. I'd already ordered the tomato soup, while Baier and Mulvaney had ordered other soups.

We all started on our soups, but the president kept saying how good the clam chowder was. He was in sales mode. I was on my fourth spoonful of tomato soup when three staff appeared and took away our bowls. They were promptly replaced with clam chowder.

'Don't worry, Joe,' he added, 'you're not fat. Have the clam chowder.'

That was the second presidential order I followed in the service of my country. And it was great clam chowder.

* * *

Playing golf with Trump that day gave me an insight into how his mind worked. The experience would be immensely helpful for my later dealings with him.

Contrary to what many people think, Trump has a very engaging mind. He feels threatened by and is somewhat distrustful of self-proclaimed experts (especially in politics), but when he knows that someone hasn't got any particular agenda and he gets to know you, he'll be very open. He's constantly asking for people's opinions – both for intel and, I suspect, to use as his own if he approves.

I've also played golf with Bill Clinton, who is one of the nicest guys you'll ever meet. He is terrific company, tells great stories, and he's very funny and curious. He was also constantly asking questions and seeking opinions.

I once asked Jack Lew what it was like dealing with Bill Clinton and Barack Obama. He said Obama always wanted to read a brief. He approached issues like a lawyer. He'd tear throughout written briefs, briefly discuss them and then make a decision. A lot of people loved Obama's style, Jack said. Bill Clinton, by contrast, would want to talk an issue through, and road-test an outcome. He was verbal. Neither approach was right or wrong: they were different ways to lead.

In truth, all presidents and prime ministers learn on the job. No person possesses all earthly wisdom and knowledge on the day they first enter the Oval Office or the prime minister's suite in Parliament House.

The challenge for all of us is the number of decisions we have to make, each minute of the day. From the logistics of picking up the kids to the mundane business of shopping, paying bills and interacting with friends and family. It can be mentally exhausting. For leaders it's no different – but the decisions they make have a bigger impact on more people.

Golf, for most US presidents, is relaxing: for a few hours they get some mental respite from all the decision making. The fresh air and low stakes make golf an escape from the intensity of being the world's leader, and gives them a chance to spend time with people they like. It's often been remarked on that Trump played a lot of golf during his time as president, but Dwight Eisenhower played far more. In fact, most US presidents have been golfers. I now understand why it matters.

A few hours playing sport with someone can reveal so much about them. In my role as ambassador, I had to be constantly thinking about how to pursue Australia's best interests in the highly unpredictable political and diplomatic environment of Washington, DC, and the golf course was a valuable forum for engagement. I was the only ambassador that got the opportunity to play with Trump.

Diplomacy, like golf, has its rules and traditions, and you can never predict exactly what will come at you next. The only thing that was clear at the end of my first year of dealing with Trump and his administration was that there was no playbook for this game. In that sense, the times suited me.

CHAPTER 6

CRACKING WASHINGTON

The first rule of the ambassadors' club, tennis diplomacy and DC derangement syndrome

Washington, DC is a tough town. There's a lot of tradition and a lot of protocol – and there's definitely a hierarchy. Initially, I did not appreciate what I was getting into. Despite my extensive experience in Australian politics, I was pretty innocent about the ebb and flow of all those international relationships that had been built over time. In many ways, Washington is the ultimate power scene – and I was never into 'scenes'.

At first, I felt like a deer in the headlights – or perhaps a kangaroo. I had no training, no experience, and not much knowledge of what an ambassador did other than to go to the airport and meet ministers. I promised myself that I would never be a bag carrier for politicians visiting from Australia. Cocktail parties and small talk were anathema to me. Speaking in polite riddles about the outcome of a bilateral meeting was turgid. I would rather go to the footy or play golf with my mates. From my perspective, everything in life had to have a purpose and an outcome. Otherwise, move on.

Once our family had settled in at the ambassador's residence, amid the madness of the snowstorms in February 2016, I had to begin work as soon as possible. I was not only responsible for the approximately four hundred people working in the Australian embassy (and their families), but also for the entire Australian diplomatic corps in New York, Houston, Los Angeles, Chicago, San Francisco and Honolulu. Moreover, we had military personnel in thirty-two US states, and I was also responsible for them and their families. This might sound odd coming from someone who was once treasurer of Australia, but it felt like a different level of responsibility compared with all my previous roles.

Early on, a friend gave me a book called *This Town*, written by Mark Leibovich, a Washington-based reporter with *The New York Times Magazine*. I wasn't sure whether it was supposed to be an instruction manual or a guide on not what to do, but it scared the hell out of me. It was about networking in Washington, DC and detailed all the cocktail parties and events you had to be seen at. Not to mention getting in magazines and associating with the right clique.

I was exhausted just reading it. Melissa and I had spent the last twenty years attending events in Australian politics, and we had no desire to do it all over again. *Oh my God*, I thought. *I'm going to be going to every cocktail party and dinner that's going on around town. I can't do this!*

I also found myself living in the beautiful but rather intimidating ambassador's residence. White Oaks is a grand home, and pretty overwhelming. With six full-time staff, ten bedrooms and various living rooms, it operates like an upmarket reception centre with a family home bolted onto it.

White Oaks has been home to the Australian ambassador since Sir Richard Casey arrived in 1940 to found the legation. The mansion was built in 1923 by a property developer, and rented to wealthy tenants for the first few years of its life. The most famous, as I've mentioned, was General George C. Patton.

The house sits just a few hundred metres from the amazing Neo-Gothic National Cathedral, and just a few kilometres from the White House. Its gardens are simply gorgeous and are adorned by only a handful of the original white oak trees from which it takes it name. These gardens are like an oasis, offering respite from the sirens and noise of the world's most powerful city. During our time at the ambassador's residence, I planted an oak sapling with each of my three children in the gardens. I hope they survive the years.

Of course, over the years Australian governments have thought about selling the property, as it has always been prime real estate. What a mistake that would have been. But just to make sure it never happened, one of my predecessors, the highly respected Dennis Richardson, invited Prime Minister John Howard and President George W. Bush to plant a tree in the garden in 2006. Every prime minister since Howard (and there have been a few) has done the same. The plaques accompanying these trees will, I suspect, ensure that Australia never relinquishes the property. Just to make sure, we have listed the property on Australia's National Heritage Register. It is, after all, Aussie territory.

In Washington, it is essential that there is something special about your ambassadorial residence. The grandness of the French and British residences was impossible to match, while the homes of the Japanese and the Italian ambassadors had a refined beauty and history. While Australia had an incredible venue for parties and events, it was just another nice DC ambassador's house. It would probably rank in the top fifteen in the city. Some countries – read: the Gulf States – had built modern palaces, and would hold huge events for people all the time. Australia couldn't compete with that.

But there was one thing the Australian residence had that no one else had: a grass tennis court. This may not sound like a big deal, but it was actually the only one in Washington, DC.

Washington society demands there be something new and exclusive. Sport always has a big pull. People are going to dinners and lunches all the time, and want something to cut through the diplomatic niceties. My predecessor thought White Oaks' tennis court was past its use-by date, and was content to let it be incorporated into an extended garden. But I could see it might become our point of difference, something that would allow us to get the cut-through we needed.

One of my first meetings in the United States was with Peter Lowy. Peter had been living in the United States for years, running the Westfield empire. He frequently travelled to DC and visited members on the Hill and administration officials. Peter said to me and others that the grass tennis court could be one of the most significant tools for an ambassador in Washington, DC. 'You have to rebuild that grass tennis court,' he told me.

I agreed, but pointed out a big problem: money. 'When I was treasurer, Peter, I cut the budget,' I said. 'I made tough decisions. I can't just arrive in Washington, DC and the first thing I do is rebuild a grass tennis court at my home!'

'Well, I'll pay for it then,' Peter shot back.

'Really? Alright, let me run it by the bureaucrats.'

Characteristically, the department quickly found ways to say no. I suspect the message from Julie Bishop was: 'Control Joe Hockey!' Some in the department wanted to do the redevelopment, but others did not. Most could see the benefits of it, but even so they didn't want to go through with it, despite the fact that Peter Lowy was happy to foot the bill. In the meantime, my kids and their friends were playing soccer on this dilapidated old tennis court.

In classic bureaucratic tradition, we settled on an agreement to have a 'tender' for the repair of the court. I was very confused as to how you could have a tender for someone to *give* you money, but we did, and, unsurprisingly, Frank Lowy won.

We then embarked on the process of rebuilding the grass tennis court. By the summer of 2017, when it was ready to reopen, all of a sudden several members of the Trump administration and members of Congress all wanted to come around and play. This turned out to be significant, because a number of those people, who at that stage were mid-level in the administration, ultimately became very senior and would be influential contacts.

We held a grand opening tennis tournament, with Australian tennis legends Rod Laver and Fred Stolle as guests of honour. The pair, especially Laver, were gods among American tennis fans. Laver, who is just about the nicest guy in the world, even put on a coaching clinic. It was the biggest event in Washington that summer, and a roaring success.

The point of the tournament was to showcase our Aussie innovative philosophy in a way that we could not have done with just another ambassadorial party. We did similar things with golf, hosting days for guests with the help of Greg Norman and Jan Stephenson; we'd donate the proceeds to American military veterans. One year, a 98-year-old veteran won a golfing prize. He had served on Iwo Jima in World War II. When Trump's chief of staff, Mick Mulvaney, and the Democratic governor of Virginia, Terry McAuliffe, attended the event, along with other senior members of Congress and the administration, it proved that the effort and expense had been worth it.

These events were always great days. The environment was intentionally relaxed, and guests were never pressured about issues. I emphasised to my staff that there was a place to do business, but we were also likely to make more friends if we created events that people wanted to be at without it feeling like work. We wanted a tone that matched our national character: warm, friendly, relaxed and casual, with a lot of good food and drink, and always plenty of fun.

It was my thinking that we needed to create a space where people could remove themselves from the transactional environment of Washington, DC, where everyone constantly wants something from everyone else. It became well known that you could come to an event with the Australians and be confident it would be light and fun.

Importantly, when it was time to get business done, we were in a better position to approach someone with whom we had shared such a positive experience.

* * *

When we first moved into the residence, we felt as though we were living in a big hotel. Like most Australians, Melissa and I weren't used to having staff, some of whom were living right next to us. We weren't very comfortable with that, not because they were staff, but because it was strange having other people in our home all the time, especially after guarding our privacy for so many years when I was in politics. Over time, we got more used to it, and White Oaks started to feel like home.

Having familiar art on the walls made a great difference. The Beazleys had a significant personal art collection, which of course they'd taken back home with them, so the walls were pretty bare. At an early dinner we hosted with senior representatives of the FBI, I noticed one of our guests looking around at the empty picture hangers.

'Yep,' I said pointing to the wall and shaking my head. 'Washington must be a pretty rough town. It must be hard to get decent policing in this city. My predecessor took off with all the art!'

The FBI agents looked at me, bemused, unsure whether I was joking.

I eventually convinced the National Gallery of Australia to change their policy and lend top-quality Australian art that fitted the character of the home to key diplomatic missions. I did have to raise the money from the private sector to ship it over, but it was nice to have some good Australian art in the ambassador's residence. It made for a good talking point, as well as making it more of a real home.

While I love being a host to my friends, entertaining as an ambassador didn't come naturally to me. It involved a lot of small talk, and – if you haven't noticed by now – that's not really my thing. This was epitomised by one of the last parties we hosted during my time at White Oaks.

I forget the reason for the function now (perhaps it was also lost on me then), but we were all sitting at the long and grand table in the formal dining room. It seated about thirty people. Melissa and I tried to engage with people from one end of the table to the other, using different techniques to try to get everyone to tell us a little about themselves. I arrived at the last guy at the end of the table. I was tired, and he must have seen through my routine. He just looked at me and said, 'Don't worry, Mr Ambassador. We both know we're never gonna see each other again, so let's cut the small talk and just have a great time with a couple of drinks.' It was hilarious, but it was also the truth. I wish people acknowledged that more often.

When an ambassador leaves office, their successor usually honours the commitments they have made. So my four-year wine and food consumption odyssey started with an unlikely dinner: Kim Beazley had offered to host a fundraising dinner for the supporters of the National Cathedral Choir. The average age of the people at the dinner would have been well over sixty-five. All were wealthy individuals supporting the amazing choristers at Washington's lauded National Cathedral. They were a very elegant bunch.

We began a discussion about the differences and similarities between Australia and the United States. The topics drifted across the predictable subjects of language, trade, the arts and sport. Somehow we moved on to corporal punishment in schools. (Schools were a fitting subject, actually: over time, Melissa would go on the board of our boys' school in Washington, St. Albans, and I would join the board of our daughter's school, the National Cathedral School.) Most were aghast at school punishment, and I had a few choice stories to share from my school days. My father, too, was one who took the old phrase 'Spare the rod, spoil the child' literally. 'When I was a boy,' I said, 'Dad used to take off his thong and whack me with it.'

At the time I had no idea that, in America, a thong was not what they call a flip-flop but, rather, a very discreet piece of female attire. Some of our guests looked shocked; others stared awkwardly at their soup. I was confused by the reaction but just moved on.

The conversation then turned to Australian gun laws. Almost all Americans know that we have tough laws in Australia, and I noted that I was very proud to be a member of the government that had made and delivered those landmark gun restriction reforms. 'Your gun laws are legendary over here,' one woman noted, and a number of people at the table agreed that Australia's gun laws were enviable. This was nice to hear (because I fervently agreed) – but I soon became aware that the temperature of the conversation was rising. A few voices were being raised, and soon there was a palpable sense of friction among the dinner guests. All of a sudden I'd lost control of the conversation. I was now hosting a loud argument about guns in America rather than which was the most favoured hymn of the Episcopalian choir at Easter.

Breaking through the noise, the elderly gentleman sitting next to me piped up loudly: 'Well, I'm from Virginia and I always carry a gun. Including now.'

The room fell silent. Melissa's eyes opened widely in reaction to his statement, and I saw her look across to where our kids were playing in the living room. She waited until I had moved the discussion on to politics (which, in hindsight, was hardly pouring oil on troubled waters), and then she left and made sure that the nanny took the children to a secure room in the house.

Others didn't seem so shocked at that guest's revelation, but for us it was a rude awakening. Welcome to America. Still, it was part of our journey to understand the psyche of the American people. There is nothing 'normal' in America – and that is the great joy of the nation.

Melissa and I were invited to a vast number of events, dinners, fundraisers and cocktail parties over the four years we were there, but most of the real friendships we made were through our engagement with our children's schools, both of which were near the National Cathedral. They're very good schools with a long history of turning out high achievers, including many household American names. As a result, you nearly have to sacrifice your first-born child to get an interview for the others. It's a gruelling process. Melissa used every means she could think of to try to get our children in when we arrived, which was halfway through the school year. The parents we met turned out to be some of our best friends and a key part of our contact with the community.

We were invited by one parent to the first formal function we attended in DC. The National Children's Hospital Fundraiser is a grand black-tie event where the elite of the city gather to support one of the most accomplished children's hospitals in the world. As I said, Melissa and I had no desire to go to a series of fundraisers but this was one we wanted to support. It was similar to the work we'd done in Australia with the Humpty Dumpty Foundation for sick and injured children; my trek up Mount Kilimanjaro was a fundraiser for them.

We walked into the Hyatt Hotel that night and it immediately struck me that we knew basically no one. This had not happened in about thirty years of such events back home. I mean, I used to be the treasurer of Australia, and I'd chaired the G20 – I was, to borrow a phrase from *Anchor Man*'s Ron Burgundy, 'kind of a big deal'. Now, all of a sudden, I realised that no one knew who I was. Hoorah!!

Believe it or not, a huge relief immediately washed over me as I realised I didn't have to be 'on' that night. We didn't have to worry about who was looking over our shoulders or making the rounds. We were anonymous, and I could just be myself and have a few drinks and a laugh. I could just say, 'Hi, I'm Joe and this is my wife, Melissa, and I'm the new ambassador from Australia.' And probably for that reason, it turned out to be one of the most enjoyable events I attended during my time in Washington.

Sitting down, we realised the event was also a pretty serious fundraiser. There were messages from a raft of political leaders, including Barack Obama and Hillary Clinton. The MC was Fox News's Bret Baier, whom I would later join on the golf course with Donald Trump. Baier's son had serious heart issues and was treated in the children's hospital; he and his wife, Amy, are amazing supporters of the charity.

At one point, Baier began a live auction. The first item was a dinner with the Thai ambassador for eight people, which sold for US$6000. Then there was a dinner with the Emirati ambassador, which sold for about US$8000.

Baier then came over to my table, camera crew in tow, and said, 'I've got a new Australian ambassador here.' By this stage I'd had a couple of drinks, and I said, 'It's great to be here, we're having a great time.'

Then Bret turned up the heat on me. 'So, Ambassador, are our friends in Australia going to donate dinner?'

'Well, of course, of course we will, Bret,' I replied. Then I delivered my spiel about how we had a great house that General Patton had lived in many years ago, which gained the attention of the room. 'We'll have twenty guests over to the residence,' I continued. 'We'll have great food, and great Australian wine. But they have to promise one thing: don't be boring. We don't do boring in Australia.' The place erupted in laughter.

The bidding started, and to my surprise the final bid on our dinner was US$22,000. Then the runner-up said they'd also pay US$22,000 if we put on a second dinner. I agreed, so we raised a total of US$44,000, which made a big impression on the crowd. I was feeling pretty chuffed.

At the first break of the event, the Emirati ambassador, Yousef Al Otaiba, a highly experienced and influential ambassador in DC, came and introduced himself. 'Congratulations,' he said, 'that was quite an arrival in Washington, DC.' After we had a chat, he went up to the stage and wrote out a cheque for a donation of US$1 million. I walked up to him, put my arm around him and said, 'Okay, you win!'

The charity auction became quite a story among the diplomatic corps: I had arrived with a bang, if unintentionally. I was struck by the competitiveness of the town. Everyone has to win. But I knew that the best way I could cut through in DC was by just being myself. Avoid the red carpet, and engage with people as friends and mates.

From that time on, I went to a couple of other big events or functions at other embassies, but they really weren't for me. We held lots of small dinners and lunches at our own residence, with an Aussie chef, food and great Aussie wine.

At one point we were holding three or four dinners a week to build up our network. In Washington, most people want to leave events by 9 p.m., so it was doable. Another benefit was that most Americans don't drink at lunch (at least, it was a benefit unless you really felt like a drink). I learnt that they were always shocked when they came to Australia and found people drinking at lunch. When I first went over to New York for lunch with Rupert Murdoch and his impressive chief executive, Robert Thomson, they served fresh juices at lunch. So I adopted the practice of fresh juice at my lunches. I did, however, draw the line at hosting breakfasts: Joe Hockey does not do working breakfasts.

I was determined not to eat for Australia (I failed), but there was still some drinking for Australia going on (I excelled). The real danger with diplomacy is you drink to celebrate with the people you like, and drink to cope with the people you don't.

There was a big cellar at White Oaks, and I can't pretend it didn't get a good workout. But I was disciplined about taking breaks, and not drinking at lunch was a big help. My alcohol intake was also reduced by the fact I wasn't going to as many events as I could have. It would be easy to drift into alcohol addiction as an ambassador: you could very comfortably drink your way through an entire posting.

Washington, DC is a transactional town, which doesn't necessarily suit the Australian approach to life. The golden rule in Washington is you never have a meeting without having either something to ask for or something to give. You never just have a catch-up. And there's an expectation that you schedule well in advance, even if it's just with friends. Everyone seems to schedule their life down to the laundry drop-off. The town does not deal well with spontaneity.

Part of the reason is that it's a city with a lot of outsiders. There are a vast number of people living there who hold a public office, and many try to maintain a formality they think befits their role. Few are comfortable to let their hair down and be themselves.

Outsiders also contribute to the really poor driving in the capital. I can safely say that DC drivers are the worst in America, and probably some of the worst in the world. If you're going to have an accident in Washington, it usually involves someone from out of town trying to navigate the roundabouts or the confusing road system. Or else they're driving while holding their mobile phone and smoking weed.

When we arrived, I replaced the small ambassadorial car with the biggest car I could get: a Cadillac Escalade SUV. The beauty of the car was that it was so big that when the kids were squabbling in the back, they couldn't actually reach each other. This thing was a monster that got about 5 kilometres to the litre. I needed a big car for the big family, but in truth I'd always wanted to have a big American truck. This was to be both the family car and the ambassadorial vehicle.

Of course, DFAT did everything they could to stop me getting that damn truck. They wanted me to have a smaller car, like Kim Beazley had. Even before I came to Washington I had told them I wanted this particular car. I explained to them I couldn't fit all the kids, the nanny, our dogs and all the rest into Kim Beazley's car, which only had to accommodate himself and Susie. In an escalating argument of Cold War proportions, DFAT even rented one of the Cadillacs to demonstrate that it would not fit in the garage of White Oaks. I told them it could sit outside all day for all

I cared. In the end, I won and we got the Cadillac. And it proved cheaper for taxpayers than its predecessor.

After four years, we were all pretty over living in the ambassador's residence. It had begun to feel like a big RSL. Too many functions, and too many people in our daily lives. Despite everyone's best endeavours, it was exhausting constantly having people in your home, doing the same tours of the residence and having the same conversations. We wanted to be in a home again, not a residence.

* * *

I was lucky to have good friends among our closest diplomatic allies. The New Zealand, Canadian and British ambassadors were all excellent at their jobs and great allies of Australia – as well as was possible in the competitive diplomatic environment.

For the bulk of the time I was in DC, the New Zealand ambassador was Tim Groser. He had been a minister for trade in John Key's government, and, like me, had resigned from a cabinet position to take up the diplomatic role. Groser was a great believer in free trade and one of the architects of the Trans-Pacific Partnership; at one point he was in the running to be the director-general of the World Trade Organization. Tim is a hugely engaging man and an indefatigable advocate for New Zealand's interests. The ANZAC spirit, I think, runs very deep, and I would support him and his interests whenever I could. In particular, we partnered together in advocating for the TPP.

Of course, it was difficult for a country the size of New Zealand to get traction in Washington. Despite this, Tim did a really good job. As a former cabinet minister, he had the chutzpah to walk up to the Hill and get the meetings he needed. Real political experience mattered in Washington, because you were respected as someone who had won elections and held senior office. It was a major error of judgement for the Kiwis to replace him with a public servant, no matter how senior and experienced his successor.

Of course, there's respect for the title of 'Ambassador' in Washington, but there are just so many of them in the city. Not just active ambassadors either, but retired ambassadors who retain the title for the rest of their lives. My American colleagues were always amazed that Australian visitors would call me Joe rather than 'Mr Ambassador'. I couldn't have cared less, as long as we got the job done. The fact that only ambassadors were invited to the presidential inauguration shows the privileged status they hold in DC.

But there is a hierarchy, and it's based on the size and scale of the nation you represent. And it's just a fact that New Zealand and, to some degree, Australia don't have that level of influence. Access is everything in Washington, and so the access to the Hill that Tim and I were able to win made a big difference. The fact that both of us were senior political figures in our home countries was invaluable with Republicans and Democrats alike.

Neither Tim nor I had anything like the budgets of major powers, and spending money matters in Washington. While seeing the Emirati ambassador casually write out a million-dollar cheque at a fundraiser was an eye opener at the time, I would see a lot more of that during my time in DC. The Saudis, the Emiratis, the Qataris and the Bahrainis, in particular, all had enormous amounts of money to throw around.

This was confirmed by my failed idea for a Super Bowl party at the embassy in 2017. I had relatively humble plans of an Australian-style Grand Final day celebration, and hoped to get a bunch of ambassadors and congressmen along. I soon discovered our plans looked pretty meagre compared to what the Saudis ended up doing for their Super Bowl party. The itinerary was as follows: the ambassador brought in a Boeing 747 from Saudi Arabia, picked up a whole lot of influencers in Washington, had a party in an aircraft hangar, flew them to the *actual* Super Bowl, and then brought them all home that night. Beer and snags it was not.

There were obviously different groupings in the diplomatic class, based on tiers of influence and alliances. One group – with the top trade and (to a degree) military relationships with the USA, included the Canadians, the Mexicans, the French and the Japanese. Then came the Chinese and the Russians, who were obviously hugely important but not exactly best mates with the Americans, for obvious reasons. Then you'd have the Arabs, who were definitely their own grouping, although often hugely distrustful of each other. Israel was a group unto itself, and had one of the most influential ambassadors in Washington.

Then there were trusted partners, and this was a group in which Australia was on the top tier of relationships. This was really the intelligence alliance with the United States known as the Five Eyes: it comprised the United Kingdom, New Zealand, Australia and Canada. At an operational level, our intelligence and defence agencies have deep links, and that was a huge help for us.

The Canadian ambassador, David MacNaughton, was an outstanding friend. He and his wife, Leslie Noble, became great mates of ours. It helped that David and I had a lot of common interests. We're both interested in business, we're both centrists, and we're also both ambitious but mediocre golfers. David hadn't served in parliament, but had supported Justin Trudeau's Liberal Party for years. While globally Canada's position is not dissimilar to Australia's, in America it carries a lot more sway. It's the United States' biggest trading partner, and vice versa. In fact, it's the largest bilateral trade relationship in the world.

But the relationship between Donald Trump and Prime Minister Trudeau saw the US–Canadian relationship decline to its worst standing in a long time, and David was dealing with that every single day. He also had the challenge of having his prime minister in the same time zone; it was a blessing for me that Canberra was asleep during my office hours (well, some of the time). This avoided knee-jerk phone calls in reaction to the latest Trump tweet, interview or news conference.

The UK ambassador, Kim Darroch, was a little different from others in that he was a Foreign Office lifer. He was a very good diplomat in the classical British tradition of Whitehall, an astute and loyal servant of his country. Like me, he had expressed an interest in Trump's campaign early on, and we'd attended the Republican debate and conventions together. We sat next to each other at Trump's inauguration, and he was often good company. But Kim would become quite agitated with me when Australia got access to Trump ahead of the United Kingdom, and this continued when we managed to avoid US trade sanctions.

Unfortunately for Kim, he resigned after his diplomatic cables were leaked in July 2019, making front-page news in both countries. Darroch described the Trump White House as 'clumsy and inept', and claimed President Trump 'radiates insecurity'. Trump, of course, got out on Twitter calling Kim 'a very stupid guy' in a series of tweets.

Given my own experience with leaks from the Trump administration, I was particularly sympathetic to Kim's plight. The whole thing was a genuine diplomatic crisis between the United Kingdom and the United States. Trump had previously expressed a preference for the former UK Independence Party leader Nigel Farage to serve as the British ambassador. Kim was caught in a particularly nasty domestic feud over the Tory leadership and Brexit. By July 2019, Prime Minister Theresa May was on the way out, and Johnson, who was about to become prime minister, was not backing his embattled ambassador. Meanwhile, the new foreign secretary, Jeremy Hunt, like Johnson a prime ministerial contender, was backing Darroch.

Kim was caught in a perfect storm of international and domestic political crises. He resigned five days after the leaks were made public. Kim is now Barron Darroch of Kew, a peer in the House of Lords – no such luck for retired Australian ambassadors!

He later told me the details that a very senior and select group of people in the United Kingdom with top-level security clearance had access to those cables. I assured him that the sharpest knives always come from your own side. While my advice may have been informative for him, it wasn't very calming.

This is why I never wrote or sent one observational cable as ambassador under my name. This was important to me. I told Prime Minister Turnbull, other government ministers and department heads that I was happy to talk any time on a secure phone. Obviously, people in the embassy expressed views in cables from time to time, but I wasn't going to be the author. I had formed the view that, given my past life as a politician, if I wrote any cables, I couldn't rely on all the people reading them not to share them with the media.

When it came to our somewhat murkier diplomatic brethren, another way of dealing with them was just to avoid them. I didn't have many dealings with the Russians, for instance. I generally worked from the premise that most diplomats are spies anyway. Having dealt with the leadership of China while in government, I wasn't inclined to spend time with the Chinese ambassador, either. There's a hierarchy in China, which is strictly adhered to, and there were a number of ambassadors – in particular the career ambassadors from other countries – whom I knew didn't really have the ear of their presidents or prime ministers.

The standout ambassadorial player in DC was the Israeli ambassador, Ron Dermer. He'd been on the scene for several years already, and it was widely known that he spoke directly for Benjamin Netanyahu. Dermer is the classic Israeli representative: hugely smart, says what he thinks, and unafraid of pushback. He would serve seven years as Israel's ambassador, and was only replaced at the beginning of the Biden administration in 2021.

Dermer was the ultimate power player in Washington. He famously arranged for Prime Minister Netanyahu to speak to Congress without seeing President Obama. That shredded the diplomatic rule book, and there was a huge amount of blowback from the White House and Democrats generally. But Dermer dealt with it in his own, perhaps uniquely Israeli, kind of way.

* * *

Having a love of sport is a great asset in diplomacy, as sporting and social occasions afford more relaxed networking opportunities. One club we joined as a family was the famous Chevy Chase Club in Maryland, established in 1892. It was expensive (personally, as I fully funded the memberships) and quite a process, but it was worth it so that, as a family, we could do things together and have an experience unlike anything available in Australia. The exclusivity and cost of these clubs runs contrary to Australian egalitarian values, and I understand why people might dislike the idea of them, but it was an amazing experience. It was somewhere we could go for meals and to meet new people, and a place where the kids could play sports and make friends.

Iggy, in particular, got into ice hockey and won two championships with the club. (I just love the fact that there is a hockey trophy inscribed with the Hockey name on the winning team!) Unsurprisingly, he adopted the Washington Capitals as his NHL team, and we sometimes went to the Verizon Center (later Capital One Arena) to see them play. At our first game, against the Philadelphia Flyers, Iggy was pestering me to get a Capitals jersey to match his. In the merchandise store, I handed over my credit card, preparing to pay something equivalent to the GDP of a small nation.

'That's not a real card,' said the store clerk.

'What? Yes it is,' I replied.

'Joe Hockey? That's not a real name!'

'It is! That's my real name!'

'C'mon, really? Joe Hockey?'

In the end, I showed the clerk my drivers licence to prove that I wasn't part of some fake credit card NHL merchandise buying ring.

Excited, he then called over his fellow clerk. 'No way! Hey, Larry, you gotta get a look at this! I've got Joe Hockey here! This guy's name is Joe Hockey!'

At this point, and upon discovering that I was the Australian ambassador, they got so excited that they brought down the owner of the Capitals, Ted Leonsis, to meet us. The whole thing turned into something of a diplomatic coup!

* * *

Washington, DC is the centre of the political universe. It becomes even more important when you have a global crisis and the world needs leadership, like a global pandemic, an economic crisis or a war. When politics matters, Washington, DC matters – and politics matters almost all the time. Despite this, most Americans hate Washington. That's something Donald Trump understood. It represents the business of the state, and Americans are inherently suspicious of the state and those who earn a (very healthy) living from it.

It's fascinating to consider the people Americans do lionise. Hollywood celebrities, sports celebrities, celebrities for the sake of being celebrities. I grew up on a diet of American television and movies, so I'm as guilty as anyone of having a bit of a fascination with celebrities – most Australians are the same. Everyone loves a story, and through its easily translatable history, and with a decent dash of help from Hollywood, America perfected the concept of celebrity worship.

I'm a big fan of *The Jerry Springer Show*. It fascinated me: who were these odd and sad people who would get up and reveal these excruciatingly embarrassing details of their lives for a chance to appear on television? And what did it say about me that I was addicted to the show?

Early on in my parliamentary career, I used to share a house with Brendan Nelson, Ross Cameron and Bob Baldwin. Four Liberal MPs in a house in Canberra. Brendan had just come out of a devastating marriage break up, and he was sleeping out in the back shed. There he was, a future opposition leader, defence minister and education minister, using a bucket for a toilet and with no running water. When parliament was sitting, we'd all get home about 10.30 each night, and part of the way we used to unwind was to have a glass of red wine, eat paddle pops and watch *Jerry Springer*. It just made us laugh – it was exactly the sort of release that we needed after a long day. Four MPs sitting on a couch yelling, 'Jerry! Jerry! Jerry!'

When I came to America, I attempted to meet every celebrity on my sometimes shameful list. (Another embarrassing love I have is for the band Nickelback.) Jerry Springer was near the top. To my surprise, he accepted my dinner invitation in New York, and it remains one of the most interesting dinners I've ever had. I was so excited to meet Jerry – and he couldn't believe that an ambassador wanted to meet him.

Springer is an extremely interesting man. He's a former Democratic mayor of Cincinnati – no small achievement, given it's a city of 300,000 people. He also used to work for Bobby Kennedy. We ended up talking politics almost the entire evening. Towards the end, I admitted that I wanted to ask him about his famous TV show as I was a fan.

'Well, you know, it is what it is,' he replied. 'My wife watched the show with me just once and was so appalled she never watched it again.' When I asked him where he found these people, he just laughed and said, 'Oh, they're out there.'

Still a Democrat with strong convictions, Springer didn't like Trump at all. He also pointed out an interesting quirk of history: every incumbent president, he said, who had been challenged in a primary after his first term in office had gone on to lose the next election. I was dismissive, but his argument bore out. Trump was challenged by two fellow Republicans (albeit briefly) and went on to lose the 2020 election.

Celebrity really does matter in America, even in the serious surrounds of Washington. I even managed to surprise some Americans with my own celebrity connections. Arguably Australia's greatest ever actress, Cate Blanchett, who had been a neighbourhood friend in Sydney, began performing on Broadway in a production of *The Present*. She was kind enough to come and meet with a series of business leaders and other American friends after the show. It's amazing what a celebrity mate can do for your credibility in America.

Some of my own run-ins with celebrities were accidental and somewhat embarrassing. I was introduced to the *Breaking Bad* star Bryan Cranston at a Google function but had no idea who he was as I'd never seen the show. He was a great guy and spent about forty-five minutes telling me all about the show and why I just had to watch it. I was impressed that he was still hustling for viewers, given that it seemed *Breaking Bad* had won every award and broken every record in modern television. As it turned out, Cranston starred in one of the best American movies ever made about politics: he gave a phenomenal performance in *All the Way* as Lyndon B. Johnson, one of the most fascinating but often underrated US presidents.

It's hard to overstate how much celebrity matters in the United States. Perhaps the obsession there has something to do with how the culture articulates the American dream. If you're on television (especially reality television these days), on the front of magazines or on the celebrity news websites, it means you've made it in popular culture. And that means you've made it in America.

The power of celebrity goes a long way to explaining how someone like Donald Trump could be elected president of the United States. There is a myth that Trump was the first celebrity to become president: this forgets that Ronald Reagan, to give just one example, was a former Hollywood actor. And he not only won two presidential elections but became one of the most effective and successful presidents of the twentieth century.

Another celebrity president in the United States is probably inevitable. Trump was not alone. More recently, we have witnessed the rise of celebrity state governors, including the action movie star Arnold Schwarzenegger in California and Minnesota's former WWF wrestler Jesse Ventura, who had a shock win as an independent. In fact, Trump endorsed and offered financial aid to Ventura during his campaign, and closely studied Ventura's successful 'anti-politician' style. (For his part, Ventura was initially a big supporter of Trump, but later came out against him, calling him a 'conman president'.)

Perhaps what was unique about Trump's celebrity victory was what he was famous for: really, he was famous for being famous, and he made money out of that. Most Americans knew Trump from *The Apprentice*, the reality television show in which he coined his famous catchphrase: 'You're fired!' Trump's business success depended on his selling an image of what success looked like. Trump's celebrity was premised on selling what celebrity is – and in doing so he further fuelled his own business success.

If Joe Biden does not run again in 2024, it may well be that the Democrats' best hope of beating Trump – assuming he decides to run – will be their own celebrity candidate.

CHAPTER 7

DINNER AT THE WHITE HOUSE

Prime ministerial visits, the state dinner and Trump's bathroom

The National Governors Association (NGA) is a kind of peak body for US state governors. The strength and influence of governors in the country cannot be underestimated: almost 40 per cent of presidents had previously served as a governor. The COVID-19 crisis has proven just how much power they exert, which extends well beyond the power of the equivalent state premiers in Australia.

The NGA comes together twice a year, holding a meeting outside of Washington in summer, and then one in Washington in February. The chair rotates annually between Democratic and Republican states. I was keen to pursue greater integration of politics and business between our two nations, and I decided that the NGA would be a good means for doing so. I wanted the bilateral relationship between Australia and the United States to reach a new high-water mark.

The summer 2017 meeting had featured Canadian Prime Minister Justin Trudeau as a keynote speaker, and we organised for Australia to be invited to host the February 2018 event in Washington, DC. The NGA was very keen for our prime minister to be their next keynote speaker.

I flew to Nevada to meet with Governor Brian Sandoval, the Republican who was the 2017–18 NGA chair. As with the G20, I didn't want the event to be conducted as it had been in the past.

If Malcolm Turnbull was going to come all the way here, I told him, I wanted to make it worthwhile. First, we would need to lock in another meeting with President Trump. Second, if we were to engage with this forum, I argued that we should have a truly bilateral opportunity that would involve state premiers and chief ministers travelling from Australia to participate in meetings. And it would be a great opportunity to have a business roundtable involving senior business leaders from Australia and the United States. Sandoval loved the idea.

Of course, saying you'll get the prime minister, all the premiers and chief ministers, and the top business leaders from Australia to attend a forum in the United States is one thing; achieving it is quite another. Balancing competing calendars, agendas and egos between Canberra, Washington and the business leaders took a mammoth effort by our embassy staff. In the end, we managed to get all the premiers to commit except two; South Australia and Tasmania would both be having elections at the time.

Along with the premiers, we had secured the involvement of business leaders including Anthony Pratt, Kerry Stokes and Andrew Forrest. On the American side, we had almost the entire contingent of state governors, leaders of US companies with significant interests such as Hilton, Marriott Hotels, CBS and FedEx. On top of all that, Malcolm Turnbull would address the forum, and President Trump would host talks with him the day before the event.

At one stage, the Americans started discussing having the first official state visit under the Trump administration with Australia. That would have been a very significant honour, and would have gone a long way towards signalling that all was forgiven. But Malcolm Turnbull couldn't decide whether it was a good idea or not in the lead-up to the next Australian election. I was a little ambivalent as well. It wasn't clear that relations between Trump and Turnbull were fully repaired. My instincts told me it would be better to have another bilateral engagement and then look at a state visit down the track. (As it turned out, in early 2018 the French were offered the first official state visit, and it didn't go well.)

I did manage to organise for Turnbull to stay across the street from the White House at Blair House – the president's official guest house. It's a building made up of a series of linked terrace houses, with a magnificently elegant interior. Malcolm wanted to stay an extra night, and even though the protocol is that you stay only two nights, I got him a third. My concierge skills proved useful.

* * *

I had struck up a good relationship with Gary Cohn, who was Trump's chief economic adviser, and director of the National Economic Council. Gary was a former chief financial officer at Goldman Sachs, and I'd met him when I chaired the G20. Even though he was nominally a Democrat, Gary had found himself at the epicentre of the White House, developing and implementing Trump's economic policies. In particular, he had a big hand in the tax reforms that Trump drove through the Congress.

Ahead of Trump's lunch meeting with Turnbull, Cohn came up to me with an air of controlled concern. 'Joe, about half an hour into the meeting, the president will run out of conversation with the prime minister,' he said. 'At that point he'll just start going around the room pointing at people, asking them if there's anything they want to raise. Do you have anything you want me to raise?'

Never one to waste a good opportunity, I thought we might take the chance to get President Trump in front of the Aussie business delegation.

'Well, there's the business delegation we brought over – perhaps he could meet them? It would be great if you could raise it with him.'

'Well, you know, we've got a press conference … it's going to be tight.'

'Leave that to me,' I said.

So we were sitting in the lunch meeting, and about half an hour in, just as Gary had predicted, Trump had nothing more to say. Gary piped up: 'I was speaking to Joe, and they've got this business delegation.'

'Who's in the business delegation?' Trump asked.

The room seemed thankful that something had grabbed his attention.

'Well, Mr President, we've got Anthony Pratt on our end,' I told Trump.

'Oh, I know Anthony; he's committed to build more factories here, invest billions on the back of my win. Who else have you got? You got Greg Norman?'

'Yes, Mr President, we've got Greg Norman,' I said, doing my best to sell the delegation to the president.

'That's great! Hey, I want to see them. I want to see Greg!'

He was calling out Norman's name like he was in the next room.

'Well, we've got them here, Mr President, but your office said it would be too difficult to do,' I explained.

'Don't worry about that, I want to meet them. Bring them to the press conference and I'll meet them in the East Wing after,' Trump declared.

I went down and corralled the forty-odd members of the delegation, making sure they all got into the front rows of the press conference. For all the delegation members, it was a magical experience. I then had them line up around the wall of the very large reception room. Then Trump burst in, full of praise for everyone. Melania was with him, and both she and the president met each member of the Australian delegation for an individual handshake and chat. Everyone was gobsmacked. Then, to top it all off, Vice President Pence came in as well. The delegation happily lined up to get photos with all of them. For our business leaders, it was unparalleled access to the president of the United States, and they went away thrilled.

Most significantly, they endorsed the narrative to the world, and in particular the Australian media, that the Australia–United States relationship was back on track. It was clear to all that we had extraordinary access to the world's most powerful (and unpredictable) leader.

Trump was at his best that day: charming, engaged, curious and (mainly) focused. Serious military supply deals, mining and investment deals were done. This included the president's announcement that the US Navy would commission USS *Canberra*, in honour of HMAS *Canberra*, which was irreparably damaged by Japanese torpedoes at the Battle of Savo Island. It was the second incarnation of USS *Canberra* and a genuine honour. The ship would be built by Austal USA in Mobile, Alabama, by a subsidiary of the Perth-based Australian shipping giant Austal. This had been suggested by US Secretary of the Navy Richard Spencer. Richard and his wife, Polly, became close friends to Melissa and me. He is a great guy and accomplished businessman, and I subsequently invited him to become the global chair of my business after I completed my ambassadorship.

Trump also announced that day that the recently retired Admiral Harry Harris would be the new US ambassador to Australia – although it didn't ultimately happen. As the former head of the United States Indo-Pacific Command, Admiral Harris would have been a great choice, but he was soon nominated to become the US ambassador to South Korea. Understandably, Australia played second fiddle to that more strategic requirement at a pressing time.

I was not overly concerned about the absence of a US ambassador to Australia. In fact, it made my job easier. I was the sole direct interface between Australia and the US government leadership. That gave me more control over the relationship. In fact, even the White House deferred to me on issues relating to Australia before they sought the advice of their own embassy. That was regrettable for the US chargé d'affaires in Australia,

James Carouso, who was a wise and respected diplomat. But he was a State Department careerist, which inevitably meant he was distrusted by the Trump White House. Australia was merely under his watch until a permanent replacement was found for Ambassador John Berry. Finally, after more than two years without an ambassador, Republican lawyer Arthur B. Culvahouse Jr was appointed. Culverhouse was establishment GOP, and was highly respected by all. He'd been in charge of vetting the GOP nominees for vice president in 2008, having previously worked for Ronald Reagan's White House as chief legal counsel, as well as in George H.W. Bush's administration.

I've always been intrigued by the extensive vetting processes that the two major US parties put their candidates through before they are nominated for a candidacy or office, and I asked Arthur what his stock killer question was for vice presidential candidates.

Arthur told me: 'If the president were incapacitated, and you were advised that Osama bin Laden had been positively identified in a town, and you had to make a decision to order a missile strike that would take him down but at the cost of innocent civilian casualties – what would you do?'

That was a cracker of a question, I thought. 'How did they respond?' I asked.

The quality of the answers varied, apparently, but the worst answer was to not make any decision.

'Who gave the best answer?' I wanted to know.

'Sarah Palin,' he said in a flash. He recounted her response: 'I would immediately order the strike based on the best available information, then I would drop to my knees and pray to God for forgiveness for the sacrifice of innocent lives.'

At the press conference that day, Trump was effusive in his praise for Australia. He made reference to our '100 Years of Mateship' (it was 'a term that you use very beautifully', he said), recalled the USS *Intrepid* event as an 'extraordinary evening', and described our countries as 'a bulwark of freedom, security and democracy'. Turnbull was equally praiseworthy, describing them as 'great friends' and the two nations as possessing 'no closer friendship'.

At one point, Trump got his two favourite Australians, Greg Norman and Anthony Pratt, to stand up in the middle of the press conference and take a bow. It was classic Trump. It was hugely rewarding for me and my team to see such incredible progress after what had been a full-blown diplomatic crisis a year earlier.

Sadly, as happens too often in America, a pall was cast over the event by a mass shooting that had taken place a couple of days earlier at a high school in Parkland, Florida. Seventeen people had been killed by a lone gunman carrying a semiautomatic rifle. The victims were innocent kids and teachers going about a normal school day. This was the largest high school massacre in US history, surpassing the Columbine tragedy some years earlier.

At our press conference, Trump gave a garbled response to the inevitable questions about gun control. He promised 'more background checks', and at one point seemed to advocate training teachers to carry guns to protect students. Turnbull was asked by an American journalist about Australia's effective gun laws, and he gave as good an answer as you could in the circumstances: they're our laws, they work, we like them, but America is a different place with a different constitution, and we're not going to tell Americans what to do.

The next night, at the Australian embassy, we had about 350 guests for the NGA function. We had Australian premiers and chief ministers, along with the vast majority of US governors, and fifty of America's and Australia's corporate leaders in the room. Prime Minister Turnbull was also there to address the event, and gave a good speech on the importance of the United States staying true to its values on free trade. At this point we were still holding out hope that Trump might change his mind on cancelling the Trans-Pacific Partnership.

Combined with Turnbull's meeting with the president, the event gave Australia a serious boost in our bilateral engagement with the United States in both the government and business sectors.

* * *

The warm relationship continued over the months ahead, until we cracked the biggest diplomatic tribute a US president can offer a foreign nation: a state visit, with a formal state dinner at the White House. It was one of my finest moments in more than two decades of public life.

Once again, I had my friendship with Mick Mulvaney to thank for this, but Melania Trump also played a large part in making it happen. Melania had a deep affection for Australia and was very keen to make a presidential visit happen. Both Donald and Melania wanted to come to Australia, and at various points discussions about a visit were reasonably advanced.

Malcolm Turnbull, however, had mixed feelings. He wasn't set against it, but I felt that we should be actively encouraging it. Turnbull had already come to the United States twice, of course, having successful visits both times. Unfortunately, the message I got back was that there was no enthusiasm for Trump to come to Australia because there would be a mixed reaction in the Australian community. I have to say, I was pretty disappointed. The United States is our number one ally, we were celebrating 100 Years of Mateship, and, for all Trump's failings, he was looking after Australia in the White House in a manner that was not being afforded to other close allies. Nevertheless, I continued pressing for a state visit by our prime minister.

A state dinner, of course, is meant to be for a nation's head of state. And Queen Elizabeth II is Australia's head of state. Because of this, I was told, the Australian prime minister couldn't be honoured with an official state dinner. But Mick Mulvaney, being of Irish heritage, and I disagreed pretty strongly with that line of thought. Discussions about a state dinner had started in 2017, but we couldn't resolve the head of state issue ahead of Malcolm's visit in 2018.

As it turned out, President Emmanuel Macron of France beat us to it, being welcomed to Washington on a full state visit in April 2018. It was a big honour for the French, who were looking to carve out a greater leadership role for themselves in Europe, with the British departing the EU and the impending retirement of Germany's influential Chancellor Angela Merkel.

Macron was one of the few in Europe who had cultivated any type of relationship with Trump, and there was the usual media chatter about a 'bromance' upon the French president's arrival. There were French flags all over Washington, and a real buzz in the town around France and Macron, followed by the first state dinner. This continued until Macron addressed Congress and basically dumped on Donald Trump, which was extraordinary.

Macron was trying to play both sides, but it was a clumsy and costly mistake. There are ways to manage these situations, and Macron was trying to establish his liberal bona fides by attacking the right. It wasn't only insulting for Trump, but for the United States, which had just done Macron the honour of a state visit. The relationship between Macron and Trump deteriorated after that, which is the opposite of what you'd hope for after such an engagement. The Trump administration was burnt by that experience, and became cautious about organising another state visit.

And then the Liberal Party decided in August 2018 to dump Malcolm Turnbull as prime minister and replace him with Scott Morrison. This did not go down well in the White House.

Despite my 'run-ins' with Malcolm (to put it mildly) in politics over the years, we had a good working relationship as prime minister and ambassador. He understood that the Trump administration was unique and needed to be handled differently. As PM, he gave me a great deal of freedom to do that. Malcolm also did a good job salvaging and then building a personal relationship with Trump after what was, let's face it, an appalling start. After that disastrous first phone call, Australia went on to be one of the few nations to have a series of political and economic wins during the Trump presidency.

Trump also began to like Turnbull. Trump views the world through the prism of wealth. To him, how much money someone has is the best indicator of both their success and their intelligence. Turnbull was a wealthy deal maker, and that meant Trump felt he could deal with him. He'd also dealt with billionaires.

Not long after Morrison became prime minister, I was at a diplomatic event at the White House and the president made his feelings clear about the change in Australia's leadership.

'Why did you guys get rid of Turnbull?' he asked, genuinely confused. 'I was just getting to know Turnbull, and now you guys have another one. Why do you keep changing your prime ministers?'

This was the narrative he was being fed by his advisers on Australia, and it was very hard for me to come up with a satisfactory response. Frankly, like many others, I thought the prime ministerial revolving door was an embarrassment. All I could do was laugh along as Australia was compared to the old days in Italy, Israel and Japan, each of which had notoriously short-lived governments.

When Morrison took over, I immediately came under pressure to secure a meeting for him with President Trump. Morrison was desperate to get guarantees that we'd be able to hold on to the tariff exemptions and other benefits won under Turnbull. If Morrison lost any of those benefits, it would've been taken as an instant judgement about his capacity to handle the international scene – which, to that point, had been very limited.

Trump, however, wasn't having a bar of it. Trump didn't like losers, and he'd already been briefed that Morrison was going to lose the next federal election, due in 2019. The president also believed it would be a waste of time to meet Morrison if there was going to be someone new in the chair the following year.

Nonetheless, I had a job to do: I needed to get Morrison a meeting. I saw an opportunity in Buenos Aires. There was going to be a G20 summit there in December 2018, and Trump would be making a relatively rare appearance on the international stage. He had eschewed other global conferences like APEC and Davos. I went into overdrive with everyone I knew in the White House. I rang Mick Mulvaney, and pushed him for a favour.

'The president really needs to meet our new prime minister,' I told Mick.

'I don't know,' he said. 'He's got a really tight schedule, and he's meeting Shinzo Abe, and you know ...' He listed all the reasons he could think of for Trump to avoid a meeting.

'Mick, it would be egregious for the US president not to meet the new Australian prime minister if they're in the same freakin' room,' I implored.

'I'll see what I can do,' he said eventually.

Later that day, I got a phone call back from Mulvaney. 'You owe me,' he said, sounding like a man who'd just taken one for the team. 'I got Morrison fifteen minutes with the president.'

'I do owe you,' I said. 'Thanks, mate.'

Fifteen minutes was enough time for Scott Morrison to have a quick conversation and a few photos with Trump. It was all he needed at the time to demonstrate that he could indeed land a meeting with the US president.

The reports out of the G20 were a little embarrassing for Morrison. During the meeting, Trump had again pressed for an explanation as to why Turnbull was ousted and how Morrison had ended up as his country's leader without winning an election. The president either really didn't understand how this worked (unlikely), or wanted to emphasise the point that he thought his meeting Morrison was a bad idea (quite likely).

Either way, Donald Trump walked out of that meeting under the impression that he'd never have to meet with Scott Morrison again. He, like so many others, thought Morrison would lose the 2019 election.

But after Morrison claimed an astounding victory against the odds, he became Donald Trump's global bestie. Whether Morrison wanted it or not, Trump was all over him – Trump loved nothing more than being associated with a winner. So, following Morrison's 2019 election win, a relationship was established between Morrison and Trump that allowed us to push ahead with plans for a state dinner. But the message from Morrison's office was that they didn't want to have *just* a state dinner. That would be fantastic, they told me, but they also wanted to do other things as part of a broader US trip.

* * *

As dull as organising a prime ministerial visit might sound, it can actually be quite an interesting exercise as you try to get the balance of engagements right. We'd already organised meetings in Washington for the prime minister with a range of people, and in fact his schedule was starting to look quite cramped. Everyone likes to have a full diary, but it can lead to exhaustion. I thought it was more important to have meaningful and considered meetings, rather than rushing from one to the next.

There were some ongoing discussions with the White House, but Melania really took over the organising of the state dinner. Much of the event was a mystery to us. We had, as it turned out, very limited input into the guest list. Of course, there was some jostling to get onto the guest list; I suggested a few names to be invited, but not all of them were.

There was a controversy about Brian Houston, which became a mini-crisis prior to the dinner. The day before the dinner, *The Wall Street Journal* reported that the White House had vetoed Morrison's attempt to have the Hillsong Church founder, who was also a spiritual guide to the prime minister, added to the list of invitees. I had very limited visibility of that issue, but Morrison would later admit he did try to have Houston invited. The fact is there were a lot of people put forward who didn't make it onto the list.

The final list was an eclectic mix, not just businesspeople. It was a varied group of individuals from all walks of life. And some people, we knew, would just reject any invitation because it was Donald Trump, so they were taken off the list. I didn't want the White House to be embarrassed by rejections.

Finally the day arrived: 19 September 2019. Scott Morrison flew in on the RAAF's new prime ministerial plane, which was a reconfigured Qantas Airbus A330. As it landed, I reflected on the decision Tony Abbott and I had made to upgrade the Australian government's air fleet, which was a no-brainer from a safety and efficiency perspective. Standing at the airport watching this plane land, I couldn't help but think back to how I'd provided for it in the 2014 budget. It seemed ironic, given the pain I went through with that budget, that I was standing here and watching Morrison as prime minister emerge from one of the upgraded planes. The A330 was one stop to Washington, and offered a far more comfortable ride than the noisy RAAF Boeing 737s. Those things mattered in international diplomacy.

Like Turnbull before him, Prime Minister Morrison stayed at Blair House. On the morning of the state dinner, we had a number of meetings, followed by the Marching of the Colors, which was attended by thousands of people on the White House lawn. It was an extraordinary display of US military pageantry, with hundreds of Australian flags all over Washington and an official welcome by President Trump.

The Australian contingent then moved to the White House to begin official talks with the president and vice president. Of course, Trump being Trump, he couldn't help getting in front of the media. What was supposed to be a five-minute doorstop press conference with Morrison in the Oval Office turned into a forty-minute media extravaganza. All the while, Mike Pence, all the security agency heads and I were waiting around twiddling our thumbs next door.

Eventually we got in and had a very engaging conversation about the Indo-Pacific region, with a focus on the shared military and intelligence relationship. At the beginning of the meeting, Trump said he couldn't wait to show us what an amazing dinner Melania had put together for us, and how we were going to have a fantastic time. He then expressed his disappointment that Rupert Murdoch was not well enough to attend – although Lachlan and Sarah Murdoch would be there.

The president sat back in his chair and began to smile. 'Why don't we get him on the phone? Yeah, that's it. We'll get him the phone.' He called out to his assistant: 'Hey, can you get Rupert on the phone?'

Someone appeared with a Diet Coke, and moments later the assistant rang through. 'Mr President, I have Rupert Murdoch on the phone.'

Trump's eyes lit up and he looked at Scott Morrison. 'Come over, Scott, come over, bring your chair here and I'll put him on the speaker phone.'

Scott Morrison moved to Trump's desk and sat near the speaker phone as Trump pushed a button. 'Rupert!' Trump chortled, as if he had an old college pal on the line.

'Hi, Mr President, how are you?' Murdoch replied in his unmistakable Australian/American twang.

'I've got Scott Morrison here, Rupert,' Trump said.

'Oh, hello, Scott,' replied an avuncular but still unwell Murdoch.

Trump then looked up at us with a grin. 'Hey, Rupert,' he said. 'I have a question for you: what's your favourite country, the United States or Australia?'

At this point Murdoch began to mumble. 'Umm, well … you know, Donald … mmm … How's it going there, Scott?'

Donald Trump has a mischievous sense of humour. He's a very funny guy, and good company – when he wants to be.

From the White House meeting and a joint press conference with many warm words exchanged, we returned to our residences to prepare for the formal dinner – which turned out to be one of the most extraordinary nights of my life. Melissa and I arrived at the White House looking our best, on what was a perfect September evening in Washington, DC.

Greeted by President Trump and First Lady Melania Trump, we made our way through a series of entrances at which stood marines bearing Australian and US flags. There was a gaggle of press in the foyer, and small bands around the garden. It was as close to walking the red carpet of the Academy Awards that I'm ever likely to get.

Our state dinner was the first to be held in the impressive outdoor Rose Garden since President Roosevelt had hosted a dinner there during World War II. Trump's entire cabinet was in attendance, as well as Vice President Pence, the heads of the Armed Forces, as well Supreme Court judges and a smattering of congressman, congresswomen, senators and governors. There were also high-profile Trump advisers, including Kellyanne Conway and Rudy Giuliani.

Aside from Prime Minister Morrison, there were no Australian government ministers in attendance, but there were a few heads of department and the chief of the Australian Defence Force, General Angus Campbell. There was a stronger business focus from our side, with the likes of Andrew Forrest, Gina Rinehart, Kerry Stokes, Lachlan and Sarah Murdoch, Shemara Wikramanayake, Andrew Liveris, and of course the president's favourites, Anthony Pratt and Greg Norman. *The Washington Post* and CNN would publish a full list of the attendees the next day.

President Trump invited Scott and Jenny Morrison, along with Melissa and me, to the private East Wing of the White House for a personal tour and a glass of champagne. The ensuing conversation was a good example of Trump's sometimes obsessive curiosity about certain subjects. Despite being a huge risk taker in his business life, he was a pretty cautious guy when it came to his personal habits: he was notoriously a clean freak who didn't drink alcohol (I suspect he had water in his champagne glass). He was obsessed with the dangerous animals we had in Australia, and kept asking how we could deal with this in our everyday lives.

'You have the brown snake – that's like the most poisonous snake in the world!' he said at one point.

'One went over Joe's boot on our farm,' Melissa offered.

'What? What the hell? What happened?' said a horrified Trump.

I relayed the story: we were on our cattle ranch in Far North Queensland one afternoon when I noticed an enormous brown snake heading straight for me. I stopped and it slithered straight across my boot.

'What would've happened if he'd bitten you?' asked Trump.

'Well, Mr President, I wouldn't be here. You have about twenty minutes to get help for a brown snake bite, and we were at least an hour away from the nearest medical help.'

Appalled but amazed as to why we would choose to live in a country with such dangers, he continued to fire questions about our near-death experiences with Australia's native fauna.

Melania was unrelentingly charming, and we talked at length about their son, Barron. He was just a little younger than my eldest son, Xavier, so we shared our concerns about sport and school and so on.

We were engrossed in this conversation when President Trump called out from the next room: 'Where's Melissa? Where's Jenny? I have to show them this new bathroom.'

I walked out of the Lincoln Bedroom to see what all the fuss was about, and headed into the Queen Elizabeth Bedroom (as Trump called it). There was the president, showing Melissa and Jenny around the bathroom, which was replete with new gold fittings.

'I love this en suite! Look at these amazing taps! We've just had this one renovated,' Trump said, like the true real estate man that he is at heart.

It was a surreal moment, watching the president of the United States show off his new bathroom to us like a contestant on *The Block*. I suppose even Donald Trump could have a 'pinch me' moment about living in the White House.

* * *

The rest of the night was simply perfect. The women present were escorted by individual marine guards to their seats. Simultaneously, an orchestra played on the roof above the Oval Office as a choir of at least forty men and women, trumpeters, an assembly of violinists and a gaggle of assembled guests looked on in awe.

As we walked past the Oval Office, I could see, sitting on the uncluttered Resolute Desk, the statue of Corporal Leslie Charles Allen that we had presented to President Trump earlier in the day. Known as 'Bull', Corporal Allen was an Australian stretcher bearer during World War II who received the US Silver Star for Bravery after rescuing twelve US soldiers at the Battle of Mount Tambu, in Papua New Guinea. The statue depicted Allen carrying an injured American through the jungle on his back. It was the Americans who had recognised Allen's bravery. Australia had treated him poorly, discharging him and not recognising his valour after he suffered from PTSD during and after the war. Although the statue was likely placed on the desk for our benefit, I was chuffed that Allen's story had moved President Trump.

The dinner itself was marvellous. Every detail, from the flowers to the seating, from the food and wine to the music, reflected the warmth of the American people and the generous hospitality of President and Mrs Trump. Greg Norman said he'd never been to an event like it in his life. Henry Kissinger said it was the best state dinner he'd been to, and he'd seen more than a few.

When the last song of the night was played – 'I Still Call Australia Home' – most in the assembled crowd were overwhelmed. Many Aussies had tears in their eyes, so moved were they that the American guests were so proud to be our mates.

In true Aussie style, when the event ended a few of the Australian guests hung around in the forlorn hope that Donald would appear and invite us for a few follow-up beers in the Oval Office. Alas, we were ushered out by the Secret Service in an efficient pincer movement.

Without doubt this event marked the high-water mark of Australian–US relations during my time as ambassador. We had come a long way since Trump's disastrous phone call with Malcolm Turnbull at the beginning of 2017. This was the moment when, despite all the madness and chaos of the Trump administration, I was confident we had navigated a way through for both our nations.

But there was a question lingering at the back of my mind that I couldn't shake: How long would it last?

CHAPTER 8

TRADE WARS

Fighting tariffs, losing the TPP and stayin' alive in Tokyo

About a month after that beautiful September evening at the White House, I was asked to give a speech at Westminster College, in Fulton, Missouri. The Cherry-Price Leadership Lecture has the aim of 'shining the spotlight on the character traits of successful leaders of our time'. The real lineage of the Westminster College leadership speech, however, can be traced back to one of the greatest and most influential political speeches for Western democracy in the last seventy years. It was, following the end of World War II, the venue of Winston Churchill's 'Sinews of Peace' speech, which became popularly known as his 'Iron Curtain' speech.

In it, Churchill warned that the evil of Nazism had been supplanted by the USSR's influence upon European governments: 'From Stettin in the Baltic to Trieste in the Adriatic, an iron curtain has descended across the Continent. Behind that line lie all the capitals of the ancient states of Central and Eastern Europe.' The speech was really about what the West had to do in order to maintain the primacy of liberal democracy. Churchill was articulating the importance of bands that tied together democratic, peaceful and prosperous nations – as opposed to dictatorial, violent and poorer regimes.

While under no illusions as to my oratory skills in comparison to Churchill's, I was inspired to devote my speech to the importance of free trade. I gave it the name 'The Sinews of Prosperity'.

There is no doubt in my mind that free trade has been one of the most important 'sinews' of peace and prosperity since World War II – and, in particular, since the end of the Cold War. Although far from a perfect creation, it has undoubtedly been a force for good in the world. My belief in the virtues of free trade is one of the core values that have guided me through my political career.

I am, by virtue of my family background and my career, of a cosmopolitan worldview. Having seen so much of the world, I cannot imagine why someone who lives in another part of the world should be denied the benefits afforded to us in prosperous nations. Of course, most of the world's population – billions of people, indeed – do not share the prosperity we enjoy. But free trade does not cause this inequality. In fact, free trade consistently demonstrates that it is a key solution to global poverty. Given the strength of my views on the subject, I was in no mind to hold back that night at Westminster College.

To give a memorable speech you need the right environment. Not unlike a sportsperson, who will always perform their very best in front of a big crowd in a rowdy stadium, orators also hanker for the atmosphere an event can bring. Lincoln's speech at Gettysburg was in front of a crowd of soldiers and families, most of whom could not even hear what their president was saying. Churchill's finest words were invariably in the bear pit of the British parliament. The House of Commons at Westminster is small, crowded and tiered with bleachers that make it the perfect amphitheatre for rhetorical battle.

In this small town of Fulton – population 12,000 – I stayed in the same bedroom at the same small B&B as Winston Churchill had all those years before. When I took to the lectern, it was in a grand environment: a church, formerly situated in London, designed by the great English architect Christopher Wren. After being severely damaged in the Blitz, it had been brought to America and reassembled, brick by brick, in Fulton.

The occasion was not lost on me. As an orator, Churchill gave truth to words, and that was what I wanted to do as well.

I had come to the conclusion that the Trump administration's increasingly protectionist trade policies, which included tariffs on some of its closest allies, ran against Republican Party philosophy and American values. Not only this, they threatened the global order of peace and prosperity, previously built and led by the United States.

'Ladies and gentlemen, if you abdicate leadership, you rarely get it back,' I told the audience. 'So the US must not allow itself to walk away from its trade leadership role in the world, otherwise it will inevitably pay a very significant price. Its role is crucial because it's American values that matter.'

I argued that the United States under Trump should have joined a slew of trade agreements and organisations, opportunities that previous administrations would have jumped at. These included the Trans-Pacific Partnership, the Regional Comprehensive Economic Partnership (RCEP), and the Asian Infrastructure and Investment Bank. I also spoke out about Trump and his leading trade advisers' obsession with trade surpluses.

'I have heard suggestions – and perhaps you have heard them too – that to "win" in trade with another country, you need to sell more to them than you buy from them – that is, that you should have a trade surplus. I disagree,' I said. 'The argument put by protectionists in favour of tariffs and quotas is akin to saying that instead of spending my time working for my employer, I should make my own food and sew my own clothes. Trust me, most of us don't want that. It doesn't make sense.'

I pointed out that the United States had a trade surplus worth US$29 billion a year with Australia, meaning that we had a substantial trade deficit with the United States. This, however, didn't worry us in the slightest. Conversely, we had a substantial trade surplus with China because of their need for our resources. But neither a trade surplus nor a trade deficit with the world's two largest economies prevented us from pursuing a free trade agreement with each.

'Of course, free trade can be contentious,' I went on. 'In my country it enjoys bipartisan support. It doesn't stop the critics, though. They usually come out to argue for special favours for particular industries, that other hardworking Australians are expected to pay for. The critics trade on sentimentality and fear, rather than hope and opportunity. The sensible middle ground of society understands that when we trade freely with other nations, our nation gets richer. Protectionism discourages growth and rewards mediocrity.'

I also wanted to articulate the dangers of Donald Trump's tariffs, pointing to their destabilising effects both domestically and internationally: how they were fuelling the rise of nationalism in America and in other countries that felt attacked by isolationist trade policies.

'Isolating an economy from trade and commerce with other countries is a political tool that should be used very cautiously,' I said. 'If a nation becomes economically isolated, then history proves it can end up accelerating domestic nationalism, fuelling outward-facing aggression.'

At its heart, free trade was an American story, I argued, and for America to turn its back on free trade was for the nation to abdicate its leadership role globally. 'You are still the world's largest economy. Your dollar is the world's reserve currency. Your capital markets are the engine room for global commerce. So I find the debate here in the United States on free and fair trade rather baffling. Being open to the world made America great in the first place. It will keep you great.'

Unlike a few other speeches I had given during my time as ambassador, there were some in the media paying attention to this particular address. 'Joe Hockey Savages Donald Trump's "America First" Trade Mercantilism', screamed a headline in *The Australian Financial Review*. 'US Ambassador Joe Hockey has unleashed a blistering attack on Donald Trump's isolationist attempts to dismantle more than 60 years of global economic order,' wrote the *AFR*'s Washington correspondent, Jacob Greber, who went on to describe my speech as a 'stunningly blunt' one.

The Sydney Morning Herald said I had 'denounced Donald Trump's trade war with China' in a 'scathing speech', while SBS News said I had given a 'stark economic warning to Donald Trump', claiming I had said the trade war was a 'precursor to war'. (I hadn't quite said that, but clicks are clicks, I suppose.)

The bluntness of my attack on the Trump administration – and it was coming from the top representative of an ally that only a month earlier had been honoured with a state dinner – was immediately felt within the US administration. And, like clockwork, just a day later, I would receive some angry feedback from the White House.

Picking up the phone, I braced for the swift backlash. Matt Pottinger, the deputy national security adviser, was on the phone. 'What are you doing?' he demanded. 'I thought you were on our side.'

I replied that I was on the side of our shared values, and one of those was free trade.

'But why are you attacking us?' he persisted. 'I mean, you don't even get to China until about page nine!'

'Hang on,' I said. 'I gave this speech at Westminster College in Fulton, Missouri. It's not like it was given in Shenzhen. And secondly, I believe in free trade. That's something I've always been committed to. Australians support free trade, and it's in Australia's interest to continue free trade. We produce four times more than we consume! And we support free trade even though we run trade deficits because that's the right thing to do, for us and for the rest of the world. I thought the president and all Republicans shared that view.'

'We do,' Matt acknowledged, and not long after that he hung up the phone.

My much-loved grandmother Rose Hockey attending one of my St Aloysius' College cadet retreats in 1982. I developed a deep respect for public service and fate prevented me from ending up at the Royal Military College, Duntroon.

My first trip to New York as a young lawyer in 1989. I formed an early bond with Wall Street and later rang the bell at the NYSE.

At the birth of my eldest son, Xavier, in 2005. Raising our amazing children remains my proudest achievement. Prime Minister John Howard welcomed Xavier to the world with a statement to parliament.

Mum and Dad – my great heroes. My father, Richard, overcame incredible adversity: as a child he spent five years in a Jerusalem orphanage and then went on to become a successful businessman. While working in his Bondi corner store, he won the heart of local beauty queen Beverley; they married in 1963.

Above: Addressing the G20 in Brisbane, 2014. Chairing and reforming the G20 was one of my best experiences as Treasurer.

Left: At the G20 with then US Federal Reserve Chair Janet Yellen (she went on to become secretary of the Treasury under President Joe Biden). I've always found her humble, open to advice and willing to share her knowledge.

Below left: Handing down the 2014 federal budget. It was much maligned, but history has demonstrated it was the right thing to do for Australia.

Below right: Former Labor Prime Minister Julia Gillard during a visit to DC in 2017. Politics is a blood sport at times, but political foes like Julia demonstrate the ability to get over feuds and move on with mutual respect.

Above left: With President Barack Obama in the Oval Office, receiving my ambassadorial credentials, 26 January 2016. Obama was always a good friend of Australia, although we would clash over Australia's relationship with China.

Above: Walking along the White House colonnade with Melissa, Adelaide, Ignatius and Xavier, on the day I received my ambassador's accreditation. It was very important to me that the family be there, given the sacrifices they'd made during my political career. The Babbage-Hockeys left an impression that day!

Left: My wife, Melissa Babbage. Always the first person I go to for advice and whose faith and support has never faltered.

Former US presidents George W. Bush and Bill Clinton – two very good presidents, for different reasons. Both men are some of the best company I've ever enjoyed among world leaders – or on the golf course.

Left: Speaking during an ANZAC Day memorial service in 2018, at the National Cathedral in DC – one of my favourite places to spend quiet time during my tenure as ambassador.

Below left: Our Christmas card, 2018. During my years in politics, I had missed so much family time and could, fortunately, be with Melissa and the kids a lot more as ambassador.

Below: The Australian ambassador's residence in DC. Alas, my attempts to make this promotional Indy car my ambassadorial vehicle were unsuccessful.

Bottom: Trying out a flight simulator for the F-35 – Australia's best defence.

With former New Jersey Governor and Trump advisor Chris Christie in 2017. Chris and I get on extremely well. He is a consummate communicator and was a great contact for me and my team in the Trump campaign.

Meeting with US President Donald Trump in the Oval Office. Trump may have been the most controversial president since WWII, but Australia achieved arguably the best policy outcomes of any foreign nation during Trump's tenure.

Donald and Melania Trump greeting me and Melissa at the White House state dinner in September 2019. Australia was one of only two countries honoured with an official state dinner during Trump's term – and the event was a great success.

Meeting former US Navy Indo-Pacific Commander Admiral Phil Davidson in Pearl Harbor, Hawaii, on the HMAS *Hobart* in 2018.

My first personal meeting with US President Donald Trump was at Trump National Golf Club in Virginia in April 2018. We were joined by Fox News' Bret Baier (centre right) and Trump's future chief of staff Mick Mulvaney, both of whom became my good mates.

Trump talked and played tough through the game but was always good company. I needed to sink this mammoth putt on the final hole to win. It's the greatest shot I've ever sunk, not least because it meant I had just beaten the president on his own course. Trump wasn't thrilled about losing, but he respected me for it.

At the US–Mexican border. Trump's famous border wall with Mexico became a symbol of his presidency, but I was told he borrowed the idea from *The New York Times* columnist Thomas Friedman.

The end of the wall – unfinished business for Donald Trump.

Addressing the US National Governors Association. The theme '100 Years of Mateship' was celebrated throughout my time as ambassador – and beyond. It was an incredible aid to help Americans understand the depth of the Australian–US relationship.

Right: With 'outback wrangler' Matt Wright and a giant python at the NGA event. Snakes were a bit of a recurring subject with the Americans, and Donald Trump was obsessed that a brown snake had once slithered over my boot.

A selfie with Olivia Newton-John on the day she was awarded an Order of Australia. Olivia is a long-time American resident but will always be a permanent ambassador for everything Australian. She is a national living treasure (literally, she was awarded that too).

Osaka G20 in June 2019. Dinner with President Trump and Prime Minister Morrison and a host of senior US officials, including Mick Mulvaney, Mike Pompeo, Steve Mnuchin and our nemeses on trade policy, Bob Lighthizer, Wilbur Ross and Peter Navarro. It was a weird dinner, but we didn't come out any worse off.

The beginnings of Bondi Partners, our strategic advisory and funds management business. With CEO Alex Tureman in our Washington, DC office. There's still a lot of my father's business sense in me today.

Matt Pottinger is an exceptional friend of Australia and a man of integrity. He knew where we were coming from, and I knew he respected our position. Nonetheless, the White House was shocked that a friend and an ally such as Australia would speak out about these core beliefs.

Not long after that conversation, another envoy was sent to placate me. 'We believe in free trade,' I was told, 'but we also want fair trade.'

'So do we,' I said. 'I guess that means we're ideologically aligned. But all the recent cases point to you guys going off in your own direction.'

Nothing illustrated this better, I said, than the US refusal to engage with us on the future of the World Trade Organization (WTO). Robert Lighthizer, Trump's formidable cabinet-level trade representative and a fierce protectionist, had enormous influence in this regard. He'd shamelessly python-squeezed the WTO by not agreeing to the appointment of new appellate judges; the result was that it didn't have a quorum of judges and couldn't move forward.

'This is all the Bretton Woods framework that you guys created, America created,' I said. 'Now you're abdicating responsibility, and you're confusing the world. You led the establishment of the International Monetary Fund, the World Bank and the WTO, and now you're undermining them. And don't get me started on the TPP! You were advocating for that as well, but now you're in reverse. What's the world meant to think? Some of us are determined to be the good guys. Some of us are going to be consistent. If it makes us unpopular with you from time to time, so be it. But we are your mates, and in our country, if you care about your mates, you'll be honest with them when they go off course.'

So ended my rant. I felt pleased. That was a show of real power on behalf of my country. The type of power that I had built over almost four years in the United States. I think real power is exercised when you can get your way without selling your soul.

The fact is we were successful during this era. The reason was that we were consistent and reliable. Some people think you're more influential when you're popular. There's some degree of truth to that. I can't deny it, having been both very popular and somewhat unpopular over twenty years in Australian politics. But while popularity is seductive, it is also fleeting. One day you are up and the next day you can be down and out. Lasting influence is about achievements and not wasting power when you have the opportunity to use it. Certainly, don't pass up the opportunity to exercise your influence when it's in your nation's best interests.

* * *

When I was Australia's treasurer, I'd rarely found a closer ally on free trade than the United States. Although our free trade agreement with the United States was completed under the Howard government, its effects began to accelerate under Rudd and Gillard, and then under Prime Minister Abbott.

As hard as President Obama's officials played on the Asian Infrastructure and Investment Bank (AIIB) and, later, the TPP, they were relative pussycats compared to the big US corporations when they wanted something to go their way. As treasurer, by far the biggest brawl I had with a company was with the food and commodities giant Archer Daniels Midland (ADM), concerning their takeover bid for Australian agricultural icon GrainCorp.

The $3.4 billion bid for full control of GrainCorp obviously made sense for ADM and the GrainCorp board. But the question I had to ask as treasurer was whether it made sense for Australia. An ADM takeover would have handed 85 per cent of the Australian east coast grain market to an American company. It was also one of the most complex decisions our Foreign Investment Review Board (FIRB) had been charged with making.

I had inherited the bid decision from Labor when we were elected in September 2013. The ALP would have supported the deal, and new shadow treasurer Chris Bowen was pushing for it to go through. ADM had also thrown in a $250 million sweetener in the form of upgraded rail infrastructure. By October 2013, the takeover process had been running for almost a year.

Some very senior businesspeople dealing with ADM had come to me and said, 'Look, you shouldn't let this happen.' Suppliers, buyers, farmers and community leaders, too, all opposed the transaction but were scared to say so out loud. The National Party's MPs were overt in their opposition, as was the National Farmers' Federation. Outside of ADM, there was no real advocacy for the sale in business circles, other than the vague assurance that it was 'a good deal'.

The requirements under the *Foreign Acquisitions and Takeovers Act 1975*, which regulates the FIRB, state that the treasurer of the day has absolute discretion to block a foreign investment transaction that is 'contrary to the national interest'. And that phrase is not a defined term, which gives enormous discretion to the treasurer.

Because of the public opprobrium, I decided to find out more about ADM. I learnt that in 1996 it had been hit with a US$100 million fine by the US Department of Justice for criminal antitrust (or cartel) behaviour, stemming from its role in an international conspiracy to fix prices and eliminate competition in food additives. That was the largest fine for criminal antitrust behaviour in US history, and several senior executives had been sentenced to jail. In 2013, ADM had been forced to pay US$36 million in fines after the US corporate regulator, the Securities and Exchange Commission, found that its subsidiary had paid US$21 million in bribes in Germany and the Ukraine. What was more, ADM seemed like bullies in their approach towards not just GrainCorp but the farmers; they were handling community relations really badly.

At the same time I was considering the deal, I was due to go to the United States on one of my first trips as treasurer in October 2013 – first to Washington, DC for a G20 finance ministers' meeting, and then to New York. I had specifically said I didn't want to meet any of the interested parties in New York. I was not going to get involved with GrainCorp or ADM or the farming groups. My view was that the FIRB process had to run its course. If they made a decision I didn't like, then I could overrule them.

Despite this, when I arrived in New York strange things began to happen. I was making the rounds to see prominent business leaders, including Jamie Dimon at JP Morgan, BHP chairman Jacques Nasser and Dow Chemicals boss Andrew Liveris. It became obvious pretty quickly that they were strong advocates for the ADM bid. Everyone was telling me it was a good deal. Could that be an incredible coincidence? I couldn't understand how ADM knew I was meeting with Dimon, Nasser or Liveris, but my political antennae suggested a campaign was afoot.

When ADM representatives started arriving for my more intimate gatherings with business leaders, I became agitated. And when their lobbyists started asking me questions about the deal at my public speeches, I became angry. I was being harassed, and I didn't like it.

There had been one too many coincidences. We did the predictable security searches and found that someone had breached my personal online diary.

When it came to a company character test, ADM had now done more than enough to fail. It confirmed for me what others had suggested. The treasurer's discretion to reject foreign investment in Australia was there for exactly this purpose.

Treasury Secretary Martin Parkinson and I decided it was necessary to meet with the CEO of ADM, Patricia Woertz, to put to her what had happened and inform her of my decision concerning the GrainCorp takeover bid. Woertz flew from New York to Canberra, and we met in Parkinson's office at the Treasury. I directly asked her to withdraw her bid, and she said she couldn't do so under US law; she had to continue. To which I replied, 'I'm going to reject your application.' Woertz was shocked. I told her that, for a range of reasons relating to the behaviour of the company, I was invoking the national interest test.

But the drama of the ADM bid was not over yet. I was preparing to make the formal announcement that I had rejected the bid, only to be told by the Americans that I was obliged to inform the US government first. 'On what basis?' I asked. It was brought to my attention that under the Australia–United States Free Trade Agreement, an undisclosed side deal had been struck between former trade minister Mark Vaile and US trade representative Bob Zoellick. The Americans produced a letter signed by the pair stating that if any US company were knocked back under the authority of the FIRB, there had to be a consultation with the US administration. I was shocked that this side deal had never been made public, and that I hadn't even been informed of it by my own department.

I rang Australia's then ambassador in Washington, Kim Beazley, and said: 'Can you speak to the White House? I'm about to knock back ADM.' Beazley said he would get in contact immediately. That was enough consultation, as far as I was concerned.

Beazley did a great job in DC. He was expedient and knew the difficult politics of the issue. In response to a White House query as to why the deal had been rejected, he used diplomatic language to send the clear message that the company had integrity issues. No further questions were asked.

A couple of days later, I made the formal announcement, and despite being attacked by some in business, media and the opposition, the relationship with the United States survived and we all moved on.

* * *

The attempt to have the United States sign up to the Trans-Pacific Partnership was a long, painful and, ultimately, Sisyphean task. Every time I seemed to get close to a final agreement, poor timing or plain bad luck would crash down on our diplomatic efforts.

The real irony was that the TPP should never have been a hard sell for the United States. To the great credit of President Obama and his administration, he was a champion of the agreement. It was consistent with the global trade policy and values of the United States right up to that very particular moment in history.

The TPP started life as a Trans-Pacific Strategic Economic Partnership Agreement, an agreement between four smaller Pacific Rim nations: New Zealand, Chile, Brunei and Singapore. Its goal was to govern a range of economic policy areas, but most notably it mandated a reduction (indeed, virtually an elimination) of trade tariffs among the group members. It was in part the brainchild of Tim Groser, the future New Zealand ambassador to Washington.

By 2008, a series of other, larger countries joined the agreement, including Australia, Canada, Mexico, Japan and, the biggest hitter of all, the United States. The aim was to have a comprehensive agreement on trade, remedies and arbitration, competition, intellectual property and financial services between member states. A central tenet was the elimination of trade tariffs among signatories by 2015. It was to be the precursor of a fully fledged APEC free-trade zone.

While the goal of tariff abolition by 2015 was never reached, a final agreement for ratification by the member nations, including the United States, was being circulated by then. The TTP accord would still need congressional approval in order to be ratified. This, of course, coincided with the rise of not just Donald Trump but also Bernie Sanders.

The growth of populism on both sides of politics in the United States fuelled discontent about the TPP. It turned an agreement that should have, and previously would have, enjoyed bipartisan support into one that could barely be uttered by a candidate in US politics.

Opposition to the TPP in the United States started on the left of the Democratic Party in the run-up to the 2016 campaign. The emergence of Bernie Sanders as a viable presidential candidate saw opposition to global trade deals move from the fringes of the left wing of the party and into mainstream Democratic thinking. The idea that a decaying America was losing hundreds of thousands of jobs to other nations in a 'race to the bottom' because of free trade agreements became a theme of Democrats' language – even if it was barely based in fact.

While similar opposition had been building on the right to more free trade deals, it was Donald Trump who became the champion of trade scepticism in the Republican Party. Despite the obvious hypocrisy of a New York billionaire opposing free trade, candidate Trump sniffed the electoral populism of the issue and ran with it – hard.

Opposition to the TPP during the 2016 election campaign therefore became one of those central issues – which also included pulling out of Iraq and Afghanistan – on which the far right and the far left agreed. It was championed by populist leaders on both sides striving to lock in their political base during the primaries.

Trade deals, in Trump's language, became synonymous with giving China a free ride. For all the anti-China and anti-TPP rhetoric that made up much of Trump's campaign, and later his trade policies, the great irony of opposition to the TPP was that it was partly there to negate the general reliance upon trade with China in the Asia-Pacific. Were the United States to sign up to the TPP, the effect would have been to lessen, not increase, China's economic influence in the world.

The last domino to fall was Hillary Clinton. She was pushed into opposing the TPP because she could see the popularity of Sanders' position within her own party, and of Trump's within the Republican Party. It was a self-evidently ludicrous position for Clinton, who in the 2000s and the 1990s – both as a senator and when her husband was president – had championed US free trade deals throughout the world. But in 21st-century America, populism has become an essential requirement for high office. It was all the more ridiculous because President Obama was still championing

America's involvement in the trade pact. Clinton's newfound trade populism left the president holding the baby, and gave Democrats and Republicans suspicious of the deal in Congress an excuse to vote against it.

Despite this general opposition to the TPP, it was one of my first tasks as ambassador to try to get it over the line with the Americans – and I was determined to do so.

I started a dialogue with Denis McDonough, President Obama's chief of staff, and began to formulate a strategy. It was obvious that we'd need to try to get it through Congress during the remaining months of Obama's presidency, as neither major candidate would support it in the next four-year term.

Next I went to see Republican majority Senate leader Mitch McConnell, to discuss the prospect of getting Republican support for the TPP prior to the election of a new president. But McConnell was adamant that the deal was dead. 'You know Donald Trump's come out against it,' he told me. 'And you know Hillary has said she's against it. And that's it.' He sounded resigned to the TPP's failure.

I decided it was time to draw on the legislative tricks I'd learnt during my years in parliament. It occurred to me that we may be able to get a bill through Congress during the 'lame duck' session – the scheduled sitting period after the 8 November 2016 election but before the swearing-in of a new president on 20 January 2017.

McConnell was sceptical. 'I don't think you'll get it through the lame duck session,' he replied, arguing that not enough Republicans or Democrats would stick their neck out for the TPP and risk the ire of the new president.

My conversations with Trump's campaign strategists made it clear that he wouldn't be moved away from his opposition to the TPP. It had become an article of faith for Trump. It was one of the few consistent policy positions he held – and, maddeningly, he was persuasive when articulating his opposition to the deal.

I felt we could still move Clinton's position to one of tacit support – at the very least, she might ignore the legislation if it was passed while Obama was still president. If we could somehow get it through the lame duck session, Clinton could wash her hands of it when she came into the White House. It would be 'Obama's deal' – which, in fact, was how Clinton's campaign described it to us.

The net effect, however, would be the same. Clinton would not overturn America's involvement in the TPP once she was president because she wasn't actually ideologically opposed to it. She could campaign against it publicly and still turn a blind eye as it was ushered through Congress before she took office.

I put the plan to Denis McDonough and awaited a reply from the Clinton campaign. To my amazement, we were informed by the White House, with a wink and nod, that Hillary would indeed turn a blind eye to the TPP legislation going through Congress in the lame duck session.

A couple of days later, in early November, I received another call from the White House chief of staff. McDonough informed me that Obama had decided he would try to execute the plan on the very day of the election. Denis told me I would have to be ready to move quickly, as Australia would have an important part to play in getting the United States to approve the TPP.

There were a few reasons we were being so closely informed by the White House of the TPP strategy. One was that it was a huge priority for the Turnbull government, and therefore a top issue for me as ambassador. Australia and New Zealand were the tireless proponents of the TPP on Capitol Hill.

Another was that Australia – more specifically, its Pharmaceutical Benefits Scheme – had become a sticking point for one US senator, Orrin Hatch. The Republican from Utah had served an incredible forty-two years in Congress, making him the longest-serving senator from his party in history. He was eighty-two years old, but there wasn't much you could do in the Senate without first getting it past Senator Hatch.

Hatch had decided he didn't care for the TPP. By some coincidence, he was also very close to big pharmaceutical companies in the United States. According to donations records, Hatch received US$238,000 worth of campaign contributions from pharmaceutical companies and the health products industry in the 2017–18 electoral cycle alone. He, of course, held earnest fears for US drug companies' intellectual property rights when they engaged with Australia's socialist-sounding Pharmaceutical Benefits Scheme.

The protection of a drug's intellectual property expires five years after it is approved for use in Australia. That means that the company that invests in and makes the drug gets exclusivity on production and pricing until the five-year exemption ends. After that, biosimilar and generic drug manufacturers can produce and sell the same drug to consumers at much cheaper prices. Drug companies hate the time limit, but it's a great outcome for consumers. The pharmaceutical company lobbyists had wound Senator Hatch up so much during the negotiations of the TPP that nobody could unwind him even now that a compromise had been reached. For him, Australia was still the enemy.

I agreed with the White House to provide Senator Hatch with a letter on behalf of Australia to allay his concerns about the TPP and the US pharmaceutical companies' intellectual property issues. Hatch was still clear that he wouldn't support any legislation before the election, but once he had received this assurance in writing from Australia, he indicated he wouldn't oppose it going through Congress in the lame duck session.

On the day of the presidential election, Denis McDonough called me again. 'Are you ready to go with the letter?' he asked. 'We're going to move on this tomorrow.'

I assured him that it was in hand: I would go to the Capitol to see Hatch when I received their say-so.

The plan, however, had one fatal flaw: it was premised upon Hillary Clinton winning the election. A loss by Clinton was an outcome that Obama's office had not seriously countenanced. Now, from where I was sitting, a Trump victory seemed a real possibility, but this plan was the only hope we had of getting US acceptance of the TPP.

As fate would have it, that night Donald Trump was elected the 45th president of the United States. Trump's victory killed off America's involvement in the TPP, and what would have been an extraordinary diplomatic coup for Australia.

On 23 January 2017, just three days after being sworn in as president, Donald Trump signed a presidential directive removing the United States from the TPP. It will be a long time before the US revisits the issue, if it ever does.

* * *

If you'd told me before I left for Washington that avoiding US tariffs on Australian steel and aluminium would be one of my greatest victories as ambassador, I'd have said you were mad. In fact, if you had nominated US tariffs as the most pressing trade issue globally, the consensus would be that you were barking crazy. Tariffs on China? Maybe. But tariffs on the rest of the world, including on America's closest allies, based on a confected threat to America's national security – really?

I first started hearing rumblings that Trump was going to slap a tariff on steel imports when President Xi Jinping of China visited Mar-a-Lago in April 2017. Trump had been making threats of this nature against China throughout the election campaign, but by the time of Xi's visit, it had become apparent that he was considering tariffs on the rest of the world as well.

To understand how America found itself in this position, you have to know the people Trump had surrounded himself with. An old guard of steel protectionists had managed to get Trump's ear on trade.

In 2017, Trump appointed a youthful Wilbur Ross (aged seventy-nine) as his secretary of commerce. Ross was a long-time steel protectionist who had made his fortune with the International Steel Group. He would acquire failing steel companies for next to nothing, restructure them and then sell them off at extraordinary profit. He managed to sell ISG in 2005 for US$4.5 billion.

Ross was joined by Bob Lighthizer, whom Trump appointed as the United States' trade representative, a Cabinet position and the equivalent of our minister for trade. Lighthizer was a Washington, DC attorney who'd had the foresight to get into politics as far back as the Reagan administration, where he'd previously been the deputy trade representative. As I would later learn, Lighthizer had also worked as Wilbur Ross's lawyer for many years. They were a formidable pair.

At the same time, Ross and Lighthizer were being encouraged by Peter Navarro. An economist and failed politician, Navarro rose to prominence as one of the earliest and most aggressive anti-China public intellectuals with a non-fiction treatise called *Death by China*. (With a title like that, I won't ruin the ending for you.) As it turned out, Trump was a fan.

Navarro was first appointed a trade adviser to Trump at the end of 2016, before the new president had been sworn in. His brief was to go after any perceived US trade imbalance, targeting China in particular, by all means necessary. He was then appointed to the new position of director of trade and manufacturing policy in 2017.

Navarro was a bit of an oddball. He was a bit like the painter in the old US sitcom *Murphy Brown* – he never left the White House. But then, out of nowhere, he would just pop up unannounced at the most frustrating moments. Although a comparatively reclusive ideologue, he nonetheless had Trump's ear on trade and China, and exerted ridiculous levels of influence, much to the chagrin of all sensible people in the West Wing.

With these three in charge of Trump's trade policies, the United States was taking a great leap backwards. Frankly, I was appalled. I had been used to dealing with Obama's trade representative, Michael Froman, who had been an indefatigable advocate for fair trade. He was a formidable negotiator – indeed, Kim Beazley had warned me that he was both very aggressive and way too blunt. I'd met him when I was chairing the G20, though, and I knew he was smart, aggressive but also very fair. He believed in free trade.

All of sudden, along came Lighthizer, who, armed with Ross's knowledge of the steel industry and with Navarro's intellectual backing, took on a prosecutorial role in Trump's administration to weaponise tariffs against China and the rest of the world.

The sad truth was that Trump believed tariffs were 'great'. He had a long history of protectionism dating back to his early property developer days. He was convinced they were a useful tool and ticked several important boxes: that they protected US industry, that they were popular in the US industrial heartland he had just won, and that bringing back tariffs would mean America stood aside from what Trump believed were largely meaningless or damaging international agreements. Most significantly, Trump thought they raised tax revenue for his administration. In short, he believed they were good politics and would also make money for the United States.

In fact, this last point was the key to understanding Trump's support of tariffs: he viewed them as a backdoor way of raising taxes. If America made money from them, where was the harm? It was very difficult to convince him of the downside of tariffs – especially as he refused to believe they had any material impact on prices.

Gradually, Trump began to weaponise tariffs under Section 232 of the Trade Expansion Act. The section was actually a national security initiative, allowing the president to use an authority delegated by Congress to impose tariffs or quotas on imports that 'threaten to impair the national security'. The law doesn't require evidence of injury or proof that the goods are being traded unfairly (like dumping or subsidies). In other words, the discretion of the president to implement such tariffs is extremely broad.

As soon as Trump started flagging that he would introduce tariffs on steel and aluminium, we sat up and took notice. The once proud Australian steel industry was already struggling under the weight of Chinese dumping, with the Whyalla-based Arrium having recently gone under and picked up in a fire sale by GFG. Our main export was now through BlueScope's rolled coil steel, which was converted into the popular Colorbond product in the United States by its American subsidiary. We didn't export a lot of aluminium to the United States, but our global exports were still worth around $300 million per year and the prospect of a tariff was very concerning and unnecessarily punitive against a close ally. Compounding the difficulty was that BlueScope, our main exporter, was not well organised in their lobbying efforts in Washington, DC.

Australian companies that deal in the United States just don't think much about regulatory risk, and therefore don't invest in protecting their interests in Washington, DC. Australian business was working from the premise that America was a predictable and consistent regulatory environment. This is simply not the case anymore. It can be volatile, and at times pose sovereign risk – and this was especially so when Donald Trump was in charge.

In January 2018, Trump ordered new tariffs on all imported washing machines and solar panels. The only significant supplier to the United States of solar panels was China, so that tariff automatically increased the cost of panels to American consumers. For Trump, it was a win against climate change alarmists, a win on tax revenue and a win against China. Of course, the Chinese simply opened factories in Thailand, Vietnam, India and Indonesia to get around the tariffs. So, in the end – and as predicted – the tariffs didn't work as intended.

On 1 March the administration announced that it would be imposing a 25 per cent tariff on all steel imports and 10 per cent on all aluminium. While Australia and close allies such as the European Union and Canada were exempt from the immediate orders, the tariffs would be applied to all supplier nations by May. I quickly got a phone call from Prime Minister Turnbull, who told me we needed to save steel and aluminium exports and stop Australian companies from being stuck with these tariffs. I agreed, and we went to work on winning Australia a permanent exemption.

The political impact in Australia of Trump's announcement was significant, although the commercial impact was actually negligible. The issue morphed into a question of whether or not Donald Trump liked us after 'that phone call'. Our success on tariff exemptions would be interpreted as an indication of how favourably we were viewed in DC and how close we really were to the United States. It was giving critics of Trump (and of me) an opportunity to say that America, at the first turn of events, was going to be as aggressive to Australia as the rest of the world – that we were no different from anyone else.

We started prosecuting the case against tariffs hard. Turnbull worked on Trump personally, and I pushed hard into the White House and the rest of the administration. Turnbull had been lobbying Trump on the matter since the previous year, and during his February 2018 trip to Washington he had continued to press Australia's case. Fortunately, we had allies in the administration who actually believed in the fundamentals of free markets. Strong advocates for our cause were Trump's chief of staff, Mick Mulvaney, Treasury Secretary Steven Mnuchin and chief economic advisor Gary Cohn.

Defense Secretary General Jim Mattis was another great supporter of Australia's exemption claim, but it was the Pentagon leadership who were our greatest advocates. According to the legislation, the tariffs were being imposed on national security grounds – but how could the United States possibly argue that Australia was a national security threat to its people? To their great credit, Secretary Mattis and the chair of the Joint Chiefs of Staff, General Joseph Dunford, made this point clearly and loudly to Trump and his team. Mattis and Dunford were not the sort of people you would readily deploy in tariff and quota negotiations, but they were compelling. As the matter progressed, Secretary of

State Rex Tillerson weighed in on our side too (although he was gone by the end of March), and in the latter stages Vice President Pence became personally involved as well.

It might sound a bit corny, but our argument was framed by the concept of mateship. The more we talked about mateship and our shared military history, the more compelling the argument was that Australia should be made exempt. It was self-evident that there could be no possible justification for tariffs against Australia on national security grounds.

I also kept making the point that it would be tremendously damaging to the image of the United States in Australia. If the United States were to say that Australia was a security threat, it could seriously damage the Australian people's view of our American allies. Imposing tariffs ran completely against the United States' own interests in the region. Here they were, encouraging us to be more active in the Pacific – and of course we had been sending soldiers to Afghanistan and Iraq, risking Australian lives alongside American – and they had the gall to claim we were a security threat? That was why they were imposing tariffs? This was twisted logic, and a bridge too far.

Nonetheless, the pro-tariffs team were shameless. They didn't mind what tool they used, as long as they could get those tariffs in place. There were so many nefarious interests at play. Eventually – and thankfully – there were enough fair-minded people around Trump making it clear that this just did not stack up as a national security issue.

It was the last day of April, and I was sitting in my office with the cable news channels going in the background. The short-term exemptions against the tariffs would run out the next day, so we were nervously awaiting Trump's next announcement. The president was doing one of those televised cabinet meetings that wasn't quite a press conference, but not a briefing either.

Trump was sitting there, surrounded by cameras, having a go at all and sundry. He launched into a monologue: tariffs were justified and should apply to everyone. Momentarily my heart sank – had we failed? But then, in classic Trumpian fashion, he went on to contradict his previous statement. Almost quietly, he said that close allies such as Australia did have a compelling case to be made exempt – and he then casually announced that Australia was exempt.

I jumped out of my seat and punched the air, yelling, 'Woo hoo!' and spilling my coffee all over my lap. I must have looked and sounded like Homer Simpson. We'd done it! There were televisions down the corridor outside my office, and all the embassy staff were standing around them cheering like we'd just landed someone on the moon.

Australia, Brazil and Argentina were exempted from the tariffs in the end, but Australia was the only nation exempt from both tariffs and quotas. Of course, we didn't crow publicly about our victory, but it was an incredible achievement.

It also raised the ire (once again) of my friend Kim Darroch, the British ambassador: 'How on God's earth did you do that?' he asked. The United Kingdom wasn't our only surprised rival. I started to get calls from around the world, asking for advice on how to escape Trump's tariffs. Some of the United States' closest allies like Canada, Mexico and the European Union were having tariffs placed on them – but we'd dodged the bullet! Not only had we managed to keep in place a refugee deal Trump hated, but we'd also got ourselves exempted from these new tariffs. We'd become the benchmark in Washington, DC for diplomatic success with the Trump administration.

I felt for some of my closest diplomatic colleagues throughout this period, and helped them where it was appropriate. In particular, my mate David MacNaughton, the Canadian ambassador, was really feeling the heat over tariffs. He's a strong negotiator and has an impressive intellect, but there was no ideological alignment between Justin Trudeau and Trump, which made David's job particularly difficult. Canada is a significant aluminium and steel exporter to the United States, and it was clear that Trump was threatening Trudeau with tariffs in a show of regional superiority.

Our early victory on tariffs wasn't the end of the matter. At times, our exemption was challenged. When push came to shove, I agreed with Trump's tariffs team – Ross, Lighthizer and Navarro – that we would not exceed our agreed levels of exports; that is, that we wouldn't take advantage of our tariff-free status. The irony was that, in the following year, the tariffs and quotas against the rest of the world led to a spike in Australian exports of aluminium and steel, which meant that, at certain times, we did exceed that agreement.

Unfortunately, by mid-2019 Trump started to be pushed again by his gang of three to revisit the issue, and tariffs once more loomed on the horizon.

* * *

It was 4 a.m. when I got a knock on the door. It was one of the house staff. 'Mr Ambassador, it's the prime minister's office on the phone. They need to speak to you urgently,' I was told.

'What is it?' I said. A wake-up call like this always made me fear the worst.

'They need you to go and meet Donald Trump in Japan. Your plane leaves in four hours.'

This was bad news.

It was 26 June 2019, and a day that was supposed to have gone differently. That day I was to be flying to Miami to catch up with one of my life-long idols: Barry Gibb from the Bee Gees. We had arranged the lunch at his home a few months earlier, and I was all set to fly down to Florida that morning. I hadn't been this excited about a trip in a long time.

I went downstairs and got on the phone with one of the PM's advisers.

'We want you to go to Osaka and meet Trump at this G20 dinner with Morrison,' I was informed. 'We need some help. The prime minister really wants you there. We've got you booked on an 8 a.m. flight to Japan.'

Standing in my pyjamas, still half-asleep as I tried to process this information, I said the first thing that came into my head. 'But I'm supposed to be meeting Barry Gibb for lunch!'

The adviser, who didn't seem to know or care who Barry Gibb was, continued in my ear. 'Look, Joe, we think we're being ambushed.'

That woke me up.

'Morrison is set to meet Trump for this working dinner during the G20, but Trump's bringing *everyone* with him. Trump is going to have all the cavalry there. We've only got Morrison, and maybe Mathias Cormann [finance minister] and Simon Birmingham [trade minister] can change their plans to get there.'

There was something alarming about the way the plans for this meeting had developed over the last few days. After all the trouble we'd had securing a first meeting for Morrison in Buenos Aires late the previous year, now all of a sudden Trump wanted to have a working dinner with him? Morrison had just won an unexpected election victory, and initially I thought this had changed Trump's attitude to the now apparently popular Australian PM. But as the date drew closer, we were informed that the president wanted to meet Morrison as soon as he arrived in Osaka. And Trump's people kept adding to the guest list: Wilbur Ross and Bob Lighthizer would be there, we were told. Morrison's team were worried. 'Oh, hell,' one adviser said. 'They're going to dump our tariff protections.'

The final straw – and what had prompted my last-minute invitation – was the news from the White House that Ivanka Trump and Jared Kushner would be joining the dinner. We later found out that the date of the Americans' dinner with the Chinese delegation had been moved, so perhaps it was simply that they needed to fill a big table – but who knew? I couldn't get a clear read from the White House on what they were planning.

Meanwhile, the prime minister's office was worried. Even with Finance Minister Mathias Cormann and Trade Minister Simon Birmingham at the dinner, they simply weren't prepared for full-blown trade negotiations with the United States, and needed some more firepower in the room.

So I wearily repacked my bag for the 8 a.m. flight to Osaka, rather than my planned 9 a.m. to Miami. I broke the news to Barry Gibb: he was gracious, and I suspect not as devastated as I was.

Arriving at the airport, I was crammed aboard an appalling United Airlines flight: I was seated backwards on a utility bench seat all the way to Osaka. The day had started badly and was only getting worse. I quietly sang 'How can you mend a broken heart ...' to myself as the plane took off. Fellow passengers groaned. I am no falsetto.

That dinner in Osaka would be one of the more bizarre encounters I'd ever have with Donald Trump – and that's saying something.

Arriving in a rather dishevelled state after an exhausting sixteen-hours-plus flight from Washington via San Francisco, I got to the hotel and tried to prepare for the dinner with Trump. I only had about two hours before it started. I did what I could under the circumstances, but it was always hard to prepare with Trump. Would we be lauded, or would we become the latest sacrifice on the altar of tariffs? In the grand tradition of politics, I prepared for the worst and hoped for the best.

I met up with Morrison, Cormann and Birmingham prior to the meeting; all three of them were pretty concerned about what was about to take place. Like me, Cormann and Birmingham were last-minute dinner guests, and felt underprepared. So while we did have the prime minister, two cabinet ministers and the Australian ambassador present, it wasn't as if we had a grand plan.

As we walked into the dinner that night, it did feel like an ambush. At the table were Trump's A-team: Ivanka and Jared (looking like something from a *Vanity Fair* photo shoot, as usual), my mate Mick Mulvaney (who had gone suspiciously quiet in the lead-up to the dinner), Wilbur Ross (doing his best impression of the emperor from *Star Wars*), Bob Lighthizer (grinning like a man who was about to screw us), Secretary of State Mike Pompeo and Treasury Secretary Steven Mnuchin (fortunately both good friends of Australia) and National Security Adviser John Bolton (who would be out the door by September, and would then become one of the most vocal ex–Trump administration critics). Most alarmingly, Peter Navarro was there. I wasn't sure whether I'd get a handshake or a wedgie.

Of course, in the middle of this there was The Donald, with that unmistakable Cheshire Cat grin.

All Trump wanted to know from Morrison was how he'd won the election. 'You're a winner! Amazing work. How'd you do it?' he asked. 'They wrote you off, but you're winner!'

In true Trump fashion, he asked a question and then answered it himself. 'Did nobody like your opponent?' he said, rather insensitively. But then the answer: 'He said nasty things about me so he must be a loser!'

President Trump loved the analogies to his own victory. Not only had Morrison won an election against the odds (like Trump, of course), but he had done so as one of the few vocal supporters of Trump. This was vintage Trump. The president now had a story, and he could relate to Morrison. Trump only wanted to be associated with winners, and Morrison was now a winner.

The media were ushered in for a photo shoot. These were the very first pictures of Trump in Japan. The public comments Trump made were hilarious. Despite not even wanting to meet with Morrison the previous year, now he was hailing the political genius of the man he claimed to have backed all along.

'US President Donald Trump has praised Scott Morrison for his "tremendous victory" in the May election and declared that he knew the Prime Minister could win,' *The Sydney Morning Herald* reported. '"He didn't surprise me but he surprised a lot of people,"

Mr Trump said. "I knew him. So I said, you're going to do very well. And he did," Mr Trump said.'

As the dinner progressed, it became pretty clear that this was going to be a one-man show. At one point Trump held his black pen up in the air for the rest of the table to admire. 'These are black Sharpies. These are my favourite pens. The best pens!' he said, holding aloft the $3 writing tool as if it were Excalibur.

The president then moved on to the issue of the Boeing 737 MAX. The new jet was still grounded following two crashes in Ethiopia and Indonesia earlier in the year. Trump had disagreed with the decision to ground the planes. Instead, preferring to see the issue primarily as a brand problem, he even favoured a name change for the 737 MAX.

'I rang the CEO of Boeing, Dennis Muilenburg, and he assured me this is a safe plane,' Trump told the table. 'I said, "I think this is a safe plane too, but maybe change the name now."'

Morrison had given a speech the week before signalling Australia's desire for the United States and China to end the trade war, and he continued to press these themes in the dinner. We stressed the importance of global free trade, and in particular the TPP, and made clear our opposition to tariffs, while of course continuing to appreciate the fact that we'd been exempted.

We moved on to talk about diplomatic issues in the region, and as the dinner went on, with Trump waxing lyrical throughout, it became apparent that we weren't going to have our tariff protections removed. We'd been bracing for a punch that never came.

Did the Americans change their plans at the last minute? Was the dinner just an intimidation tactic? Or was Trump just paying Morrison and Australia a compliment? Who knows. But we walked out of that dinner with the same trade deals that we had when we walked in, and with a prime minister whose standing in the eyes of the US administration was increased. That was a win.

Later that night I had a drink with Cormann and Birmingham. The three of us were relieved, and shared a laugh about what a bizarre dinner it had been. The next morning I got on a fast train to Tokyo, and flew straight back to Washington. I've still never met Barry Gibb.

* * *

With Morrison enjoying a newfound bromance with Trump in the wake of his election win, there was much we could do to take advantage. I'd been working on some plans with Anthony Pratt about a prime ministerial visit to one of his US factories during Morrison's state visit.

There were a lot of parallels between Pratt and Trump. Both had wealthy and successful fathers who'd given them responsibility for growing the family business. Say what you will about Trump, but the guy is a successful businessman. At heart he will always be a real estate guy, but his real genius was understanding the value of branding. Trump sold the idea of what it looked and felt like to be a billionaire, and in the process he became one.

Anthony Pratt became a billionaire as well, although under less glamorous circumstances. He'd been thrown in the deep end by his father to establish a US arm of Visy – what would be called Pratt Industries in the United States. It's now the fifth-largest packaging company in the country, and the largest privately held cardboard and recycling company in the world.

Back at the dinner on USS *Intrepid*, Pratt had pledged to invest billions of dollars as a result of Trump's policies. Now he was delivering on that promise. He'd built a new recycled paper mill in Wapakoneta, Ohio, employing hundreds of local people. So Pratt and I suggested that Prime Minister Morrison and President Trump visit the factory together.

Logistically, it was a huge challenge. Wapakoneta is famous as the birthplace of astronaut Neil Armstrong ... and that's about it. Nonetheless, Pratt grabbed the opportunity and did everything he could to make it happen. On our end, my chief of staff, Alex Tureman, a life-long Democrat, did an extraordinary job dealing with the logistics of getting Trump and Morrison together in a town seemingly smack bang in the middle of nowhere.

Alex found a way to route Morrison to Wapakoneta on the way to Chicago, the PM's next stop. Getting the US president there, however, would prove a much tougher logistical feat. Trump was already due to meet the Indian prime minister, Narendra Modi, in Texas that same afternoon. The 'Howdy, Modi!' summit would take place in front of an extraordinary crowd of 50,000 at the home of the Houston Texans NFL team. But Wapakoneta's airport was tiny, and there was no way that Air Force One, a Boeing 747, could land there. This meant Trump had to fly to Texas, do the rally, board a smaller plane and fly to Ohio, and then head back to Washington, DC that night.

This meant Trump would spend less time with Prime Minister Modi and more time with Prime Minister Morrison. It was a measure of our influence that President Trump agreed to the arrangement. Because of air space restrictions around the movement of the president's plane, not only were they flying in from different locations, in different planes, but Trump and Morrison had to land at different airports at different times before meeting at the Pratt factory. All this on pretty short notice.

As Morrison's motorcade approached Wapakoneta, we drove through huge, empty fields that are so characteristic of the Midwest. All of a sudden, jutting out of the plains like the Emerald City, was Pratt Industries' shiny new recycled paper factory.

Thousands of screaming locals lined the roads, many with MAKE AMERICA GREAT AGAIN or KEEP AMERICA GREAT AGAIN paraphernalia and waving American and Australian flags. There were differing accounts, but it was possibly the first presidential visit ever to Wapakoneta. It was certainly the first combined visit of the US president and the Australian prime minister.

Contrary to what some in the media and the ALP leadership would later claim, Prime Minister Morrison and I were not part of a 'Trump rally'. The people who were there for the visit that day were all workers and their families. They were genuine Trump fans because Trump had delivered jobs to their community. An Australian, Anthony Pratt, had just opened a new factory in the town on the back of Trump's corporate tax cuts, and it provided well-paying jobs to locals. The impact on the town was already very significant. This was what Trump promised, and it had been delivered. Was it any wonder these people were Trump fans? This was his heartland.

For Morrison, it was a perfect demonstration of the alignment between US and Australian business interests. Yes, Pratt was an unabashed Trump fan, but so what? That was his right. Truth be told, at one stage we did have to tone down his expectations: Anthony wanted to issue caps reading 'MAKE AMERICA AND AUSTRALIA GREAT AGAIN', but we made it clear that this was a visit, not a rally.

On the back of the state dinner, it was an extraordinary thirty-six hours. We'd locked in the affection between the United States and Australia's new leadership, and for me that was a source of satisfaction. Institutionally, the United States needed to know that we were with them, and that's what mattered to me.

CHAPTER 9

THE MUELLER INVESTIGATION

Our man in London, and how Australia almost brought down Trump

I had never heard of Robert Mueller. He was described to me as being a trusted and independent legal brain with Republican instincts. But unbeknown to Mr Mueller, he nearly blew up the relationship (again) between the president of the United States and the government of Australia. The whole experience of the Mueller investigation and Australia's unsuspecting role in it was surreal from beginning to end.

It will likely not surprise you if I say that Donald Trump is a phenomenal hater. He never forgives and rarely forgets. And few things riled him more than attempts by his critics to suggest that his campaign had worked with the Russians to steal the 2016 presidential election from Hillary Clinton.

At first that suggestion seemed absurd to me too, but later evidence would demonstrate there was little doubt that Russia had interfered in the election. Trump, however, never accepted this reality. His position seemed to be that if he did accept that interference had occurred, it would delegitimise his administration in the eyes of his enemies.

But even Trump's most ardent critics could never demonstrate a direct link between Trump himself and Russian interference in the campaign. Despite the Mueller investigation demonstrating contact between Trump's campaign and Russian state actors in at least one meeting, there was no direct evidence of Trump's or his campaign's role in the hacking of the Democratic campaign or in any fake news campaigns.

It all became a bit absurd when allegations against Trump emerged involving 'golden shower' romps with Russian prostitutes and secret deals with Vladimir Putin. The so-called Steele dossier had been put together by former British intelligence officer Christopher Steele, who had been hired by a private polling and research company, Fusion GPS, to investigate Trump's connections with Russia. It would cause my British colleague Kim Darroch a great deal of heartburn with Trump and his administration, given Steele's connection with British intelligence. Leading media outlets initially wouldn't go near it, even after being briefed by Steele in June 2016, including *The New York Times*, *The Washington Post*, *The New Yorker* and (initially) CNN. But after CNN ran some details, the online publication Buzzfeed – in a classic example of modern media FOMO (fear of missing out, for the uninitiated) – published the whole dossier. A feeding frenzy ensued.

The whole episode demonstrated a central failing of those aiming to tie Russian interference allegations directly to Trump: overreach. Every time the media released another supposed 'smoking gun', closer examination would debunk it or, at the very least, bring into question its veracity. Trump and his supporters could then point to the 'fake news media', whose hysterical reactions cemented their view that Trump was being unfairly targeted. Needless to say, overreach is a common problem in politics and the media, and has ruined more than one career.

But despite the questionable veracity of some claims against Trump by his detractors (and there were many), the allegation that his campaign had colluded with Russia was a serious one, and even Trump knew it had to be taken seriously. Trump's closest advisers, both inside and outside the White House, urged him to defuse the claims quickly and decisively when he took office. The president tasked one of his favourites, Attorney General Jeff Sessions, with investigating and hosing down the allegations once and for all.

However, only a few months into 2017, the investigation into the allegations of Russian interference became a personal and political disaster for Trump. In a career-ending decision, Sessions recused himself from making a decision about an inquiry into the interference. Sessions' recusal followed reports of two meetings he'd had in 2016 with Russia's ambassador to the United States, Sergey Kislyak. My view of this was that there was no doubt Sessions was doing the correct thing from a legal standpoint, if not a political one. It spoke to his integrity, especially given there was no evidence that the meetings concerned any questions of interference in the campaign.

Still, Trump wasn't much interested in Sessions' integrity, and the move shocked and infuriated the president. He would never forgive his one-time key adviser and political mentor for that decision, which he felt started a chain of events that resulted in the launching of a hugely damaging FBI investigation. Sessions' recusal empowered Deputy Attorney General Rod Rosenstein to launch a special investigation. In May 2017, Rosenstein appointed former FBI director Robert Mueller as special counsel to head up the investigation.

There could not have been a more trustworthy public servant than Robert Mueller. A director of the FBI for twelve years, Mueller was the second longest–serving person in the role – behind none other than J. Edgar Hoover. Mueller was also a registered Republican, and had been appointed to senior positions under presidents George H.W. Bush, Bill Clinton, George W. Bush and Barack Obama. Combine this with the fact that he'd fought with the US Marines during the Vietnam War, and a more all-American figure could not be found if they'd appointed Captain America himself.

When you google Robert Mueller's name, you get back more than 75 million results. That's a fair indication of the interest in Mueller and his report. In the last five years, there have been millions of words devoted to reporting and analysis of the Mueller report itself, its internal machinations, its key characters and, of course, its observations on President Trump.

My own experience of the Mueller investigation was much more immediate. After all the work we'd done to rebuild Australia's relationship with Donald Trump, we were suddenly faced with the diplomatically terrifying situation of being blamed by the president for this investigation into his legitimacy. Moreover, I was a large and obvious target for Trump's attacks. To understand why this investigation threatened our standing with the president, we need to turn to one of my old colleagues in government: Alexander Downer.

Downer was Liberal Party royalty. And as with the British royals, high office seemed to pass from father to son in the Downer family. His grandfather, Sir John Downer, was premier of South Australia in the 1880s and '90s, and later served in the Senate. His father, Sir Alexander 'Alick' Downer, was a minister in the Menzies government, and then became Australia's high commissioner to the United Kingdom. Alexander Downer himself was Australia's longest-serving foreign minister in the Howard government; he seemed to have a genetic predisposition towards high public office.

Our relationship had always been cordial, if a little mischievous. Late at night I liked to have a cigar in my ministerial office in Parliament House, and the stench of cigar smoke would waft down the corridors. Of course, when security arrived, my staff would deny any smoking and sigh that it was probably Downer (again), and inevitably he copped the consequences. Having said that, he threw me under a few proverbial buses over the years, too. But he was always a genuine man with sound values.

My first inkling that Australia was involved in the complex affair came when I learnt of the involvement of Downer, who back in May 2016 was our high commissioner in London. In his role Downer had come across a member of Trump's campaign through an Israeli intelligence contact. George Papadopoulos was only in his late twenties at the time, and had been presenting himself around London as Donald Trump's campaign adviser on foreign affairs. The Israeli operative who lined up Downer's meeting with Papadopoulos was the partner of an Australian DFAT official. The pair had been made aware of Papadopoulos boasting, while in London, that he was getting some emails that would provide dirt on Hillary Clinton, thanks to the Russians. He had also been publicly criticising, and demanding an apology from, British prime minister David Cameron after he called Donald Trump 'divisive, stupid and wrong'.

Much as I had in the United States, Downer had surmised that he should probably meet with this fellow who was putting himself out there as Donald Trump's adviser on foreign affairs. After all, what if Trump succeeded in gaining the Republican nomination, or even won the presidency?

There was no doubt that there was, shall we say, an unsavoury breed of adviser hanging around the Trump campaign. But this was born of necessity, rather than a specific recruiting tactic. The GOP primary contest was in full swing, and other, more mainstream candidates had snapped up the most experienced Republican operators, as well as the youngest and brightest. Trump had been left with a kind of D-team of eccentric characters and some dead-set weirdos, many of whom would later face or serve time in prison: Papadopoulos himself, campaign chairman Paul Manafort and the infamous Roger Stone, to name a few. None of this, however, could detract from the fact that they were advising the favoured Republican presidential candidate, and thus a possible president of the United States.

So, through the Israeli and DFAT operatives, a meeting was arranged between Downer and Papadopoulos. The pair met at a Kensington wine bar, along with Australian embassy official Erika Thompson. Papadopoulos would later claim this was a boozy night out with Downer, but it was nothing of the sort. Downer would later confirm, in an interview with *The Australian*, that a mere gin and tonic was consumed at the after-work catch-up.

Downer did, however, glean some interesting information from the young adviser. Papadopoulos claimed he had been aware that the Russians were in possession of some 'material that could be damaging' to Hillary Clinton, and may use it in the lead-up to the presidential election. This piqued Downer's interest, but much of the rest of the discussion was devoted to Trump's views on various trade and foreign policy issues affecting Australia, the Trans-Pacific Partnership and China chief among them. Downer has also said there was no indication from Papadopoulos that Trump was involved or had knowledge of the Russian 'Hillary' file.

Finding the conversation worthy of a report to Canberra, Downer sent a diplomatic note to various people on the meeting with Papadopoulos, and made mention of the Russian 'dirt file' on Clinton. Much of the rest of the cable was concerned with Trump's other views on foreign affairs, particularly as they pertained to the Asia-Pacific region.

Papadopoulos would eventually plead guilty to lying to the FBI, serve a few weeks in prison and be forced to cooperate with the Mueller investigation. It turned out his dealings with the Russians extended back to March 2016. He had met an academic in Rome, Joseph Mifsud, who in turn had facilitated meetings with Ivan Timofeev, a director at the Russian International Affairs Council, a front for the Russian foreign ministry. Papadopoulos then took it upon himself to broker a meeting between Paul Manafort and Timofeev.

I heard of the encounter between Papadopoulos and Downer two months later, in July 2016, when the presidential election was reaching a fever pitch. Trump was preparing to accept the Republican nomination, while Clinton was ready to do the same for the Democrats.

On 22 July, the media organisation WikiLeaks, founded by Australian Julian Assange, released a stunning trove of 20,000

emails hacked from the Democratic National Committee
(DNC). This was just three days before the Democratic National
Convention, and so was a clear attempt to inflict maximum
damage on Clinton and her campaign. If there was any doubt
about that, another tranche of emails was released just days before
the presidential election in November.

In that sense, the hack and the WikiLeaks release were very
successful in achieving their aim. Among other things, the emails
demonstrated the DNC's institutional bias in favour of the Clinton
campaign and against that of Bernie Sanders. Central to this was
DNC chair Debbie Wasserman Schultz. In emails to other DNC
staff and media, she mocked Sanders' campaign chief and made it
clear that the Vermont senator 'isn't going to be President' and said
he didn't understand the Democratic Party. Sanders, of course,
was independent in the Senate, not a registered Democrat.

Sanders, his team and his supporters were, understandably,
furious. It confirmed every suspicion they had about how the
Clinton campaign was operating in unison with the DNC to make
sure Sanders never got the Democratic presidential nomination. To
Sanders' supporters, the DNC machine and the Clinton campaign
were one and the same, and they felt these emails proved it.
Wasserman Schultz resigned before the convention, and several
other senior DNC officials did the same not long after. The DNC
issued a humiliating apology to Sanders and his campaign.

Of course, all this also helped Donald Trump no end. It played
to his characterisation of his opponent as 'crooked Hillary'. The
scandal was also running in parallel to another email scandal –
her use of a private email server while secretary of state – which
had long dogged Clinton.

Immediately, the source of the hacked DNC emails was
investigated, and US intelligence officials wasted no time in
looking to Russia. It was widely known that Vladimir Putin
despised Hillary Clinton from her time as secretary of state, so
the hacking claim was not implausible. Subsequent reviews by the

US Department of Homeland Security, the Director of the Office of National Intelligence and the CIA would find with 'confidence' that the cyber-attacks against the DNC were directed by the Russian government.

Meanwhile, back in London, Alexander Downer took notice. Hadn't that Papadopoulos fellow been bragging about the Russians holding 'material' that could be damaging to Clinton? Downer got in contact with the acting head of the US mission in London and asked for a meeting. After being alerted by the US embassy of the possible breach, FBI representatives and other senior intelligence officials in London were also present to meet with the former Australian foreign minister.

There was extraordinary haste in the FBI's response to the Downer report. A case investigation was opened immediately; this was one of the primary reasons for Trump's anger at the FBI. Would they have opened a case investigation and sent a team to London so rapidly in the normal course of business? In my view he had a reasonable point.

I suspect the FBI was attempting to even up the ledger. No police agency wants to be a political football during a heated election campaign. They'd already had to investigate the Clinton private email server allegations, which caused her no end of grief. It's perfectly plausible that, in an effort to even the score, the FBI jumped on the suggestion that the Trump campaign had conspired to dig up dirt on Clinton in partnership with a hostile foreign nation.

While I was aware of the existence of Downer's cable concerning what he'd heard from Papadopoulos, I did not become aware of his discussion with the FBI until after Donald Trump was elected. I neither transmitted nor handed over information to the FBI about the meeting or the cable at that time. Nor was I even approached by the Americans and asked to do so.

The Mueller report would later state that 'on July 31, 2016, based on the foreign government reporting, the FBI opened an investigation into potential coordination between the Russian government and individuals associated with the Trump campaign'. This a reference to the Australian cable and Downer's subsequent conversations with the US embassy and the FBI. Of course, there were a number of ingredients in the FBI's decision to investigate the matter, but Downer's intervention was key.

I am certain that Downer acted properly in this affair. He had heard that Russia might be playing games in the US election, and, as a trusted ally should have notified the US embassy in London. At various points, a frustrated Prime Minister Turnbull, who was feeling the heat from Trump over the investigation, said to me: 'Downer should never have gone to the Americans.' For my part, I would have done the same thing as Downer. Our relationship with the United States is such that if you hear of information of that nature, you should bring it to the attention of your mates.

Downer was not, as Papadopoulos would later suggest to *The New York Times*, a spy working at the behest of the Obama administration and the Clintons. His was the behaviour of a close ally and good diplomat. It just so happened – unfortunately for Australia and our old mate Downer – that his information kicked off an FBI investigation into the man who would soon be elected the US president.

Allegations that Downer was a spy for the Clintons would have been funnier had they not been given so much credence by many in the Trump administration and his supporters in the media. This idea also began to fester into an obsession for Trump himself.

None of this paranoia about Australia's role was helped by the release of the 'Nunes memo' in February 2018. Devin Nunes was chair of the House Intelligence Committee, and the same Republican congressman I had been sitting next to the night the Trump–Turnbull phone call was leaked. The Nunes memo was part of his own secret investigation into the supposed role of the FBI in spying on the Trump campaign, which by this time had reached Byzantine heights of complexity and alleged conspiracy. For the first time it was publicly confirmed that it was the meeting between Papadopoulos and Downer in London (and not the so-called Steele dossier) that had sparked the FBI investigation. Furthermore, one of the Nunes memo's central allegations was that the FBI 'may have relied on politically motivated or questionable sources' in obtaining wiretap warrants to investigate the Trump campaign's connections to Russia. All this added fuel to the fire that was burning inside Trump to try to establish a connection between Downer, Australia and the Clinton campaign.

That fire was obvious on the day I met and first played golf with Trump. It was April 2018, not long after the release of the Nunes memo. Trump asked me outright: 'What's the story with Alex Downing? Who is he? Is he friends with the Clintons?'

'It's Downer, Mr President. And no, he's not friends with the Clintons. He was part of one of the most right-wing governments in living memory, and he would not have been acting inappropriately,' I replied, being very careful about what I said.

Trump went on to ask me about Downer's supposed relationship with the Clintons through Australian government donations to the Clinton Foundation, demonstrating that more than a bit of research into my London counterpart was taking place. 'Why did Alexander Downing give hundreds of millions of dollars to the Clinton Foundation?' he demanded.

'No, he didn't, Mr President,' I replied. 'The Clinton Foundation was doing good work in Papua New Guinea and around other places. The Australian government contributed to the foundation's work, not to the foundation itself.'

Trump shook his head and gave me a dissatisfied look, but he eventually dropped the subject and we got on with our golf. But Trump's irritation that day was a mere dress rehearsal for what happened at our next golf day, a year later at Mar-a-Lago.

* * *

By March 2019 the Mueller investigation was complete, and things had begun to look up for Trump. After Jeff Sessions was sacked in November 2018, William Barr had taken over as attorney general. In March 2019, Mueller handed his final report to Barr, who, in a letter to Congress summarising the findings, stated: 'The Special Counsel's investigation did not find that the Trump campaign or anyone associated with it conspired or coordinated with Russia in its efforts to influence the 2016 U.S. presidential election.'

The key allegation against Trump – that he and his team had conspired with Russia to gain advantage in the 2016 presidential election – was not proven, and there was no finding to that end. Trump felt vindicated and called the claim 'the greatest political hoax of all time', saying it 'should never happen to another President of the United States again'.

'NO COLLUSION. NO OBSTRUCTION. FOR THE HATERS AND THE RADICAL LEFT DEMOCRATS – GAME OVER,' he tweeted in a series of *Game of Thrones*–style tweets.

The Mueller report, however, did not completely exonerate President Trump or his campaign team. Mueller's team made clear there had been Russian interference in the 2016 presidential campaign, including the hacking of the DNC emails and a 'fake news' misinformation campaign. Most damningly, there were findings of contact between Trump's campaign and individuals connected to the Russian government dating back to 2016, including a meeting at Trump Tower between Jared Kushner, Donald Trump Junior, Paul Manafort and five people, including the well-connected Russian lawyer Natalia Veselnitskaya and a former Soviet officer turned lobbyist. Emails leading up to this meeting would demonstrate that the Russian contingent wanted to offer Donald Trump Junior material that 'would incriminate Hillary' as 'part of Russia and its government's support for Mr. Trump'.

Mueller wrote that 'while this report does not conclude that the President committed a crime, it also does not exonerate him'.

He did not state a view on whether or not Trump had committed an obstruction of justice. This was in relation to a part of the investigation that centred on a claim by former FBI Director James Comey, who alleged that Trump had asked him to drop an investigation into his disastrous National Security Adviser General Michael Flynn. In a somewhat oblique finding, Mueller made clear that a president of the United States 'cannot be charged with a crime while he is in office'. It may simply have never been within his power as special counsel to make a criminal finding against the president, although Mueller never said he would have done so if he could have.

This was indicative of a flaw in the final report, which was that it became a kind of Rorschach test for Trump supporters and haters alike. In playing a straight bat both in his findings and in his eventual testimony in front of House committees, Mueller allowed for the possibility that his report would be used as both a vindication and a damnation of the Trump presidency. When he appeared in Congress, Mueller refused to fall into the trap of extrapolating on his findings, saying the report sufficed for his testimony. Of course, this meant neither side was content. It led to allegations from Trump haters that Mueller hadn't done his job properly, and to further attacks from the president that this was a time-wasting 'witch hunt' made possible by anti-Trump forces within the FBI.

None of this was Mueller's fault. It appeared to me that he conducted himself and his inquiry with integrity and thoroughness, in keeping with his experience. Mueller was one of the few to raise Trump's ire and not get sacked by the president – despite attempts to do so. But he also refused to fall into the trap of giving Democrats and Trump's media enemies the president's head on a stick with his findings. Mueller walked away from the political carnage that his inquiry caused with his reputation and integrity intact.

* * *

In late April 2019, I was invited by Mick Mulvaney to Mar-a-Lago for a golf day with President Trump. Mulvaney had become acting White House chief of staff in January, which was a huge boost for my access to the administration and to the president himself. Given the context of the Mueller investigation, which had concluded in March, I was cautious, but I also saw it as a good opportunity to meet with the president again and clear the air over Australia's role in the investigation that could have ended his presidency.

On Thursday, 18 April, a week before I went down to Mar-a-Lago, the Mueller report was made public. Trump held to a strangely naive assumption that his enemies in the press would be forced to exonerate him after the report's findings were made public. Of course, those who had attacked him over the last few years continued to do so, and he and his team were still heavily criticised in the media. This was the backdrop against which I found myself arriving in Florida that Easter weekend. I had decided against staying at Mar-a-Lago itself in an attempt to keep a low profile. I was due to have breakfast with President Trump and Mulvaney before our game on the Saturday morning.

Keen to arrive at the right time and place that morning, I had only scanned the day's papers. The Mueller findings were all over the news again. Trump's outrage at the 'witch hunt' and his declarations of absolution had been stoking even greater interest.

Upon arriving at the golf club, I was ushered into a large dining room, filled with couples in their sixties and seventies eating breakfast and keenly awaiting the arrival of their president. Trump International Golf Club at West Palm Beach, like Trump National and all Trump golf clubs, reflects its owner's personality. This club's particular style could be best characterised as Tropicana Trump.

Seated at a table with Mick Mulvaney, I awaited the arrival of the president. Suddenly, the large dining room doors swung open and Donald Trump walked in. This was followed by a spontaneous round of enthusiastic applause from the casual guests. It was quite a sight, the president striding across the dining room in his full golf attire and MAGA red hat amid rapturous morning applause.

The president made his way over to our table. I motioned to greet him but he just stared down at me like I was a piece of burnt toast at the breakfast buffet. Then he just snapped. 'Oh, we have the Australian ambassador here,' he said to the entire room, pointing at me and shaking his head. 'We have Joe Hockey here. Yeah, the Australian ambassador.' He looked and sounded like an old comedian preparing to roast a member of the audience. 'What have I done to Australia? What have I done to Australia, Joe? Why?' he said, increasingly irate. 'You know, the whole thing started with Australia. You know, the whole thing started with Downing in London. The Australian ambassador in London ...'

And he began retelling his tale of woe in Trumpian style to everybody and nobody in particular. I could feel the anger in the room rising. It was only 8.30 a.m. on a Saturday. Way too early for this level of aggression.

He went on. 'And why would you do that? I exempt you from tariffs. I've given you a great deal on the military. I even hosted your prime minister. Why would you do that to me? What have I done to Australia?' he pleaded.

Trump had by this time worked himself up into a lather. He was not screaming hysterically – that wasn't his style – but I could tell he was genuinely furious. He looked at me and then back to his audience for moral support, repeating over again how he couldn't believe Australia had treated him this way.

The whole time I just sat there, stunned. The president of the United States was humiliating me and my country in front of the entire room. What was I going to say? Please read the Mueller report, Mr President? You're wrong about Downer? Why don't you join us for a refreshing glass of orange juice? I knew that anything I said risked escalating the situation, and then I'd be in a public slanging match with Trump – something I didn't need. At any rate, I'm not sure saying anything would've helped the situation. I was simply an outlet for his frustration at what he viewed as a close ally's role in his attempted downfall.

Trump's tirade went on for a few minutes before the president, seemingly exhausted by his own anger, quietly continued on to another table. Evidently, Trump had decided not to sit with us.

Mulvaney looked at me like he had just seen a ghost. 'Holy cow! What was all that about?' he said.

'You tell me,' I replied. 'You know, he still thinks that we started the whole FBI and Mueller inquiry.'

'Okay, well,' Mick said, 'we better just try and calm him down before we go out and play golf together.'

'Yeah, that would be good,' I said. 'In fact, I think that would be essential.'

Mick went over to see the president and tried to talk him into inviting me to join them on their Air Force One flight back to Washington that night. But Trump was still furious and didn't want me on his plane, or anywhere near him. Mick slinked back to our table with an apologetic look on his face and explained the situation – most of which the whole room had already heard anyway.

Feeling about as popular with the president as Robert Mueller himself, I summed up the situation to Mick. 'Look, I don't think I should be in his playing group today. I don't think there's any calming him down in this environment.'

'Yeah, let's play in the group behind him,' Mick agreed.

It emerged that Ron DeSantis, Florida's governor, and Louis Oosthuizen, a South African professional golfer, were slated to be in Trump's group for the day. Mick and I ended up playing in the group behind them, with Casey DeSantis, the governor's wife, who was a really good player. I was enjoying being out in the fresh air – and away from the president's fury.

Trump International was, like all Trump courses, really tough to play. We were on the first hole playing our second shots, and Trump's group were teeing off on the second hole, coming in our direction. I took out my five-iron and gave the ball an enthusiastic wack. But I managed to hook the ball, and was dismayed to see it fly towards the president. Sure enough, the ball dinged into Donald Trump's golf cart. A team of Secret Service agents turned and looked my way. I felt angry glares through their sunglasses and the sensation of multiple guns pointed at me.

I pointed to Mulvaney, grimaced and said, 'Hey, watch out, Mick – you almost hit the president!' He didn't laugh much. My only consolation was that I didn't hit the president himself. The way the morning was going, it wouldn't have surprised me if I had.

* * *

Later that night, Anthony Pratt asked me to dinner as his guest at the Mar-a-Lago club. It's a stunning resort, designed very much in the fashion its proprietor favours. After purchasing it for what now seems like a bargain US$10 million in 1985, Trump later converted Mar-a-Lago into a club. He and his family have private quarters there.

Mar-a-Lago can certainly be described as palatial, but it's unlike any palace you've ever seen. It feels like it has been designed by a kind of Hawaiian shirt–wearing Louis XIV. Versailles on a Mezcal bender.

There were about two hundred people at the dinner, which was held outdoors in the grand courtyard. Anthony had insisted on getting a table right next to the passageway through which Trump would walk to get to his own table. *The Australian Financial Review* journalist Joe Aston, also an old staffer of mine, joined us at the table as a guest of Pratt's. I was sitting next to Anthony, and Joe Aston was on the other side of him. Everyone was eagerly awaiting the president's arrival on this beautiful, balmy night.

Trump and Melania finally made their entrance, emerging from their own home, in a closed-off wing on the other side of the resort. The president walked right through the corridor past our table. Anthony and the rest of us were standing up as he passed, and the moment Trump saw Anthony he stopped to talk, embracing the Australian billionaire.

'Anthony, good to see you. You're a great guy. I love Anthony. This guy made me $2 billion,' he said, referring to Pratt's new cardboard factory. Clearly, investment in Trump's America was as good as an investment in Trump himself.

'I've got Joe Hockey, the Australian ambassador, here, Mr President,' Anthony said.

Trump looked at me with dagger eyes. 'Yeah, I know Joe,' he said suspiciously, not for the first time that day.

'Mr President, I've got a famous journalist from Australia here too – Joe Aston, a big fan of yours,' Anthony went on, perhaps trying to soften the blow of the news that a member of the media was having dinner at Trump's resort.

Trump took Aston's hand and shook it, commanding him to 'be kind to my friend Anthony. He's a great guy. Only good stories. Only good stories!' he said. Ignoring me completely, the president and Melania then went off to be seated.

The table of honour was at the top of the courtyard, ringed by a barrier of ornate brass and red ropes, the kind you might see outside a theatre. Over the course of the evening, people would go and pay homage across the roped barrier until the Secret Service ushered them away to allow the president and first lady to eat their dinner in peace. Needless to say, I decided against paying a diplomatic visit to the presidential table that evening.

As the dinner ended, Trump and Melania walked through the crowd to leave and everyone burst into spontaneous standing applause. POTUS and FLOTUS retraced their steps past our table, and again Trump stopped to talk.

'Thank you, Anthony. Good to see you, Mr Journalist,' he said with a Trumpian finger point. This time the president looked at me, almost growled, and walked off.

I didn't stay for Easter Sunday lunch.

* * *

Back in Washington, DC, the pressure we were feeling over Australia's role in the Mueller investigation only seemed to increase. My hopes of clearing the air with the president had failed spectacularly, and it seemed the issue was only intensifying.

After Attorney General Barr made the key findings of the Mueller report public, the president was feeling triumphant. Bill Barr had now been tasked with conducting his own investigation into supposed conspiracy against Trump on the part of the FBI and other intelligence agencies. Central to that contention was the legitimacy of warrants issued under the Foreign Intelligence Surveillance Act (FISA), which had allowed the FBI to tap phones and gather intelligence on the Trump campaign in 2016. Trump was intent on making his enemies pay for what he viewed as a two-year 'witch hunt'. The Empire was striking back.

'I think spying on a political campaign is a big deal,' Barr told Congress that April. 'I think spying did occur. The question is whether it was adequately predicated. And I'm not suggesting that it wasn't adequately predicated. But I need to explore that.'

In May, a month after our disastrous golf weekend, Trump publicly named Australia as one of the countries he wanted Barr to investigate over their role in what he called 'a hoax' against America.

'I hope he looks at the UK, and I hope he looks at Australia, and I hope he looks at Ukraine,' Trump said. 'I hope he looks at everything because there was a hoax that was perpetrated on our country.'

At that point, I decided to do something I had previously been unwilling to do: release to the Americans our diplomatic cable on the Downer and Papadopoulos meeting, as well as anything else that might be relevant to Barr's investigation.

During the past two years, the FBI had come to us on a number of occasions asking whether we would release the cable from Downer about the May 2016 meeting. To that request I replied with a polite 'no'. We did not want Australia to be in the middle of a domestic political bunfight about who said what to whom. Now, of course it's appropriate that US and Australian intelligence agencies work together at a professional level. But Australia should never want to take sides in US domestic political arguments.

In fact, several times very senior people at the FBI came to see me and said, 'Will you give us permission to release the information Downer gave us to the Intelligence Committee and Congress?' I continued to say no. If we gave that permission, I knew, it wouldn't be long before Downer and I were sitting in those famous witness chairs before a congressional committee. Who wins out of that? Certainly not Australia.

There was debate on this issue within the Australian government. When he was still prime minister, Malcolm Turnbull held the view that we should just release everything. But my consistent view was that we should not, and Malcolm eventually accepted that rationale.

But as the Mueller investigation concluded and Bill Barr was tasked by Trump with a running new 'counter investigation', it became increasingly apparent that my position would not hold. Trump's recent comments specifically asking that Australia be investigated and his personal behaviour towards me indicated that something had to give. In addition, Trump was flagging that he would issue a presidential directive that all documents be released, including what the FBI already had on the Downer meeting. In effect, we were facing the diplomatic equivalent of checkmate.

Since the beginning of Barr's investigation, we had met with him on a couple of occasions. The attorney general was now asking if we could release the information to him. Although he was characterised publicly as Trump's attack dog, in my opinion Barr actually brought a lot of calmness and composure to the situation. Along with Mick Mulvaney, we devised a way for us to offer up the information to his investigation, establishing that Australia was happy to cooperate and we had nothing to hide.

Like most decisions in politics or diplomacy, this decision was not made in a vacuum. Of course, a year earlier we had achieved a stunning victory in managing to be the only nation to avoid Trump's steel and aluminium tariffs. Now, in the midst of Trump's fury over Australia's supposed role in the Mueller investigation, we were hearing chatter that the president was considering abolishing our tariff protection. The fact that Trump mentioned tariffs to me during his rant at Mar-a-Lago had set off alarm bells in my head. An undertaking to the president to cooperate via Bill Barr would placate Trump – and it certainly wouldn't hurt our chances of maintaining our tariff protections.

On 28 May, I penned a letter to Attorney General Barr, copying in Mick Mulvaney, stating Australia's willingness to help with the investigation and pledging that Australia would 'use its best endeavours' and 'provide all relevant information'.

> *Dear Attorney General,*
> *I refer to President Trump's announcement on 24 May that you will investigate the origins of the Federal Bureau of Investigation probe into Russian links to the 2016 US election.*
>
> *I note that the President referred to Australia, the United Kingdom, and the Ukraine as potential stakeholders. Moreover, I note that he has declassified intelligence material to support your investigation.*
>
> *The Australian Government will use its best endeavours to support your efforts in this matter. While Australia's former High Commissioner to the United Kingdom, The Hon. Alexander Downer, is no longer employed by the government, we stand ready to provide you with all relevant information to support your inquiries.*

On 2 June 2019, just five days after my letter was sent to Attorney General Barr, *The New York Times* reported: 'The

Trump administration considered imposing tariffs on imports from Australia last week, but decided against the move amid fierce opposition from military officials and the State Department.' There was no mention of the Mueller inquiry.

We would go on to meet Barr and attorney John H. Durham, who was appointed to lead the investigation; we would meet with Department of Justice officials six times over the next four months to discuss how Australia might help. As per our undertaking, we provided Barr's office with relevant parts of the cable and some other information that, as it turned out, had not been made public.

The secretary of DFAT, Frances Adamson, was at one point quizzed about this at Senate estimates hearings back in Canberra. By accident or design, it was revealed to the hearing that I made a 'proactive offer' to the Americans to cooperate with the Barr investigation. Despite opposition senators hoping to elicit some criticism of my decision, in fact it drew praise from DFAT.

'I would say that Ambassador Hockey's forward-leaning approach on this ... was exactly what I as DFAT secretary would expect him to do,' Adamson told Senate estimates in October 2019. 'An inquiry had been launched, Australia had been mentioned by the president, the foreign minister had indicated our willingness to assist. That's what he [Hockey] was doing, effectively saying we're here, we're ready to help in whatever way you want.'

With the success of the state dinner in September 2019, the United States–Australia relationship under Trump and Morrison seemed at its highest point since the time of George W. Bush and John Howard. Throughout Morrison's entire visit, there was barely a mention of the Mueller investigation. Things, it appeared, were going swimmingly.

That was until another bloody story leaked.

On Monday, 30 September, only a few days after Prime Minister Morrison had completed his trip to the United States, *The New York Times* published a story claiming Trump had personally contacted Morrison prior to his arrival in Washington and asked

Australia to aid in the attorney general's investigation. 'President Trump pushed the Australian prime minister during a recent telephone call to help Attorney General William P. Barr gather information for a Justice Department inquiry that Mr. Trump hopes will discredit the Mueller investigation, according to two American officials with knowledge of the call,' *The New York Times* reported.

This was accurate. But given that I'd already written to Barr and offered to provide 'all relevant information' for the investigation, the president was not asking for anything that we hadn't already agreed to do. The prime minister's office said as much in their media responses to *The New York Times*: 'The Australian government has always been ready to assist and cooperate with efforts that help shed further light on the matters under investigation. The P.M. confirmed this readiness once again in conversation with the president.'

However, the story took on added importance in the context of the impeachment proceedings that had been commenced against the president by congressional Democrats in late September. The impeachment inquiry would not be, as the Democrats had hoped, based on findings by Mueller. Quite simply, there were not adequate findings in the report to support impeachment. Rather, they would take a new tack, focusing on a conversation the president had had with Ukrainian president Volodymyr Zelensky in July 2019.

As he had with Morrison, Trump said he wanted the new Ukrainian president to assist Barr's investigation. The first thing he wanted was for Zelensky to assist Barr with an investigation into the whereabouts of the DNC email hackers' server. This was to explore a new theory being promulgated by former New York City mayor Rudi Giuliani – now Trump's personal lawyer – who claimed the hackers originated in Ukraine, not Russia.

But the primary issue Trump was concerned with was the role of Hunter Biden, the son of the likely 2020 Democratic presidential candidate Joe Biden, in a Ukrainian energy company called Burisma Holdings. Burisma's boss was a Ukrainian energy oligarch being investigated for corruption during the Obama years; he was never prosecuted and is believed to have left Ukraine in 2019. Hunter Biden was on Burisma's board, which in itself raised red flags for Trump.

There was some evidence that the Ukrainian anti-corruption prosecutor Viktor Shokin had been removed from office at the behest of Joe Biden when he was vice president. Biden and Obama advisers would later go on the record to confirm they did use US$1 billion in aid as leverage to achieve, among other things, the removal of Shokin, but said it was because the prosecutor was not cleaning up corruption in Ukraine. Shokin himself was also accused of corruption, which he denies.

A new Ukrainian anti-corruption prosecutor, Yuriy Lutsenko, started to pursue a line of inquiry against the Bidens, including claims they were part of a conspiracy to profit to the tune of millions of dollars by preventing corruption charges against Burisma's boss. Joe Biden denied this, and a subsequent report by Senate Republicans found no evidence that he had pressured Ukraine to fire the prosecutor in order to protect his son.

Trump's view was that Lutsenko was his guy in Kiev. But when Zelensky was elected in 2019, he dumped Lutsenko as prosecutor.

Much of the conversation between Trump and Zelensky in July 2019 concerned getting Lutsenko reinstated and allowing him to pursue the Bidens. On the call, Trump claimed that 'the prosecutor was treated very badly and he was a very fair prosecutor.' 'There's a lot of talk about Biden's son, that Biden stopped the prosecution and a lot of people want to find out about that so whatever you can do with the Attorney General would be great,' Trump said to Zelensky in a transcript of the phone call that was later released. 'Biden went around bragging that he stopped the prosecution so if you can look into it ... It sounds horrible to me.'

Not long after the phone call, the conversation between President Trump and President Zelensky was reported to Congress by an anonymous whistle-blower. It kicked off what would become the third impeachment of a US president by the House of Representatives.

So what did any of this impeachment inquiry, which seemingly had its roots in a corruption investigation into a Ukraine gas company, have to do with Australia? Well, central to Trump's impeachment charge was that the president was soliciting foreign interference to affect the outcome of the 2020 presidential election by encouraging the Ukrainians to go after Joe Biden. Therefore, when Trump urged Scott Morrison to help Barr with his investigation, some in the media and some Democrats were trying to mount a case that Trump was, once again, encouraging a foreign power to interfere in a US election campaign.

The situation was as infuriating as it was surreal. Although we had astutely avoided being seen to influence American politics over the last two years, and although there were no negative findings against us in the Mueller report, Australia was now being used as part of a new and improved bid to impeach Donald Trump. *The New York Times* was clearly making the case that this phone call could constitute foreign interference:

> *Mr. Trump's discussion with Prime Minister Scott Morrison of Australia shows the president using high-level diplomacy to advance his personal political interests.*
>
> *The discussion with Mr. Morrison shows the extent to which Mr. Trump views the attorney general as a crucial partner: The president is using federal law enforcement powers to aid his political prospects, settle scores with his perceived 'deep state' enemies and show that the Mueller investigation had corrupt, partisan origins.*

It wasn't subtle. Some Democrats were happy to follow the *Times'* lead, while some Trump hardliners were doubling down after the story, making matters even worse. Senator Lindsey Graham of South Carolina, chairman of the Senate Committee of the Judiciary, had been gunning for Australia on behalf of Trump, propagating the idea that Downer was 'ordered' to meet Papadopoulos in London back in 2016. Two days after *The New York Times* story, Graham took it upon himself to write, and then publicly release, a letter from the judiciary committee addressed to the prime ministers of Britain, Italy and Australia:

> *I write to request your country's continued cooperation with Attorney General Barr as the Department of Justice continues to investigate the origins and extent of foreign influence in the 2016 U.S. presidential election. That the Attorney General is holding meetings with your countries to aid in the Justice Department's investigation of what happened is well within the bounds of his normal activities. He is simply doing his job.*

The senator had written to the United Kingdom because of its connections to the Steele dossier, to Italy because of disappearing academic Joseph Mifsud, who had supposedly lined up the Russian contacts meeting with Donald Trump Junior (Barr himself had recently visited Italy as well), and, of course, to Australia because of the Downer–Papadopoulos meeting.

As interventions intended to support Trump go, it was a massive own goal: it drew more attention to Barr's attempts to seek help from foreign powers, and so could well have made other countries less likely to cooperate. Furthermore, when it came to Australia, Graham was factually wrong. He accused US intelligence and law enforcement of '[a]ccepting information from an Australian diplomat who was also directed to contact Papadopoulos and relay information obtained from Papadopoulos regarding the campaign to the Federal Bureau of Investigation'. In claiming that Downer was 'directed to contact Papadopoulos and relay information' to the FBI, Graham was repeating a falsehood about Australia's role in the Russia probe, one that had already been rejected by the Mueller investigation. It fed into a dangerous conspiracy theory that our high commissioner in the United Kingdom was acting in a sting operation at the behest of the Obama administration and/or Hillary Clinton's campaign and the FBI, in a bid to set up Trump and delegitimise his future presidency.

Coming from a senator who was chair of the judiciary committee, this was a statement I could not let stand. I had spent more than two years studiously avoiding Australia 'becoming the story'. Australia was not to be used as a tool in US domestic politics, by politicians or by the voracious media, ever obsessed with the Trump/Russia conspiracy. But at this point I felt I had little choice but to fire back. Australia was the story now, whether we liked it or not. Both *The New York Times* and Senator Graham were placing us at the fulcrum of an impeachment investigation into the president of the United States. To borrow a phrase from Leon Trotsky: 'You may not be interested in war, but war is interested in you.'

I decided to pen my own letter to Senator Graham, responding to his untrue claims about Australia. For maximum impact, I would then tweet it – he had done the same – along with my original letter to Barr pointing to Australia's willingness to assist his investigation.

'I note that we have been public about our willingness to cooperate,' I wrote. 'We gave this undertaking, on our own initiative, to the Attorney General in the letter of May 28th 2019.'

I then made clear that Graham's statement about Downer was wrong, and corrected the record publicly: 'In your letter you made mention of the role of an Australian diplomat. We reject your characterisation. As you have requested, we will work closely with the Attorney General to resolve any misunderstandings in this matter.'

Seconds after I tweeted my letter that morning – with an intentionally demure caption, 'Australia's response to Senator

Graham' – it went ballistic on Twitter and in the US media. It had over 1.12 million impressions, over 300,000 interactions and 1400 retweets. It was trending nationally, including on NBC.

'Australian Ambassador Rejects Graham's Description of Diplomat's Role in Russia Probe's Origins', ran the headline in *Politico*. 'Australia's ambassador to the U.S. confirmed to Sen. Lindsey Graham that the Australian government is assisting Attorney General William Barr's investigation of foreign interference in the 2016 election – but disputed the lawmaker's reference to an Australian diplomat involved in the Russia probe's origins,' *Politico* reported.

We were fielding calls from all the major US cable networks and newspapers for interviews, and, of course, from the media back at home. At this juncture, I decided the letters and the tweet had made the point well enough, and so I wasn't going to provide a running commentary on Senator Graham – lest I fall into the trap of becoming the story even more.

Fortunately, my decision seemed to be supported by Canberra (which was just as well, I suppose), and received minimal backlash from the White House. Barr continued with his investigation and we continued to cooperate where necessary. His final report would clear Australia of any wrongdoing without our intelligence leaking publicly. Australia would also avoid playing a role in Trump's first impeachment investigation, despite the implications of *The New York Times* story. Thus we had dodged bullets from both sides while keeping our relationship with the Trump administration and the Democrats intact.

* * *

As I worked to manage the implications of the Mueller investigation for Australia, as well as the periodic rage of Donald Trump and his enemies, I was reminded of a lesson another world leader had taught me. At the time we met he was not a prime minister, but one of the world's greatest cricketers. His name was Imran Khan.

During my university days, I played cricket for the University of Sydney. It may not surprise you to learn that I was an aggressive and somewhat bombastic middle-order batsman. One afternoon, I was batting in the cricket nets at training when Imran arrived. The Pakistani superstar was in Australia in the summer of 1984/85 to play for New South Wales in the Sheffield Shield, the premier domestic competition. In order to play for the state, Imran first needed to join a local club, so he came to Sydney uni. He wouldn't actually play many games for the club, though, as he was mostly with the state side.

Sauntering around the nets that afternoon, Imran was understandably drawing attention from the other players, all trying to act cool in the presence of the player rightly regarded, even then, as one of the best fast bowlers to ever play the game. As fate would have it, he chose to warm up his bowling in my net. As Imran affably chatted to others around him, I was quietly panicking at the end of the pitch. One of the fastest bowlers in the world (he could bowl at around 140 kilometres per hour) was about to put a spear through me, and I had no idea how to handle him. To make matters worse, I wasn't wearing a helmet. I never wore one, hoping this decision might send a message of fearlessness to the bowler. In retrospect, it almost killed me.

With my mind racing, I looked up and saw Imran casually coming in to bowl off a short run-up. To hell with his superstar status, I decided; I was going to go for it. Moving onto the front foot, I smacked the ball back over his head. Imran watched the ball fly overhead and then turned back and smiled at me with his playboy good looks.

Holy shit, I thought. *Now what?*

Imran was thrown another ball and gave it a shine on his trousers. Then he stepped back another five paces and began his run-up. I started readying myself for the next ball, but almost before I was set at the crease I felt a ball flying past my face. I never even saw it. It passed like a strong wind against my cheek, and was followed by a millisecond of pure terror. I still wince thinking about it.

Imran Khan taught me two great lessons that day: never get ahead of yourself, and never take your eye off the ball. If you do, you might get your head taken off.

Diplomacy, like politics, involves an enormous amount of intrigue. The trite aphorism is true: most of the action in politics and diplomacy is what you don't see. This is, of course, why journalists bust their bonnet to find out what's going on below the surface.

During the Mueller investigation, we at the Australian embassy in Washington, DC were very transparent with the Trump administration and the US media – when it was appropriate. Perhaps the intrigue in the Trump presidency played into general obsession with scandal, on both sides of politics and in the media. They seemed convinced that Australia must know more than we were saying. We must be hiding something! But the fact was we were telling the truth about a situation that, admittedly, looked at times like a bad spy novel, except that we weren't spying on anyone.

Both in the lead-up to the 2016 presidential election and after it, I was determined that we were not going to become a political football. It was also important back in Australia that we weren't seen as a patsy for Donald Trump. I was also acutely aware that he was not popular in Australia among those whom Americans would call independents and we call marginal seat voters.

In my view, the first impeachment of Donald Trump was really about kicking off a political brawl ahead of the 2020 presidential election. If it was a success, it would have been used relentlessly by the Democrats in the campaign. But in the end, during the entire presidential election campaign between Trump and Biden the impeachment was rarely mentioned – because it fell flat. The incessant TV ads focused on every aspect of Trump's presidency, but barely mentioned the impeachment, Mueller, Russia and related issues that had dominated the headlines for almost all of his term in office. This was in no small measure related to the fact that at the end of the day, despite all the intrigue, there was nothing much there.

In fact, the impeachment had the reverse impact, making Trump more of a hero with his base. In my view there was some legitimacy to Trump's claims that, from the beginning, even before he was nominated by the Republican Party, his enemies were conspiring to pull him down. In inquiry after inquiry, the Democrats channelled their opposition to Trump into quasi-judicial processes in order to undermine his presidency. Sadly, weaponising quasi-judicial bodies and institutions against individuals for purely political outcomes has been a trend in US politics in recent years, and, regrettably, it is increasing in Australian politics too. (It's why I despise quasi-judicial bodies like anti-corruption agencies with virtually no rules of evidence running show trials against political leaders based on allegations rather than substantive evidence.) It is an unfortunate tactic that undermines public confidence in political representatives.

And I'm not leaving Trump or the Republicans out of this criticism, by the way, because they used impeachment against Bill Clinton (although the Monica Lewinsky scandal may have played out very differently in today's world), and threatened impeachment against Hillary Clinton while she was secretary of state. I have no doubt that the Republicans would have tried to impeach Hillary had she won the 2016 election. While James Comey's public announcement on the FBI's decision to restart the investigation into Clinton's email server days out from the 2016 election rang the death knell for her campaign, he was clearly trying to get ahead of a likely move by the Republicans to impeach the future president. If Comey had not investigated the former secretary of state at that time and she'd gone on to win the presidency, he would have been in the invidious position of having to either investigate Clinton as president or justify to Republicans why he would not.

This also accounted for the speed with which the FBI opened an investigation into Trump's campaign. In my view, the FBI moved too quickly in this, but it was likely done to even the score. Because of what was afoot with Clinton's email investigation, the FBI didn't want to be perceived as behaving in a partisan manner. Comey's decision-making on investigations into Clinton and Trump was being dictated, primarily, by the threat of impeachment as a political weapon. Because of this, Comey ended up being despised by both sides and had nothing to show for it.

For me, one of the great successes of the Obama presidency was that it was almost entirely scandal-free. For a modern president to avoid scandal will be one of his great legacies. The bar for Obama was much higher than for others because of the colour of his skin. Tragically, and repulsively, racism is still very much alive in parts of America. If the first Black president had a scandal-ridden presidency, it may have set back the cause of equality for years. He didn't and it hasn't.

Much the same can be said of the Biden presidency so far. Thankfully, there's not even a whiff of any inappropriate behaviour by Biden or his administration, with the Ukraine allegations failing (once again) to amount to anything. I hope this trend continues, because obsessions with scandal are sucking the oxygen out of good government. They are a cancer on trust. And all too often they are baseless.

Frankly, I lay a great deal of blame at the door of social media, which has made negative voices in society much louder than positive voices. The mainstream media have reacted to the massive growth of these platforms by becoming agents of their ugly cousin's conspiratorial instincts.

Of course, much of the time the obsession with scandal comes at the expense of policy. For the millions of words and hours devoted to Mueller's investigation, speculating on what he would report and how it would be handled, there was during that time a vast amount of policy change that had a huge impact – not just on

America but on the rest of the world too. Much of that was lost in the public discourse.

Throughout those years, the task of the Australian embassy in Washington, DC, and of our missions around the world, was not to lose sight of the things that really mattered. We would monitor the news cycle – which seemed to evolve every thirty minutes during the Trump presidency – but not be distracted or obsessed by it. That's one reason why Australia continued to have diplomatic and policy wins during this time. We didn't get ahead of ourselves, and we didn't take our eye off the ball, despite the political pyrotechnics display that was the Trump administration.

CHAPTER 10

CHINA

**Boney M., iron ore, the Great Hall and
why America is scared of China**

China has been a constant throughout my life in politics, diplomacy and now business. While the focus of my diplomatic and recent business career has been on the United States, China's role in the global economy and its significance in the Australian–US relationship demands some analysis. China has had an undeniable impact on the defence, security, economics and, now, health of Australia and the United States. China is also key in the evolution of the Australian–US relationship itself.

One of my most enduring memories of China is the disco beats of Boney M. Sitting in a drab upstairs conference room in Beijing, the hit songs 'Rasputin' and 'Daddy Cool' were playing on repeat. It was New Year's Eve 1978, and a thirteen-year-old Joe Hockey was visiting China for the first time.

My parents' adventures had taken them to the Far East, as it was known then. They had booked a spot on the first commercial tour group out of Australia, to what was regarded as a secretive and closed-off communist regime that Australians knew little about.

With the death of Chairman Mao and the economic reforms of Deng Xiaoping in the late 1970s, China was gradually opening itself up to the world. The sleeping dragon was stirring. The problem was the Chinese didn't actually have much to show you.

Or, to put it another way, they didn't yet know *how* to be a tourist destination.

China's turbulent recent history meant that many of the artifacts and knowledge associated with the country's extraordinary cultural legacy had been lost. Great collections had either been destroyed or shipped off to Taiwan at the end of the Civil War, and the Cultural Revolution had been devastating. There wasn't a lot of adventure tourism to be experienced in what was basically a third world nation. While we were taken to the Great Wall and the Forbidden City (you could hardly miss those), they didn't have much other tourism to offer. Beijing was bleak. Nanjing and Shanghai were interesting but basic. Rural towns like Wuxi were still beautiful back then.

At all times, we were escorted by two members of the Chinese Communist Party. They were there to keep us in check. In fact, much of the trip was a display of the Party's supposed economic and cultural achievements. We were taken to a farm to watch the commune in action (force-fed ducks attached to rudimentary garden hoses), and to a primary school to see the wonders of the communist education system. For entertainment, we had Chinese opera in the park. For a boy from Sydney, the entire experience was about as far from the concept of entertainment as one could possibly get.

The hotels we stayed in were ugly and spartan, with tiny, hard beds and filthy bathrooms. Compounding my malaise was some pretty awful food. I had come expecting feasts of what I understood to be Chinese food: Mongolian beef and sweet and sour pork. But we were regularly being served some grey, bony soup with a bowl of rice. Not a spring roll in sight. People were all dressed in green or blue Mao suits. There were almost no cars on the road, just bicycles. Even though we weren't always shown the real China by our tour guides, it was clear that these people were poor. Many lived the same day every day. I hadn't seen poverty on this scale before, and it was more than just confronting – it was otherworldly.

Most of the Chinese were astounded to see, for the first time, white people. As a teenager, I was a particularly attractive target: my cheeks were regularly squeezed by Chinese men and women, fascinated by this fair-skinned Australian boy.

It was a completely different country compared to the China we know today. Much of the nation didn't follow a Western calendar. We were told there wouldn't be any recognition of Christmas (there wasn't), and not to expect any celebration on New Year's Eve either. The kind tour group staff did, however, find us a conference room near Tiananmen Square in which we could have a celebration. They also found just one cassette tape, with only two Boney M. songs on it – which was why 'Rasputin' and 'Daddy Cool' were played on repeat from 8 p.m. till midnight. To this day, I can't listen to either song without having flashbacks. It's safe to say this was the strangest New Year's Eve I've ever experienced.

Despite the culture shock, I found that first trip to China fascinating, and was always thankful to my parents for exposing me to such a cultural experience at a young age.

I grew up in an immigrant household, and was always being reminded that white Australia and its culture was very small compared to what the rest of the world had. Given my father's Armenian Palestinian background, he disliked Australia's insular – at times downright xenophobic – suspicion towards 'foreigners'. When my grandmother was asked where she was from, she'd reply: 'None of your business. Unless you're Aboriginal, you're not *from* here either.'

And so my parents had always pushed back against the notion of immigrants as outsiders. Whether it was Italians, Greeks, Lebanese or Vietnamese, I was taught that these people were all contributing to Australia and our way of life. And even back then, my parents understood the importance of China and what it could mean for Australia within my lifetime.

* * *

In September 2013, on the same day I was sworn in as Australia's new treasurer, I flew to Bali to attend an APEC finance ministers' meeting. This would also be my introduction to one of my great sparring partners and friends, Chinese finance minister Lou Jiwei.

Sitting on the government plane that day, I was nervous. It was my first international finance ministers' meeting as treasurer, and I didn't have a clue what was expected of me. Treasury Secretary Martin Parkinson was with me and I turned to him for advice. 'How am I going to handle these APEC meetings? Any tips?' I asked.

He smiled and shrugged his shoulders nonchalantly. 'Don't worry, Treasurer, you'll be fine. I'm sure you'll work it out,' he said.

Thanks, Mr Secretary, I thought. *Those sound like famous last words.*

My first meeting when I arrived was with Indonesia's finance minister, Dr Muhamad Chatib Basri. Thankfully, that did go extremely well. He was a lovely bloke – a classically urbane member of the Indonesian political class, and educated at the ANU in Canberra.

Walking back to my hotel room, a traditional Balinese hut, I was feeling pretty chuffed, and I began to wonder what all the fuss was about with these international summits. And I felt that way until my next meeting – which was when I first encountered Lou Jiwei.

I was sitting in my Balinese hut and preparing for our meeting when I got a knock on the door. It was Lou's advance security team. This guy literally had a larger advance team than the president of the United States. I sat there among a group of what seemed like thirty state security guards and awaited the arrival of China's finance minister.

Not long after, Lou Jiwei entered my room. He was wearing a poorly fitting suit and his tie was slightly askew. He gave me a limp handshake and barely a smile. He sat down, crossed his legs and lit a cigarette without so much as a 'do you mind?'

Lou Jiwei was the former head of the China Investment Corporation. I knew he was a hardliner on economics, but I wasn't expecting the first thing that came out of his mouth.

'Why won't you let me buy BHP?' he asked with a dull stare.

Oh, I thought, *we're playing this game, are we?*

'Well, Minister, Qantas have just told me they want to buy China Southern and China Eastern. So I'm sure we can come to some sort of arrangement.'

He sucked on his cigarette and started laughing. 'Look, all I want to do is buy 15 per cent of all the top 200 stocks on the Australian Stock Exchange. Is that possible?' he asked.

I replied in the same vein. 'As long as we can do the same in China, I'm sure we can come to an arrangement,' I said.

We both knew he was testing the new guy, but I wasn't going to be intimidated. I was standing up to him, and I could see he respected that. We went on to have a good chat that day, and it wouldn't be my last honest conversation with Lou Jiwei.

It was no secret that when we came to office in 2013, iron ore was the oxygen of the Australian economy. Before the Coalition took government, Wayne Swan had built into the budget forecasts an iron ore price of between US$130 to US$140 a tonne over the next four years. Iron ore had been on an absolute tear, and the Labor government had assumed that would continue. But as luck would have it, not long after I became treasurer, the price of iron ore began to plummet. From January 2014, the price fell from US$135 a tonne to below US$80 a tonne, and by September this was causing havoc with the federal budget.

In the last months of 2014, we were attempting to prepare numbers for the mid-year economic and fiscal outlook. We had to adjust the budget figures urgently to account for the dramatic price drop. Between our May budget and November's economic update, we saw a 30 per cent price wipeout. But, like it or not, you have to have realistic figures in the budget over a four-year period. All my advice was that the iron ore price would continue to fall dramatically over the forward estimates, so we began pricing iron ore at the scarily low price of US$40 a tonne. That price forecast would result in a $31 billion hit to our tax receipts, and the largest fall in the terms of trade since records began.

Unfortunately, that wasn't even the worst of it. Treasury kept coming to us with increasingly dire forecasts. To our horror, it appeared the real price was going to fall to as low as US$30 a tonne in the coming year.

Treasury then advised me that if I came out with an official forecast of US$30 a tonne in the midyear review, it would be bad news for Andrew Forrest's Fortescue Metals. While they wouldn't reveal what their costs of production were, it appeared to us that they were relying on a price of US$34 a tonne. If we wrote down the iron ore price to US$30 a tonne, it could trigger a series of events that could wipe Fortescue out.

While the price of iron ore is dictated by demand, we suspected that the Chinese had been stockpiling, and that this was pushing down what Australian companies could charge for it. There were ways to manipulate the iron ore price, and the Chinese were pulling every lever.

I was heading to Beijing in October for an APEC meeting, and when I got there I made a beeline for Lou Jiwei. I needed a one-on-one conversation, so I threw everyone out of the room. Senior Chinese politicians like to pretend they don't understand English, but in my experience they all do.

I sat down with Lou and spoke clearly. 'My friend, I am on the threshold of recognising that iron ore is going to fall to US$30 a tonne,' I said.

He looked at me blithely and shrugged. 'Joe, that's your market. Not our problem,' he said.

'No, it's your market,' I replied, making it clear who was the cause of this. 'And if I lower my forecast to US$30 a tonne,

Fortescue will fall over. Then do you know what I'll do? I will merge BHP and Rio, and you'll have one supplier out of Australia.'

Now his eyes widened. 'Really, you would do that?' he said.

I looked him in the eye. 'Yes, I will do that. I'll have job losses throughout Western Australia and I need to get that price up,' I said.

Lou looked at me, puzzled. He was no doubt wondering whether I was bluffing, but probably also considering whether he wanted to be the one to explain to President Xi how BHP and Rio merged under his watch.

'What price do you want it up to?' he replied finally.

'No less than US$35 a tonne,' I said.

He looked at me, lit up another cigarette and then changed the subject.

Since that meeting, the iron ore price has never fallen below US$35 a tonne – and, needless to say, Fortescue Metals is doing just fine.

Lou's way of doing business was complicated but sometimes entertaining. He was, after all, managing an unbelievably complex relationship between the Chinese communist regime, foreign governments and Chinese state-owned industry.

It was also thanks to Lou Jiwei that I ended up addressing the top brass of the Chinese Communist Party in the Great Hall of the People.

We were in Beijing on the last day of the APEC finance ministers' meeting, and Lou wanted another favour. There was going to be an address from the Chinese premier, Li Keqiang, at the end of the conference, and we were going to meet all the members of the Politburo Standing Committee (except for President Xi Jinping himself). Lou wanted me to give a brief speech at the end of Premier Li's address.

It's not every day that you get asked to address the leadership cabinet of China in the Great Hall of the People. 'What do I have to do?' I asked.

'I want you to thank the premier for having us. Say some nice things about China and that's it. Not long. Two minutes,' he said, making the globally recognised karate chop gesture.

I agreed, and began thinking about what I would say.

The Great Hall of the People is actually a number of different rooms with twelve-metre-high ceilings in a monstrously large building next to Tiananmen Square. We filed in, and found the chairs organised in a horseshoe shape so that the Politburo members and the APEC finance ministers were looking directly at each other. At the apex of the horseshoe was a huge bowl of flowers and two big chairs. Premier Li sat on one side and I was directed to sit on the other. An interpreter appeared from behind the flowerpot, ready for Li's speech. As I looked out, I could see probably seventy cameras with a small army of Chinese journalists lined up behind them, all keenly awaiting the premier's address.

Premier Li started speaking, and his words appeared to be of great interest to the assembled Chinese media. It was long, and drew on a rhetorical tradition of which Chinese leaders are fond. It was all about how well China was doing, what China's goals were and why China is such a great country. You get the drift.

Sitting there attempting to listen attentively to the premier, I reflected on the moment. Above the assembled media in front of us was a gigantic mural of the Great Wall of China. I thought of the history of this great nation, the sacrifices of many and the current plight of its more than 1 billion citizens. While the landmass of China is not much larger than Australia's, it has a population that is sixty times ours. Many Chinese cities have more people than my entire country.

It began to dawn on me that I had an unusual opportunity here. I couldn't just stand up here and say, 'Gee, thanks for having us, guys, you run a great country.' I started thinking about all the people who had been with me on my political journey. I thought about the old ladies handing out how-to-vote cards on my behalf in North Sydney. I thought about my father getting away from tyranny in the Middle East and starting his own business in Australia. I reflected on my visit to China in the late 1970s, and on how much things had changed since then. I thought about all these things and more as the Premier went on, and on, and on.

All of a sudden, Premier Li stopped. He turned his hand towards me and gestured for me to speak. I sat there for half a second, staring at his perfectly manicured fingernails, before preparing to speak.

'Premier, thank you for your words. And thank you for hosting us here. Combined, my colleagues in APEC represent a majority of the world's economy, and your hospitality has been generous,' I said. I noticed the assembled media beginning to file out.

'I first came to China in late 1978,' I said.

All of a sudden, the Politburo members turned and looked at me, and the media stopped in their tracks.

'I remember as a young lad, thirteen years old, standing out the front of this building in awe. Back then, no building in Beijing was more than four storeys high.'

I noticed Lou Jiwei communicating his 'cut it' signal with his eyes, but I continued.

'Everyone seemed to be wearing green suits or blue suits. There were hardly any cars on the road. Most people rode on black pushbikes. There was not a neon sign to be seen. The lights were very dim at night,' I said, failing to mention Boney M. 'It has been my privilege to see the greatest economic transformation of the most people in the history of humanity.'

By this time, the CCP leadership had decided to embrace my ad-lib moment, and were nodding in furious agreement, pride written all over their faces.

'I want to thank you for embracing capitalism,' I said.

Now their jaws dropped.

You don't fully understand the power of silence until you drop a clanger like that in the Great Hall of the People while addressing communist China's top brass. Nobody made a noise or a gesture. Cold eyes stared back at me from all parts of the room.

There was one exception. From the corner of my eye I could see my friend Taro Aso, Japan's finance minister and deputy prime minister, who was slapping his thigh and smiling in agreement. Nobody else on our side did anything but look at me in stunned silence.

The attendants in the Great Hall began to usher the media out of the room, and at this point I started to worry. Looking at an exit sign in front of me, the thought of making a break for it crossed my mind. But where would I go? What was I going to do, run out into Tiananmen Square like a madman? *No*, I thought, *bugger it. I'm going to keep going.*

'Mr Premier, just a few weeks ago, Ali Baba listed on the New York Stock Exchange, the biggest public offering in world history, listing at a value of US$231 billion. And part of Ali Baba's mission statement is to facilitate the growth of small and medium-sized businesses in China. What your nation has done in a generation, no nation on earth has ever done. And we want to work in partnership with you to continue that great story,' I said.

Premier Li looked at me with a strange expression on his face. I saw him compose himself, and then he spoke. 'You're right,' he said, to my enormous relief. 'By embracing enterprise, China has lifted many people out of poverty, and our great challenge is to continue that journey. We want to continue to embrace enterprise and continue to improve the living standards of the Chinese people.'

Those few minutes in the Great Hall of the People have caused me to reflect deeply on China's relationship with Australia and, more recently, with the United States. As treasurer, I went to Washington and made a vigorous defence of China's gradual deregulation of its economy. For example, they had gone faster than almost any other country in the world at deregulating their currency, and they were never given proper recognition.

Australia has had a relationship that has drifted between being fawning and being highly critical of modern-day China. This is too broad a spectrum to manage a long-term relationship – which is exactly how China views its relationships – in the long term.

In the United States, and on Wall Street in particular, they were advocating for China when they could see commercial opportunities. When those commercial opportunities did not materialise, Wall Street became indifferent and Washington became critical.

I've also defended China in numerous speeches against the accusation that it has 'stolen' American manufacturing jobs. China lost 19 million manufacturing jobs between 1996 and 2005. Those jobs went to Vietnam, Thailand and Indonesia. Many of the manufacturing jobs lost in the United States were lost because of improved technology and the emergence of a global economy, which is exactly what the United States has long argued for.

I was proud to be part of a government that negotiated a free trade agreement with China, which was unthinkable only a few years earlier. And it was actually harder to get a free trade agreement with the United States through the Australian parliament than it was to get the free trade agreement with China approved.

At one point in 2015, when things had begun to heat up between the United States and China, President Obama flat out asked Prime Minister Abbott to stop selling Australian iron ore to China. Both the prime minister and I were astounded. Abbott just palmed it off, but I was more animated in my reply. 'That's ridiculous!' I protested furiously. What was the Americans' plan for Australia – were they going to buy *all* our iron ore? Those exports were critical, both for the economy and for the federal and the West Australian budgets. Clearly President Obama hadn't properly thought through what such a decision would mean for our country. Perhaps he was confusing us with the Saudis and OPEC – tap on, tap off. But we weren't going to trash our economy for President Obama – or any other president, for that matter.

Despite recent challenges, I believe there is goodwill towards China, and certainly towards the Chinese people, within the hearts of Australians, and in the hearts of many Americans also. I think the challenge is that Beijing is cloaked in mystery. It's very hard to read because it's so lacking in transparency and accountability. Mystery fuels suspicion. It then becomes a threat to you and your interests.

When I was treasurer, I defended the rise of China and its role in the future of global geopolitics. I was frustrated by the lack of attention paid to China at the International Monetary Fund (IMF), which is essentially a European-run organisation. The Chinese decided on various occasions not to send their senior people to meetings because all the discussion focused on Europe, the US and the global financial crisis. The World Bank, meanwhile, is very much an American club. The Asian Development Bank is heavily influenced by Japan. The OECD is, like the IMF, dominated by the Europeans; the Chinese aren't even members. There just didn't seem to be any room for China in these global institutions.

The Bretton Woods Agreement of 1944 helped shape most of these institutions, but its legacy hasn't kept pace with a rapidly evolving world. This was one of the reasons I pushed so hard for Australia to join the Asian Infrastructure Investment Bank (AIIB). My support wasn't designed to placate the Chinese. It was appropriate recognition of their role in Asia and their preparedness to support and lead infrastructure investment in the region through a multilateral forum.

President Obama was also putting pressure on us not to join the AIIB. The Americans really did a 'full-court press' (an American term I love) on this one. Obama personally rang Abbott, advising him against letting Australia join the AIIB. Secretary of State John Kerry rang Foreign Minister Julie Bishop to tell her the same thing. They didn't try me because I was pushing hard for us to join, and I was the strongest advocate in Cabinet. The Japanese government, led by Prime Minister Shinzo Abe, was also pushing Abbott hard not to be a part of it.

The Chinese had been asking us to join, and we saw it as an opportunity to be involved from the outset. The AIIB wasn't a development bank, it was an investment bank, and in my view that was a big difference. The Chinese perspective was that the Belt and Road Initiative was their development bank, while the AIIB was a partnership for building infrastructure in the region, with US$50 billion in starting capital. With Australia being the main supplier of iron ore in the region, we wanted to be a part of it, and we expected others in the region would follow. We had just signed a free trade agreement with China. So why wouldn't we want to be part of it?

Things were progressing badly in Cabinet, however – and they got worse when there was a leak to *The Australian*'s Paul Kelly on 30 October 2014. Kelly reported that Julie Bishop and I were split on the matter of joining the AIIB. According to the report, Bishop had killed off our membership by taking the American position that it was a strategic risk. The fact that this leak came out of the National Security Committee (NSC) was particularly bad.

Despite Abbott's initial decision to delay Australia's commitment, I managed to convince the NSC and Cabinet that it was a no-brainer. In Cabinet, I got the support of influential advocates like Andrew Robb and Mathias Cormann. As part of our agreement to join, we were able to negotiate better corporate governance within the AIIB. When our concerns were addressed, we went in and, as I predicted, other countries, including South Korea and Thailand, followed us. They wanted us to lead the pack. Despite all this, our procrastination was costly. We had to forgo a leadership role within the AIIB.

I was so pleased that, when we joined, I flew to Beijing for the signing ceremony in the Great Hall on Tiananmen Square. It was particularly special that mine was the first signature on the agreement – it's handy to represent a country whose name begins with A! I stood on the dais and held up the pen, a touch that China's President Xi Jinping loved, and the photo went around the world.

Concerningly, our friends in the United States and Japan did not join the AIIB because they saw it as a Chinese-led institution. I had negotiated solutions for all their legitimate corporate governance issues. In the end, their intransigence was petulant and pretty disappointing.

* * *

When I came to the United States, I gained more granular insight into the intelligence data that flows between our countries. There was a significant increase in Chinese state engagement in international commerce, and with that came more malevolent behaviour. In particular, there was a dramatic increase in the theft of intellectual property.

I was never naive about the security threat posed by China. When I was treasurer, there had been attempted security breaches against me – attempts to hack my computers or eavesdrop on my conversations – all standard stuff at those high levels of government. Fortunately, I was disciplined enough to know that nothing can be kept secret unless you're using top-secret communications devices.

There is an inherent insecurity built into governments in countries where there has previously been a civil war. Countries like China, Russia, the United States, Spain and Greece all had civil wars in the last 200 years. All those countries still carry the scars, in the form of a degree of distrust between the central government and its citizens. The tension is exacerbated if the countries also had revolutionary wars along the way. It means that no community either fully trusts itself or its government.

In the United States, checks and balances were built into the US Constitution and the nation's laws following its revolutionary war. Those laws guarantee the privacy and independence of individual citizens, particularly against the perceived power of the central government. The majority of citizens in China probably distrust the authority of Beijing. However, that distrust is mitigated by the massive advances made in a short period of time to improve the living standards of the average Chinese citizen. They don't have to like their government to know it has helped make their lives better.

It's also the case that in China, the government doesn't trust its own people. Because of that, the government has put in place laws that give the state extraordinary powers to crush dissent in the community and to control, without serious limitation, every aspect of the community. Having only one political party helps. The Chinese Communist Party sits above the state, and the state will always sit above the people.

There is not a great deal of recognition among most everyday Americans about what China is historically or what the present-day Chinese state actually is. When China began to rise, everyday Americans didn't know what they were dealing with. They did, however, know that the manufacturing plant down the road had closed and supply chains had moved to China. They also knew that cheaper goods were coming in from China. As consumers, they sucked these up like vacuum cleaners, but these goods were, nonetheless, viewed as inferior products. The same view was originally held of Japanese goods; their quality improved over time, and Chinese goods are improving too.

Australia had an engagement with China that was deeper, broader and more sophisticated than that of the United States. So I came to Washington more attuned to the relationship than many Americans were at the time. Immediately, I could sense a deterioration in the relationship between the United States and China. Part of this deterioration was marked by a change in rhetoric. From day one Donald Trump was putting 'America first'. China wasn't used to that sort of rhetoric coming out of the United States, and was fearful and defensive.

Then China saw that Trump's posturing was translating into real policy change. Very quickly the Chinese understood that

'America first' didn't mean 'China second' – it meant China came third or fourth or fifth, or not even on the list.

Early on, President Xi Jinping attempted to work on the relationship, in what was a humbling act for him. He brought his whole team to Mar-a-Lago. Trump loved the idea that he was being feted. He also respected strong leaders, and never wanted to be disrespectful to them. If he viewed someone as weak, he'd roll right over the top of them, but if he viewed you as strong, he'd respect you. And of course he loved winners. All of that meant political leaders such as Vladimir Putin, Xi Jinping and Recep Tayyip Erdoğan were respected adversaries.

Regardless of Xi's attempts to court Trump, the United States started to toughen up not only its attitude towards China, but also its rules for engagement with China. That was particularly the case under Secretary of State Mike Pompeo. As a former director of the CIA, he was naturally more anxious about China.

Australia, too, was increasingly being briefed by the United States on the threats posed by Chinese state actors. It was Chinese provocation that led to the reinvigoration of the diplomatic and military partnership between the United States, India, Japan and Australia known as the 'Quad' (short for the Quadrilateral Security Dialogue). It's all a bit contentious, but India always had some reluctance to fully engage in a formal process because they feared Beijing's reaction to what might appear a diplomatic and military encircling of China. And you can see their point of view about that.

The Indians also had a bad reaction to Kevin Rudd's 'China first' attitude towards foreign policy when he was prime minister, which was best reflected by his government's decision not to sell Australian uranium to India (which had not signed the Treaty on the Non-Proliferation of Nuclear Weapons). Rudd walked away from India, and the Indians never forgave us.

China's rulers have no regard for democracy. Freedom of expression, a fair rule of law and the rights of the individual undermine power in Beijing, and pose a threat to the future of the one-party state. As the Chinese Communist Party no doubt sees it, the rapid improvement in Chinese people's quality of life has vindicated its abolition of their personal rights.

I will never forget sitting at the G20 finance ministers' meeting with (once again) Lou Jiwei. I was on the verge of achieving my goal in setting up a Global Infrastructure Hub. Every nation had agreed to the fund except India, which had decided that we needed to 'take a more cautious approach'. They had sent a bureaucracy chief along, who was droning on about why we needed to take it all slowly. I was sitting there in the room going crazy over the Indians' inability to just agree and get it done.

Sitting next to me was Lou Jiwei, who could sense my frustration. He pointed and smiled at the Indian delegation. 'China and India have a similar-sized population. There's your democracy. How's it going for them?'

Through its own modern history, the United States has always been cognisant of the potential of China, but still communist China largely snuck up on the Americans. You would think that after the travails of the Korean War, Vietnam and skirmishes in between, America would have been wiser to the looming threat. However, President Richard Nixon's visit to Beijing in 1972, together with the gradual opening of the Chinese economy to US businesses and the end of the global threat of communism, lulled America into the false sense that it controlled the direction of the relationship. America was hubristic in its treatment of modern China.

China's rise, both economically and militarily, did not take place in a vacuum, but it did come at a time when the United States was distracted with a series of other national security and economic threats and rivals: Russia, al-Qaeda, the Taliban, ISIL, Hezbollah. Those were all understandable threats, but almost in the background China was gradually increasing its influence in the world.

America has also realised that China represents a unique threat to its dominance of the global order, both economically and militarily. No nation since imperial Britain has presented such a challenge to Americans – not Nazi Germany, not imperial Japan, not North Korea, not even the Soviet Union. These states, particularly the Soviet Union, presented catastrophic kinetic threats to the United States, but never truly represented an economic threat. It was ultimately the United States' economic scale that underwrote its military machine, and it was ultimately economics that contributed most significantly to the unravelling of the USSR.

The great economic stories of the modern era – the re-emergence of a united and democratic Germany, and the rebuilding of Japan – are still not commercially superior to the United States, and, by design, can never re-emerge as military threats. Meanwhile, with a population more than four times larger than that of the United States, China is able to combine an enormous and advanced military, vast economic and material resources, and massive supply chain control and influence to represent the greatest threat to US hegemony in over 200 years.

When Trump became president, there was a tsunami of voices telling him what China was doing and how it was undermining the United States. From university campuses to Wall Street, from Silicon Valley to Pearl Harbor, Chinese surveillance, intellectual property theft and state-sponsored cyber attacks harassed US stability. Moreover, some Chinese students and visiting workers were co-opted by the state to assist with that aggressive behaviour. Such was the concern that the director of the FBI, Christopher Wray, gave a highly unusual speech naming all the people his agency had arrested for stealing intellectual property or spying.

It was this bad behaviour, which was hardly covert, that fuelled the protectionist narrative propounded by Wilbur Ross and Bob Lighthizer. It also reinforced Trump's assertions about the Chinese stealing US jobs. The defense chiefs, too, were making a big noise to the president over the Chinese military threat. In areas like hypersonics and missile propulsion generally, China was taking the lead. The impact of those technologies is such that they could threaten the effectiveness of America's massive strategic advantage at sea through the use of aircraft carriers.

In every area China was playing catch-up. Most significantly, they have become far more aggressive in space, and it was this that motivated Trump to create the Space Force as the sixth branch of the US Armed Forces (alongside the Army, the Navy, the Marine Corps, the Air Force and the Coast Guard). The Space Force is aligned with the Air Force in much the same way as the Marines are affiliated with the Navy. At the time of its announcement, the Space Force was ridiculed, but you will notice that Joe Biden and sensible Democrats have never advocated for its abolition. In fact, in his first budget, President Biden increased the funding for the Space Force by 13 per cent to over US$17.5 billion. (That's about half of what Australia spends on its entire military.)

In addition to all this, the United States has also toughened its foreign investment laws by upgrading the Committee for Foreign Investment in the United States (CFIUS) with a tougher screening process, and putting in place additional national security assessments for investors. It has also toughened supply chain reporting and sourcing requirements, and the banking and investment rules around Chinese commercial interests. The United States has also been inching towards simply delisting all Chinese companies that are raising capital through listings on various exchanges including NASDAQ and the NYSE. In a short time, the nation has moved from concern about China and its ambitions to outright defiance and hostility.

Of course, when COVID-19 came along, it amplified that anxiety. The 'China virus', as Trump termed it, tore through America and the world at exactly the wrong time for China. One of the most formidable communicators of the last forty years, Donald Trump was never going to let the blame fall on him. The way Trump saw it, China gave 32 million Americans the

COVID-19 virus and killed half a million of those people, causing the greatest crisis in the United States since World War II.

It is true that China, through COVID-19, has done what no other nation has done in human history. The lives lost and the health effects of COVID-19, combined with the economic impact through lockdowns and travel bans, has meant the virus has affected every lounge room in every house in every city in every country on the planet. No other nation has ever had that impact on every household in the whole damn world, from Park Avenue in New York through to the favelas in Rio de Janeiro and everywhere in between. Through a virus originating in Wuhan, China has had a greater impact on the planet's population than any other nation in history.

Of course, Trump also needed someone to blame for the disastrous impact of COVID-19 in the United States, but he was given China on a platter because it was the source of the virus. The 'China threat' narrative had achieved its peak impact in the United States: China was a nation-level threat – economically, and in security and defence – but it now also posed a personal threat to the health and wellbeing of American citizens.

* * *

US antagonism and fear about China was not invented by Donald Trump, nor has it disappeared with the end of his presidency. In many areas Joe Biden has taken up where Trump left off. Biden won the election by winning back blue-collar American voters, and the substance of his rhetoric on China throughout the campaign was no different from Trump's. At times it was like they were trying to outdo each other on how anti-China they could be. Uniquely, in this age of a divided America, China has managed to unite Americans – against it. It has been left completely alienated by everyone in Washington and beyond.

China has even run out of friends in business. Many business leaders – such as Steve Schwarzman at Blackstone – did their best to build bridges with China. They identified both hope and opportunity in the China growth story. Progressively, though, most businesses have found doing business in China really difficult.

As a business partner, Beijing is hard to work with. Unpredictable policy backflips that could smash your business and industry in a split second are becoming more commonplace. The closing down of the gaming industry in Macau, and the upheaval, without notice, of tertiary education has frightened investors. Moreover, individuals such as Jack Ma, co-founder of the massive Chinese online retailer Alibaba, have been targeted by their own government.

As a result, business leaders are finding it very hard to navigate the volatility of Beijing. As business confidence fell, the number of China-sourced cyber attacks on businesses rose. The downward spiral of mistrust increased in speed. If you're being hacked by Chinese interests trying to steal your intellectual property, you're not going to rush down to Washington and say, 'Let's reduce tariffs and be friends with China.' And if the business community isn't advocating for China, then what friends do they have in the United States?

Despite our more integrated relationship with China, Australian companies have suffered the same disillusionment with the way Chinese companies do business. Australian firms would regularly complain of pitching for investment opportunities, only to have their intellectual property stolen after a meeting. There has been a conga line of large companies (not to mention SMEs) leaving China in tears after poor experiences.

Ultimately, it comes down to this: the Chinese will buy what they want. That might sound obvious, but Western business has discovered the hard way that it's very difficult to sell products or services that don't fit in with Chinese culture or the Chinese Communist Party's agenda. Media is a perfect example. Two decades ago, Rupert Murdoch and News Corp were great advocates for China. Within a few years, he'd pulled out. Even gambling companies couldn't make it work in Macau. James Packer used to tell me about how China was the next big thing, and that 'we just don't understand China'. Now he no longer operates there.

The fact is that while China can be a good customer when it wants or needs what you're selling, it can also be a very volatile business partner. Despite our integrated trading relationships in mining and commodities, and the vast numbers of Chinese students who come to our shores, the Chinese government is treating Australia appallingly. The Australian government has been doing completely the right thing in its response.

China has been immature in its dealings with Australia of late. Confected trade embargos, WTO complaints and refusals to even meet with Australian ministers are simply crazy. The Chinese leadership seems to think the best thing it can do is humiliate and bully Australia. These are also the same tactics defenders of China over the years (including me) had warned against in international forums. They are not the actions of a global superpower.

This behaviour towards Australia is only going to embolden our alliance with the United States. It will not prise us apart.

CHAPTER 11

A PANDEMIC, RACE RIOTS AND AN ELECTION

How COVID, BLM and Biden brought down Trump

It's morning in America, early June 2020. As I ride my bike down to the Mall just after 7 a.m., the scene in downtown Washington, DC is dystopian. In front of the White House, out on the section of 16th Street that will soon be renamed Black Lives Matter Plaza, I can see police in full riot gear clearing the street of lagging but threatening protestors, after yet another night of violent Black Lives Matter (BLM) demonstrations.

On 1 June a curfew had been imposed on the city between 11 p.m. and 6 a.m., but even after the curfew is lifted, the streets are almost empty. We are, after all, in the middle of the largest global pandemic for one hundred years. COVID-19 brought this city to a standstill well before BLM.

The few harried and masked faces I see hail police with placatory gestures, demonstrating their civilian status, in a need to get to wherever they are going. They must really need to be somewhere, because nobody wants to be out on the streets at the moment.

Washington in the summer of 2020 is perhaps the strangest and tensest city I have ever been in that wasn't an actual warzone. I may see nothing like it again in my lifetime.

If COVID-19 brought America to a standstill, then the BLM protests brought it to a boiling point. Almost everyone is fearful on some level. Pretty much every American I know has spoken to me about the importance of keeping a gun in their home. Even non–gun toting Democrats I've known for years are advising me to get one for my own safety.

It's going to be a long summer – and it's still five months until the presidential election.

* * *

Leading into the 2020 presidential campaign, Donald Trump had not one but three opponents. The Black Lives Matter movement, the COVID-19 pandemic and the Democratic candidate, Joe Biden. And the fact was that BLM and COVID-19 were more formidable opponents for Trump than anything Biden could have thrown at him. And if Trump had handled the first two issues differently, he may well have been re-elected. As it turned out, he failed on all counts and handed Biden a deserving victory.

The United States' tragic history of race relations, I think, is one of the keys to decoding its politics today, and this was exemplified in the impact the BLM movement had on Trump's re-election effort in 2020.

A city such as Charleston, South Carolina, which historically was the epicentre of the horrific North American slave trade, exemplifies this. Today, Charleston tries to deal with its history through monuments, museums and even a 'slavery tour'. But with a quarter of its population descended from those very slaves, how can the city's people ever truly reconcile this heartbreaking history? How does it affect present-day African Americans to live in a city founded by the slave labour of their forebears? Especially if people of their skin colour are still worse off than whites by every measure of societal wellbeing.

Even in Washington, DC, which also has a large African American population, there are reminders of slavery. At the time we arrived, there was a big debate at the National Cathedral about removing a stained-glass window that had a Confederate flag in it.

The parishioners were divided on the issue, and I was perplexed too. We were dealing with a historical building, but if the window gave genuine offence – especially as this was a house of worship – then maybe it should be removed.

Tragically, there is a large element of self-segregation in US society, which we experienced first-hand. When we came to Washington, two of our children initially went to the local public school. The school had a reach-out program to bring children from poor districts in Washington – most of whom were African American – to study at our school. The quality of US public education is very closely aligned to the socio-economic status of the local community: in this regard, school boards are essentially the equivalent of local governments in Australia, and are formed through fiercely fought elections, which are dependent on community funding. The result is that wealthier areas of America have much better public schools than poorer areas. In some states in the Deep South, for instance, the school week has been cut to four days because of the lack of funding allocated to public education. This is literally a third world standard.

Anyway, at our local public school my daughter quickly formed friendships with two African American girls. We tried several times to organise playdates, but the girls' parents just didn't return our calls. Eventually, we understood that they were hesitant because we lived in the best part of Washington, DC, while they were in a much tougher part of town and might have felt too embarrassed to reciprocate. This was heartbreaking to me.

When COVID-19 appeared, things got worse. The panic of the teachers' unions and the determination of people to weaponise the different responses of Republicans and Democrats to the pandemic resulted in extensive school closures, which disproportionately hurt the poorest communities.

We all know that home schooling was hard. But think about how much harder it was for single-parent households in poor neighbourhoods. Many families didn't have a home computer, let alone internet access. Yet even when some schools determinedly returned to semi-normal operations, some teachers refused to go back into the classroom.

The result has been that in some of the poorest parts of America, teachers and schools have lost contact permanently with up to 10 per cent of their students. This has created a new underclass of American children, many of whom have hit the streets due to poor public policy.

That America is partly self-segregated today is not entirely surprising when you reflect that, up to about 170 years ago, it was fully segregated, with an entire slave population in the South, and racial segregation continued with Jim Crow laws in many states, prompting the start of the Civil Rights Movement in the 1950s. You can see it in churches, restaurants, bars, nightclubs, golf clubs – basically, any social setting. It's an implied segregation, even though it's not necessarily intended.

It is especially apparent in the South. Bars are a good example. The idea that Black people go to this club or bar with a certain type of music and white people go to another bar with another kind of music is not uncommon. There's a lot of movement and mixing between bars, but the sense of the venues being different is still there. You're always reminded, 'That's the Black bar.' Perhaps at a certain point this is more about culture than race – after all, African American culture is a distinct and globally exported culture. Still, at its heart, African American culture is defined by the pain of slavery.

The fact that white supremacist militias and the likes of the Ku Klux Klan still exist demonstrates the genuine dangers that Black people and other minorities face in parts of the United States. Of course, American society has moved on from mainstream acceptance of a group like the KKK, but how do Black Americans feel when they look around and see a society where in general they are economically and socially still far behind white Americans, and often genuinely under threat?

It seems a statement of the obvious that the COVID-19 pandemic, with its severe and economically damaging lockdowns, heightened anxiety in an already tense United States. Jobs were being lost and business closing at a rate not seen since the Great Depression, ninety years earlier. On top of this, there was no sport, no movies, no church, no dancing, no concerts, nothing at all to cheer for – and Americans always need something to cheer for.

Then, in May 2020, footage emerged out of Minneapolis of a Black man named George Floyd handcuffed and pinned to the ground by a white police officer. Officer Derek Chauvin held his knee on the throat of Floyd for nine and a half minutes, with Floyd struggling for air. Floyd's final words before he died were 'I can't breathe.' The incident was filmed by a witness with a mobile phone.

I was shocked by the footage but I wasn't surprised by the fallout. Racial tension, poverty, job losses (particularly when on a large scale, and sanctioned by the state) and a pandemic make for a dangerous mix for any society. All it needed was a match, and George Floyd's death was a grenade.

Even Donald Trump seemed conscious of the tinderbox he was dealing with. The president initially took a conciliatory approach after Floyd's death, trying to make clear his own shock and distress at what took place. On 30 May he expressed 'the nation's deepest condolences and heartfelt sympathies to the family of George Floyd. Terrible event. Terrible, terrible thing that happened,' Trump told the press. 'I've asked the Department of Justice to expedite the investigation into his death.' Trump was also pretty clear about what he had seen take place: 'It's a terrible thing. We all saw what we saw, and it's very hard to even conceive of anything other than what we did see.'

Ultimately, though, Trump would fail in his management of the fallout from Floyd's murder. But I don't believe that his failures were motivated by racism – I don't believe Donald Trump is a racist. In fact, I think he was genuinely committed to delivering better outcomes for Black Americans. His electioneering catch-cry to Black Americans was: 'What do you have to lose?' Trump was disgusted by the ongoing failure of Democrats – who dominated US cities with large Black populations and claimed an overwhelming proportion of the Black vote – to change the lives of these people they claimed to represent. Trump's pitch was that generations of politicians had failed to help improve the lives of Black Americans, and the federal government needed a new approach.

As I see it, Trump's failures on race issues boiled down to a lack of empathy and old-fashioned political pig-headedness. Trump simply hated being told how to respond to issues by the media or by his political opponents. With Trump, it was almost like the more you told him how he should feel or respond on an issue, the more stubbornly he dug in his heels. He hated being lectured by the left-wing media, so he wasn't going to do anything they demanded.

In this regard, and *only* in this regard, Trump reminded me a little bit of John Howard. Howard had been wrongly labelled a racist, and as prime minister had failed to do as the media told him on most issues on race and immigration. On the one hand, his instinct – which told him the majority of people agreed with him on these issues – was usually correct. On the other hand, concerning issues that the left advocated for and that were ultimately correct, he couldn't be swayed. Howard's refusal to apologise, on behalf of the federal government, to members of the Stolen Generations was a classic example of this.

In August 2017, Donald Trump refused to adequately condemn violent far-right and Neo Nazi protestors, whose actions in Charlottesville, Virginia, resulted in the death of a left-wing counter-protestor. He did condemn 'violence on both sides', but also claimed there were 'fine people' among the far-right protesters.

Trump would dig in on some positions not necessarily because he believed in them, but because he just refused to be bullied into taking the position his opponents wanted him to. For him, doing that would be evidence of his weakness – and as he saw it, too many politicians were coerced in this way.

But in reality his was a stupid position – and it was a failure for which even many in his own administration wouldn't stand. These included economic adviser Gary Cohn, who publicly said Trump 'can and must do better in consistently and unequivocally condemning' extreme right groups.

George Floyd's death immediately re-energised the Black Lives Matter movement, and massive protests began in many cities across the United States and internationally. But Trump displayed an alarming lack of empathy for the protesters and their cause. As president, he didn't have to agree with the actions of BLM in order to recognise the understandable grievances of many Black Americans. As the protests against Floyd's killing spread, and some became violent, Trump made it clear that he stood with the police who were trying to take back control of the streets. The president also announced that he'd bring in the military if need be. 'These THUGS are dishonoring the memory of George Floyd, and I won't let that happen,' he tweeted on 29 May. 'Just spoke to Governor Tim Walz [of Minnesota] and told him that the Military is with him all the way. Any difficulty and we will assume control but, when the looting starts, the shooting starts. Thank you!'

Trump's support of law and order was correct and understandable. The president of the United States has to be on the side of the police, and the vast majority of Americans would have supported him on this. But the killing of Floyd had been blatant and graphic. Trump could have pointed out that there were around 15,000 law-enforcement agencies in the United States, and that it was sadly inevitable that some policemen would go too far. But in failing to condemn the police accused of Floyd's murder, as well as other potentially racially motivated violence by police, Trump set up a dichotomy: it was the police versus the African American community. He effectively forced people to take sides.

Many African Americans have experienced systemic problems with the police, and feel great mistrust and pain as a result. This is not an imagined pain, but Trump, as he tried to manage what was a national crisis, lacked the empathy to realise this. Trump gave tacit permission for, and even fuelled, the worst of human emotions in response to the BLM protests.

In politics, this can happen. One lot of media took one side, and the other lot of media took the other side. And in a divided America, this further energised both forces. Trump had somehow turned a grievous event into a left-versus-right moment. Suddenly, both sides were fighting for middle-ground support.

Trump labelled BLM as a 'symbol of hate'. At one point, he effectively put BLM organisers in the same category as other extremist groups. He also affiliated the movement to the extreme left-wing 'Antifa' group. Personally, I couldn't see any coordinated effort by Antifa to run the protests, and I wouldn't label them as an extreme terrorist group on a par with the KKK. There wasn't much evidence of Antifa being an organised terrorist group, but Trump wanted to define and destroy his opponents.

However historic and disruptive the BLM protests were that summer, they were not 'unprecedented' civil unrest in the United States. The US has seen a lot worse, even in the last half-century. Whenever people were fretting excessively about the BLM protests like it was the end of US civil society, I'd remember what George W. Bush once told me about the tumultuous summer of 1968. I was talking with the former president not long after Trump was elected and there was, even then, talk of 'unprecedented' civil unrest on US streets.

Bush recalled: 'We were in a war in Vietnam that we were losing every night on TV. Bobby Kennedy had just been assassinated. Martin Luther King Jr was assassinated a few months earlier. There were nineteen American cities on fire every night.'

Others have told me their memories of Washington, DC, back in 1968, of armoured personnel carriers facing out from the centre of the city towards the suburbs, lined up waiting for the mass invasion from Virginia to occur.

The point is not that the BLM protests were nothing in comparison to 1968, but that they exist in a historical context of civil unrest in the United States. For all the violence of 1968, it's a period now viewed as a historical turning point in the history of the nation.

On the issue of destruction of historical statues, it's worth pointing out that a lot of the Confederate statues around the United States were actually erected in the 1950s and 1960s. There was a kind of Confederate revivalist movement taking place at that time that portrayed the Confederate South as a hopeless noble cause of an American golden age. In the South, in particular, this was being done as a less subtle bulwark against growing calls for greater civil rights. Even statues built in the late 1880s drew on similar inspiration, which was the time of the Jim Crow laws that were used to disenfranchise Black voters.

From a purely historical perspective, Robert E. Lee is someone I would think worthy of some public recognition. He led the Confederate States Army and after its defeat he was instrumental in holding the Union together. His pleas for the proper treatment of his surviving soldiers prevented many years of potential civil terrorist groups from tearing the fledgling nation apart. Despite that, as one African American friend said to me, 'When I look at the statue of Robert E. Lee it would be like you're looking at a statue of Hitler or his generals. Why do we have to celebrate him? It makes me feel bad.' To be honest I'd never thought of it like that.

As much as the divisiveness and violence of the BLM protests appeared to be an existential crisis for the US, they may just as easily be viewed as another turning point in US history. In other words, America is evolving under the weight of demands from its own people and continuing to do what the United States has always done.

* * *

Great presidents have always defined themselves through their handling of unexpected crises. Think of George Washington, or Abraham Lincoln, or Theodore Roosevelt – it was their strength of character in moments of adversity that made their reputations. Often it was war, but not always. Franklin Roosevelt's success was navigating first an economic crisis and then a war. Equally, failed presidencies are often defined by failure to meet a crisis. Herbert Hoover, Richard Nixon and Jimmy Carter come to mind.

Donald Trump failed when faced with the crisis of the COVID-19 pandemic, and this failure would define his presidency and cost him re-election. If he had handled the beginning of the pandemic differently, or even the later stages, he may well have won a second term – globally, most nations have voted for political stability during the crisis. Trump was an exception to this trend.

In times of crisis, voters are less concerned about party loyalty than they are about who is steering them out of the storm. People are good observers. They watch how leaders handle unexpected, confronting situations and make judgements on their character. I think of the former New South Wales Premier John Fahey, who, when a man produced a starting pistol and fired two blanks at Prince Charles at an event in Sydney in 1994, jumped up onto the stage to take the guy out, seemingly risking his life. How would you react as a leader? Like John Fahey, or like *Seinfeld*'s George Costanza, who in one episode hilariously palmed off women and children to escape what appeared to be a burning building. People know whether they have a Fahey or a Costanza at the helm during a crisis.

Somewhere along the line – indeed, perhaps it was as the polls turned against him – Trump morphed from being an unlikely president of the United States into someone trying to be a cult hero but detached from his actual role. The problem was that nothing he did was particularly heroic.

Even during the worst global pandemic in a hundred years, Trump as president couldn't stop talking about himself.

Everything was focused on Trump the brand, Trump the persona. It was all about Trump. When he came out of hospital, still infected with COVID-19, and took the presidential limo for a drive to greet his adoring fans, most Americans could only think about the risks he was forcing others to accept: the hospital staff, his political staff, the Secret Service agents assigned to protect him, and even his driver.

Trump told Americans that he'd learnt so much about the disease by having it. The immediate reaction of a whole host of people was: 'Well, what about when I had it? Why didn't Trump care about me? He has the best people in the world advising him on COVID-19, and he only learnt about the disease by having it? He's the president of the United States – he's meant to be protecting me and my family.'

When Trump caught COVID-19, I wrote in a column for *The Australian* that if he had stayed in his hospital bed and appeared more humble and less brazen, then he might have had a chance of recovering his popularity. He might have demonstrated some empathy for others who had become sick or who had loved ones die from the virus. But any humility Trump felt after contracting COVID lasted about seventy-two hours. Instead, he claimed superhero status. 'I felt like Superman,' he said of his recovery, bragging about the fact that he'd had twelve doctors looking after him in hospital.

All this reflected the mindset that Trump seemed to bring to the pandemic generally. When it first appeared, he'd ridiculed COVID-19 as 'a bad flu'. By March 2020, he was in denial, despite the fact that the virus was already running rampant through the community.

The last social event I attended in 2020 was on 2 March at the home of Chris Liddell, deputy chief of staff to President Trump. Also in attendance were chief of staff Mick Mulvaney and national economic adviser Larry Kudlow. Together with our partners, we were enjoying what would effectively be the Last Supper of 2020.

Inevitably, the discussion turned to COVID-19. The Americans indicated they thought it would just be passing, and wouldn't be an issue in the longer term. They all thought the summer would kill it off, and that the flu was basically worse. Melissa and I were aghast. There was another Aussie couple there, one of whom was a doctor, and she couldn't believe what she was hearing. You can't spin your way out of a pandemic, and the Trump administration was in defiant denial. My mates were loyally following their president.

To be fair, there was conflicting advice about how to handle the breakout – and particularly in relation to border closures. The United States was never going to be able to entirely shut its borders in the way that Australia, being an island nation, could. Early in the outbreak, Prime Minister Morrison had moved quickly to close the borders, first with China, then with the rest of the world. Having just come through the disastrous bushfire season of 2019/20, he'd clearly learnt some lessons about getting ahead of a national crisis.

It suited Trump's political narrative to end international travel to and from China, but America still had very porous borders. It is a near impossible task to close America's borders, with the amount of necessary trade and family interaction that takes place daily. The nation's physical borders alone, with Canada and Mexico, see hundreds of thousands of people a day coming into the country.

The US Defense Force, it turned out, was the perfect COVID delivery system. Senior US officials came to believe that the effective spread of COVID in the United States came via northern Italy, not directly from China. Northern Italy, and Milan in particular, had a very productive industrial and textile industry that did an enormous amount of trade with China – and specifically with Wuhan. Hundreds of thousands of people travelled between the regions each year. And there are two US Army bases in the Veneto region of northern Italy, while many US Air Force personnel are stationed at Italy's NATO base in Aviano. Even after the United States closed its border with China, the open border with Italy allowed returning servicemen and women who had been infected in northern Italian centres like Milan and Bergamo to return to their homes across the United States. This explains how COVID-19 spread throughout the nation so quickly, rather than just through the major US cities.

US states don't have the power to close down their own borders, as states in Australia do. Ironically, when Trump attempted to close the borders of New York, New Jersey and Connecticut, the early epicentre of the US pandemic, New York's Governor Cuomo threatened to take him to court. Trump didn't want the fight and folded. The best that many US states could do was ask that arrivals quarantine themselves at home when entering the state. It was a joke, and unenforceable in practice.

There was a lot of confusion about the use of masks. Different health advisers were saying different things about the utility of masks, although we pointed out that Asian countries had used them to curb the outbreak of SARS in the early 2000s, so why not err on the side of caution.

It seems particularly ironic that Donald Trump was in charge as this infectious virus spread across the United States, as he is famously a germaphobe. He's constantly pulling out wet wipes and cleansers to ensure his hands are germ-free. When we were out at a dinner in Japan, Trump barely ate, and I saw him cleanse his hands four times with hygienic tissues he kept in his pocket. Perhaps as a result of this obsessiveness, he rarely gets sick. He's also one of those people with a genuinely strong constitution. And I suspect this played a part in his denialist approach. He thought, 'Well, if I don't get sick, you shouldn't get sick either.' His own experience is always his benchmark. He's contemptuous of people who fall ill because he holds the view that they should've taken better care with their hygiene, as he does.

I also think Trump's personal business position added to his hesitancy about calling for a general lockdown, and pushed him to open the US economy up again as soon as he could. Closing down large parts of the economy is an enormous issue for any president, but particularly one who has considerable business interests in leisure and hospitality. When Congress passed a bill to fund and help businesses as a result of COVID-19, they made the frankly idiotic decision to prohibit anyone serving in the administration from accessing that money. It was clearly targeting Trump. This may have been a political win for the Democrats, but it was a loss for America because Trump's hotels and golf courses were inevitably going to suffer.

I suspect Trump is the type of businessperson who has a lot of physical assets, a lot of debt but not a lot of cash. And his companies employed people, like everyone else's. Because Trump couldn't access the emergency package that everyone else could, he must have bled a tremendous amount of money. It provided a perverse, Faustian incentive for Trump to open up the economy quickly.

At that time, I texted Joe Scarborough, who was on air presenting his MSNBC show, *Morning Joe*, and said this was a mistake. And he came back to me on air and agreed. He was critical of the Democrats and the Congress for the move.

When Trump can't control something, it drives him crazy. He needs to be the boss. Obviously, though, a pandemic has no boss, and that drove him nuts. Now, because the president wasn't able to hold his political rallies, he started doing long press conferences in a small and stuffy press briefing room at the White House. These went for an hour or longer, and in classic Trump style they were all ad-libbed. Of course, they were scheduled to take place during the prime-time news. That infuriated my friend Brett Baier, who has one of the highest-rating news shows in America on Fox News. Brett would be ready to go to air with a prepared show every day, and then Trump would begin a press conference that would take up his entire hour.

It was one of these press briefings that blew up on Trump spectacularly. In late April 2020, speaking off the cuff, he started speculating about methods of killing the SARS-CoV-2 virus, to the obvious discomfort of one of his leading health officials. 'And then I see the disinfectant, where it knocks it [the virus] out in one minute. One minute. And is there a way we can do something like that, by injection inside or almost a cleaning?'

Health officials looked back, horrified.

'So it'd be interesting to check that,' Trump went on. 'I'm not a doctor. But I'm, like, a person that has a good you-know-what,' and he pointed to his brain.

At that point, as I saw it, the American people switched off. That was it. That was his 'Costanza in a fire' moment – the instant he became a figure of ridicule, and lost the fading veneer of respectability that the office of the president still afforded him.

The left had always been itching to portray Trump as dangerous, but he wrapped himself in the flag and relied on the authority of his office to defend himself. But when he suggested that people could inject themselves with disinfectant to cure themselves of COVID-19, it made him a laughing-stock among many who had previously voted for him. Later, Trump claimed that what he had said was a joke directed at the press. No one was laughing.

At a time of crisis, Trump was still looking to divide the nation and pick fights. It was the only tactic in his political playbook. He would pay tribute to the governors one minute and then criticise them in the next. He would embrace the medical professionals and then push them away. He even credited the Chinese for doing a good job at one point, before famously calling COVID the 'China virus'.

I had a pet black cat like that once. The cat would purr for the first three pieces of meat, and then scratch you when offered the fourth. I love cats, but that one was very hard to love.

* * *

Despite Donald Trump's significant failures handling COVID-19, the presidential election of 2020 was by no means a certainty for Joe Biden. Time and again Trump had escaped what appeared to be certain political doom because of the apparent willingness of Americans to forgive his failures. And many Americans – over 74 million, it turned out – were even willing to forgive his disastrous leadership through the COVID pandemic.

Biden understood this impulse of the electorate. If he had not run a disciplined and measured campaign, the result could have been very different. Biden's victory was deserving because, unlike many other Democrats, he never underestimated the nature of he appeal and the threat posed by Donald Trump.

In the last weeks of the campaign, Trump's enthusiasm and energy clawed back ground for the Republicans. But Biden held his nerve against the political hurricane that was Trump. The voting trends confirm the conclusion that Biden won the early campaign. In an election where a record 65 million people cast their votes through the post office and not at the ballot box on polling day, this was where the election was won.

Biden's campaign relied on his ability to distinguish himself from Trump in both character and style, but to come closer to the Republican candidate on policy. This separation even projected itself physically during a campaign held in the midst of a deadly pandemic.

Trump held mass rallies with tens of thousands of people mingling, at a time when COVID-19 was killing thousands of Americans each day. When Trump himself contracted the virus in October it proved to be only a speed bump and his campaign rallies soon resumed. Meanwhile, a cautious and respectful Joe Biden encouraged 'car rallies', and went days without appearing publicly. He understood that millions of Americans had been infected or seen loved ones die because of COVID, and countless numbers had lost their jobs in the disruption it caused.

While Trump played Superman at his rallies, Biden looked empathetic and respectful of the awful situation so many Americans found themselves in. He wore a mask, kept his public campaigning to a minimum and never contradicted the medical experts. Trump increasingly looked like some kind of mad king who thought he could will the virus away. Biden's realistic approach underscored Trump's irresponsibility.

The literal separation of Trump from Biden also meant the Democrat wouldn't be drawn into a street brawl in debates. Pulling Biden down to his level was always the New Yorker's strategy.

Donald Trump loves boxing. For years he used to sit ringside in Atlantic City or Las Vegas with the legendary promoter Don King, watching and funding championship fights involving the likes of Mike Tyson, Evander Holyfield and George Foreman. He'd pepper any conversation with boxing anecdotes. A friend told me of a meeting they once had in the Oval Office with Donald Trump. They were discussing some US technology, and the president didn't like the look of the equipment and wanted sharper aesthetics. My friend responded that it might not be pretty, but what mattered was the lethality of the punch: 'Much like Mike Tyson, Mr President.'

'I watched Tyson lose two fights. Conversation over,' Trump responded abruptly.

So Trump was a tough crowd – but he knew his boxing. I'm not sure he likes the violence much, but he is drawn by the raw competitive energy of the sport, the crowning of a winner over a loser. In boxing, there's nowhere to hide and nothing but your own skills between victory and defeat.

Trump had tried for months to take on Biden one on one, but it wasn't until 29 September 2020 that they faced off in a presidential debate, returning once again to Cleveland, Ohio. Trump felt supremely confident. He knew that if he got Biden in a debate the contrast between the pair could work to his advantage. Define and destroy your opponent. His go-to line was that 'Sleepy Joe' would be a 'teleprompter president', and wouldn't even last a full term if elected.

As it turned out, the first debate was closer than many had anticipated. It was a bad-tempered scrap, with constant interruptions and squabbling. I thought Trump won the night. He succeeded in bringing Biden down to his level. Trump drew the Democrats' grandfather figure into a nasty brawl, revealing Biden's known short temper.

The Biden camp's eventual success in getting the second debate cancelled confirmed their desire to separate their candidate from Trump. If Biden appeared with Trump, debated Trump and engaged with Trump, they knew he would end up being compared to Trump. That was Trump's game and his great strength. And by removing himself from that type of comparison, Biden could remain measured and composed.

Trump also struggled to define Biden in the public mind. Unlike his attacks on Hillary Clinton four years earlier, this time his personal jibes just didn't seem to stick. Far more Americans liked and admired Biden than voted for him. Conversely, there were a great many Americans who disliked Trump but still voted for him. This was why Trump really struggled to lay a glove on Biden in the contest over character.

Biden is a very decent man, and his story is inspiring for Americans. He suffered gut-wrenching personal tragedies with the death of his first wife and baby daughter, and later lost his elder son to brain cancer. Biden was also a known entity, and a trusted one, which is a huge advantage in any election campaign. He first ran as a Democratic candidate for president in 1988, well before many of his current voters were even born. He lost again in 2008, but then served as a much-admired vice president to Barack Obama for eight years.

Vying to become only the second Catholic president in US history, Biden appealed to the traditional working-class and middle-class Democrats in the 'blue wall' states of Michigan, Wisconsin and Pennsylvania, where in 2016 many had shrugged and voted for Trump. Biden had also, in contrast to Trump, lived a humble life – another reason why the 'Washington swamp' attacks never stuck to him.

Perhaps most importantly, Biden could demonstrate genuine empathy and compassion at a time when the nation was crying out for it. Deaths by the thousands were impacting Americans across the social and racial spectrum. For Trump, showing compassion was a sign of weakness. He failed to understand that the nation was crying out for some sympathy from their leader over what was happening to them.

* * *

When I was asked to write a series of columns for *The Australian* in the lead-up to the election, I came up with an imaginary American swing voter, a member of the group who I thought would decide the 2020 presidential election: an aspiring middle-class, non–college educated, white woman living in one of the former 'blue wall' states. I called her Mary Milwaukee from Wisconsin.

Mary worked at Walmart, earning US$11.11 an hour (20 per cent above the national average), and had a son on his third tour of duty in Afghanistan about whom she felt painful anxiety every day. She also had a daughter who wanted to go to college, but the family was unsure how to pay for it. Her husband was a truck driver, one of 3.5 million in the United States, and hadn't gone to college. Both Mary and her husband held traditional middle America views on God, freedom and family. They were patriots.

Until COVID-19 came along, Mary was pretty happy. She had quietly voted for Trump in 2016 because she felt that she had nothing to lose. Her salary hadn't changed in years and the politicians in Washington made her feel guilty about everything in her life, from her regular church attendance to the fact that she'd never made it to college. She worried constantly about her job and her personal security, and the state of the country that she would leave to her children.

Voters like Mary Milwaukee ignored Trump's tweets, his narcissism and his shenanigans because she supported his policies on the economy, on law and order, on the environment, on border control and on 'draining the swamp' in Washington, DC. She wanted her son to come back from Afghanistan, and she wanted her husband to keep his job as a truck driver. In particular, she wanted her daughter to have a chance to go to college. Her higher wages and her husband's new-found job security had made that increasingly possible. When the coronavirus hit, she believed it would soon pass and that Trump would protect her and her family. But when Trump fell ill with COVID-19, it became clear that the president was more focused on himself than on the health and welfare of Mary and her family.

This was Trump's key failure during the 2020 campaign: he didn't talk about his policies. Instead, Trump never stopped talking about Trump. The president's policies were popular among people like Mary Milwaukee, but Trump just didn't talk about them enough.

Biden also demonstrated his ability to appeal to the centre. Ultimately, this election was not about right versus left, or even Trump versus Biden. It went beyond the traditional battle formulas. Always a centrist himself, Biden overcame hopeless division within the Democrats, a key achievement.

Ever since Clinton's loss four years earlier, the Democrats had been tearing themselves apart, with the centrists facing off against both a kind of 'old left', led by Bernie Sanders, and the new 'green left' star Alexandria Ocasio-Cortez (or AOC as she's known to the kids). For the sake of the Democrats, Sanders and Ocasio-Cortez stopped attacking Biden for (most of) the campaign, and let the former vice president focus on winning the middle ground. His only real misstep on policy was a pledge to end fossil fuels for energy production in America, and he quickly backtracked on that.

Realising that he wasn't landing any punches on Biden, and becoming aware of the general pandemic trend towards postal voting, Trump knew he was losing. He then did something that was largely unheard of for an incumbent Republican president: he tried to broaden the base of the Republican vote.

In the United States, the accepted wisdom is to motivate your base to vote, and then suppress the vote of your opponent. Swing voters are not necessarily the focus. That is so very different from elections in Australia, where our system of compulsory voting means that swing voters are the key to an election victory. In this election, as early polling turnout surged, it became clear that Trump simply could not suppress his opponent's vote. He had largely lost the Mary Milwaukee swing voter in key states, so his only pathway to victory was a massive Republican turnout in a few select states.

For all his failures of leadership, for all his narcissism and the tension of a divided America at the end of Trump's term, this strategy almost worked. If the election campaign had gone on for another month, Trump may have narrowed the gap, but in the end Biden won by 7 million votes – a gap too large to beat in the final weeks.

More than 74 million Americans voted for Donald Trump. This was 5 million more votes than the next highest vote ever, which was for Barack Obama in 2008. But Joe Biden won more than 81 million votes, and secured the necessary numbers in the Electoral College.

Like anything to do with Trump, nothing about the results of the election was straightforward. For instance, among women voters Trump actually increased his 2016 margin by 4 points (despite losing to Biden 44–55), and among white women he increased his majority of the vote by 5 points (53–46.) But in the key battleground states there was enough of a swing in suburban areas among women (like my Mary Milwaukee) and (more unexpectedly) among middle-class white men to Joe Biden, and it was this that allowed the Democrats to reclaim the 'blue wall' and the presidency.

Joe Biden's victory was all the more impressive when you consider that he had to get more votes than any other presidential candidate in history to beat Trump. Inspiring the greatest voter turnout (by percentage of eligible voters) since 1900, Joe Biden won back several key Democratic states, and flipped the key Republican states of Arizona and Georgia. The Biden victory required more money, more third-party advocacy and more unity than ever before to beat a candidate who had disrupted US politics and turned the modern political battle on its head. Biden's moderate policies and unifying message vaulted him over the line in states such as Michigan, Wisconsin and Pennsylvania. But only just.

The loss in Arizona could largely be attributed to Trump's feud, even in death, with Senator John McCain. Cindy McCain, John's high-profile and influential wife, and Meghan McCain, his even more prominent daughter, were campaigning nonstop against Trump, who lost by just under 12,000 votes, a tiny margin. It was just unnecessary for Trump to be so mean-spirited towards McCain after his death. (Trump would later demonstrate a similarly appalling lack of grace following the death of Colin Powell, a true American hero and a Republican.) At any rate, the McCains got the last laugh.

Critics will say that Biden should have won by more. I don't accept that. The United States is a bitterly divided nation. Those same critics consistently underestimated Trump, viewing him as an unelectable fool, and they took his every word as a spear from an adversary. They saw no good in anything Trump did, whether it was peace agreements in the Middle East or criminal justice reform that got record numbers of Black Americans out of jail.

Joe Biden, from day one of his campaign, had framed the election as a 'battle for the soul of our nation'. And he had never once wavered from this theme. His message consistency was remarkable, and was purpose-built for a time when the nation was hurting.

Biden's focus was reflected in his nomination of Kamala Harris as his running mate. During the Democratic primaries, Harris had landed the most aggressive blow on Biden's character but he still chose her as his running mate. That's Biden the forgiver. He also knew that his choice of Harris would send a powerful message: a woman would be his legal successor for the next four years. Mary

Milwaukee may not have admitted it, because she was focused on policy first, but she was pleased to see a woman in leadership. She took it as an inspiration for her daughter.

Ultimately, the 2020 election was a repudiation of both the far left and far right of the American political spectrum. At a time of tumult, Americans gravitated towards the centre. They rejected Bernie Sanders in the Democratic primary and then voted out Donald Trump. Americans wanted respite from disruption and zero-sum politics.

Many people around the world also wanted a break from doom-scrolling Twitter for the next presidential outburst. The fact that Angela Merkel, chancellor of Germany, publicly congratulated Biden on his victory before he had even claimed the win said it all.

Every election is deemed important. Every election is crucial. Biden has been in American politics for forty-eight years. He knows his nation and his people better than most. While many people these days eschew the big hug, Biden has largely been himself in his first year in office. He shows emotion and empathy. If nothing else, being Joe Biden will be his legacy.

CHAPTER 12

TRUMP'S END, BIDEN'S BEGINNING

The Capitol riot, the 2024 conundrum and Biden's Aussie submarines

Claims of voter fraud in the United States are as old as the republic itself. Both Democrats and Republicans have alleged plenty of fraud over the years. And various inquiries, Department of Justice reports and many different courts have found that electoral fraud does exist – in a limited form. The challenge is to remain vigilant and make sure there is no opportunity for it to become widespread.

There was potential for voter fraud at the presidential election in 2020, as at all US elections, but in the event there was no real evidence that it occurred. Certainly there was no evidence that it happened on a scale that would have changed the result in the way that Donald Trump falsely claimed. Unsurprisingly, it's usually the losing party that alleges fraud at the ballot box.

The factor that most enables voter fraud in the United States – or at least the perception of it – is the complexity of the US electoral system. There are more than 10,000 different entities responsible for the administration of the presidential election every four years. The voting rules are usually set by state governments and administered by counties and cities. In many places the rules are tweaked as each election approaches.

This is completely at odds with the Australian experience, where federal elections are handled by the Australian Electoral

Commission (AEC). The AEC is an independent federal agency with administrative responsibilities for every vote, polling booth and electoral boundary. In short, it's the body that manages all aspects of federal elections and national referendums. It's pretty straightforward. Having an independent electoral agency removes the issue of political bias, either in the location or availability of polling stations and ballot boxes, or in the setting of electoral boundaries.

It stands to reason that the more complex the electoral system, the more susceptible it is to fraud. There are many mechanisms for electoral fraud, but one that Australians are not very familiar with is voter suppression. For us, this is not an issue at all: because we have compulsory voting, we don't have a choice about whether to participate or not. But in US politics, getting your supporters to the polls and discouraging the supporters of your opponent from making the effort to go out and vote has long been a goal.

In 1965, after years of activism by those in the civil rights movement, the US Congress passed the Voting Rights Act, which aimed to prohibit the disenfranchisement of voters – and especially Black voters – by discriminatory means such as reading tests, poll taxes and intimidation. (The fact that legislation had to be enacted to protect the right of people to vote, even though the US Constitution guarantees it, reflects the deep political and racial divisions that existed at the time.) Although this legislation has greatly increased voter participation in areas where it had been suppressed – particularly in the South – state legislators have never stopped attempting to keep their opponents' voters away from the polls.

A recent example occurred in Harris County, Texas, centred on the city of Houston, which is home to some 4.7 million people, making it about the size of Melbourne. Ahead of the 2020 poll, the local elections administrator set up twelve booths for early voting. The Republican governor of Texas, Greg Abbott, then ordered that there could be only one early-voting booth for each county in the state. So Harris County, with the largest population of any in Texas, was left with just one ballot box for early voting – and this in the midst of the pandemic.

It will not surprise you to learn that Harris County is a predictably Democratic oasis in mainly red Texas. In 2020, some 56 per cent of its citizens would vote for Joe Biden. After numerous lawsuits, the decision to remove the ballot boxes went to court and, on appeal, the governor's order was defeated. Another appeal was immediately lodged by the governor's office.

Another, more insidious consequence of such attempts at voter suppression is that they can create the impression that your vote will not matter, and this can turn people off voting altogether. In Washington, DC, 93 per cent of voters picked Joe Biden. This was in line with the last three presidential elections, but for an entire city of nearly 700,000 people to vote so overwhelmingly for one party is extraordinary. This has prompted claims that some DC residents are taking advantage of residency rules and casting their ballots in cities outside of the District of Columbia where their vote might make a bigger difference.

Complex ballot papers, hard-to-find booth locations and varying requirements around one's entitlement to vote are all weaponised in the United States for political purposes. In Mississippi, a foreign-born citizen needs to be able to prove their naturalisation in order to register to vote. In eleven US states, it is still unlawful for someone convicted of a felony to vote, even after they have served their sentence. Never mind that some people become felons as a result of minor, non-violent crimes, including unpaid traffic fines. It just so happens that a disproportionate number of African Americans are convicted felons. In Florida, even though Floridians voted to allow felons to vote following the 2018 elections, the state legislature enacted laws in 2019 that forced felons to pay any and all court fees before they could cast their ballot. The felony disenfranchisement clause had been in Florida's state constitution since 1838.

So much supposed 'electoral reform' in the United States is in fact pure political jockeying. Because Washington, DC has been, historically, around 93 per cent Democratic-voting, unsurprisingly it's only the Democrats who want to make the District of Columbia a state – which would presumably deliver them two additional Democratic senators and an extra member of the House of Representatives. When Alaska and Hawaii were given full state rights in 1956, it came about only because Congress accepted that, politically, the then Republican Hawaii would offset the then Democratic Alaska. As it turned out, each state completely reversed its politics over the next few decades – at least the balance remained.

So it's important to appreciate that when Donald Trump claimed that the 2020 presidential election had been rigged, he was drawing on a history of highly politicised claims about electoral fraud.

It almost goes without saying that Trump doesn't like losing. In business, on television, in politics or on the golf course, he is always up for the fight. When he loses, he usually litigates the result. At the end of our first golf game, at Trump National in Virginia, he wouldn't let me keep the scorecard. Despite my memorable victory on the last hole, he didn't want me to keep the souvenir – it could remind others of *his* loss.

Trump was always going to contest the outcome of the presidential ballot, and anyone paying attention knew this. Joe Biden and the Democrats certainly did. Trump was laying markers a year before the 2020 election, pulling from his 2016 playbook, that any outcome that didn't result in him being re-elected would be illegitimate in his eyes, and he expected his supporters to go along with him on that.

The hardcore Trump supporter base was already predisposed to believe Trump's claims of voter fraud because, generally speaking, they have a deep suspicion of government. In the case of some full-blown conspiracists – like QAnon followers – Trump's failure to win the election only confirmed the 'deep state conspiracy' that was supposedly militating against him.

And then came the violent scenes in Washington, DC on 6 January 2021, when Trump's supporters invaded the Capitol building as a joint sitting of Congress was ceremonially counting the electors before confirming Joe Biden as the duly elected next president of the United States.

Trump's real failure of responsibility on 6 January was not his decision to hold a rally in Washington that morning, but the manner in which he conducted himself there, and what he communicated to this gathering of his hardcore supporters. I still think that if Trump had acted differently that day, the riot and the storming of the Capitol could have been avoided. He had the power to defuse the situation by telling his supporters to go home or return to their hotels – but he chose not to. It was here that Trump's lack of judgement as a leader came to the fore. His disregard both for the history of the republic and for the institutions that had been built up over hundreds of years became particularly apparent.

From what I've been told by security officials, the rioters who stormed the Capitol were well organised, with a 'hard core' who had every intention of escalating the situation when they got the chance. There's also no evidence that Trump had any real insight into their violent intentions. Nonetheless, he could've stopped it turning into a rebellion against one of the key institutions of US democracy, and for that reason he will bear responsibility for the Capitol attack for the rest of his life.

* * *

An obvious question is whether Trump's responsibility for the Capitol riot will poison his chances if he makes another run at the presidency in 2024. My guess is that tens of millions of Americans will give him yet another chance, notwithstanding his history.

In February 2020, ahead of my exit as ambassador, I gave an interview to the ABC's *7.30* program. At the time, I noted that

'Donald Trump has more influence over a greater proportion of the US population than any other figure in American history'. I didn't say that lightly, and I believe it remains true today.

No other political movement in US history was a cult of personality in the way that Donald Trump's rise to power has been. Even the leadership of the civil rights movement was split between Martin Luther King Jr and Malcolm X. Trumpism, and everything it represents, is inseparable (at least for now) from Donald Trump personally. Trump is the movement and the movement is Trump. He is, of course, a marketing man, and this is his ultimate branding triumph.

In that *7.30* interview, I noted that Trump had the support of 30 to 35 per cent of the population, and recalled how he had observed in 2016 that even if he shot someone in the middle of New York, they'd still vote for him. After mounting a false campaign about a 'stolen election' and the events of 6 January, would he still be able to claim the support of up to 35 per cent of the US population? Probably not, but the entirety of that support wouldn't just disappear. These rusted-on Trump supporters were not going to be turned off by the Capitol riot – if anything, they might take it as more evidence of the 'fake news media' still blaming Trump for the nation's problems. His hardcore vote would still be around 30 per cent of voters. And among registered Republicans, Trump still has an overwhelming majority. That's an incredibly powerful voting block in the US electoral system.

As I write today, I feel it is beyond doubt that if Trump runs in 2024, he will win the Republican nomination. On balance, though, I think it's increasingly unlikely that he will run. Apart from his age (he'll be seventy-eight by then), and the likelihood that Democrats will seek to legally bar him from running, I don't think he could bear the prospect of losing again. A more likely option is that Trump endorses another candidate, anointing a successor (of sorts, although he'll be clear that there's only one Trump), which would give Trump proxy control of the Republican

Party. That candidate could be one of a number of people, but the only thing they need to do is make sure they don't criticise Trump. I think Trump would tolerate policy differences from his agenda, so long as his candidate admired and revered him.

On the Democratic side, the key questions are whether President Joe Biden runs again, and how the party fares in the midterms in 2022.

I think there's a growing realisation among both parties that Joe Biden won't run for a second term. America hasn't been in such a precarious position for a long time. The only person to give up the presidency when he had an opportunity to run again was Lyndon Johnson. Assuming Biden becomes the second, the question will quickly turn to who takes the baton.

As vice president, Kamala Harris would be an obvious candidate for the Democrats. However, her problem is likely to be the midterm elections, where there is a good chance that the Republicans could gain control of the Senate and perhaps even the House of Representatives. If that does happen, it will make governing extremely difficult for the Biden administration, and will frustrate a Harris presidential run.

If Biden does not run, he will be treated as a lame duck president for his last eighteen months in office. The Republicans will also know there's not a lot of political capital to be gained from attacking the (by then) eighty-year-old president. Their focus in Congress will be to place Vice President Harris at the middle of an administration that won't achieve anything substantial in its last two years. Republicans will weaponise Congress against her in the same ways Democrats did against Trump, seeking to destroy her candidacy and stop her from being elevated to higher office.

Beyond the obvious choices of Biden, Trump and Harris, for both parties there are four other pools of potential candidates.

The first are current or former White House administration officials. On the Democratic side you'd have the likes of Pete Buttigieg, who ran a good campaign in 2020 and still has a profile as secretary of the Department of Transport. Republicans in this category include former Trump administration officials such as former Secretary of State and CIA Director Mike Pompeo, and Vice President Pence. Pompeo will almost certainly run whatever the case, and has a chance of becoming the candidate, especially if Trump doesn't run again.

The second category includes current and former politicians and previous candidates. Bernie Sanders and Ted Cruz may run again. Marco Rubio may have another go, but I don't see a path for him to win the Republican nomination. Former South Carolina governor and UN ambassador in the Trump administration Nikki Haley is also clearly working towards a run.

The joker in the pack on the Democratic side would be Alexandria Ocasio-Cortez. If AOC runs, she would almost certainly be endorsed by Sanders and his left-wing support base. It would be highly divisive for the Democrats, but she is a talented politician and the closest thing the left has to a Trump-like cult of personality.

The third type of candidate is the celebrity. After Trump's success, it's likely there will be a few celebrities who fancy their chances. Their best chance, they will know, is in an open field, as 2024 will be if both Trump and Biden don't run. Actors Matthew McConaughey and Cynthia Nixon are openly considering running as Democratic candidates at state or federal level. Perhaps the most fascinating prospect is the former wrestler turned actor Dwayne 'The Rock' Johnson. A *Newsweek* poll found in April 2021 that 46 per cent of Americans would vote for him as a presidential candidate, and he seems to be entertaining the prospect with fundraisers and by hiring consultants. The question is whether he would run as a Republican or a Democrat.

The final category is the state governors. My instinct tells me that the next president of the United States is most likely to be a governor, whether a Republican or a Democrat. America is in an era where the White House and Congress are hopelessly divided, and politics is arguably more partisan than at any other time in history. This means very little reform is actually achieved at a federal level. State governors, meanwhile, can more readily point to a record of achievement and reform, and have good name recognition outside their own states.

The Republican governor of Florida, Ron DeSantis, may well run on a Trumpian agenda, and could find himself anointed by Trump himself. Greg Abbott from Texas may also fall into this category.

Before he lost the Virginia gubernatorial race in November 2021, I would have said Terry McAuliffe was a favourite for the Democratic candidacy, and perhaps even for the presidency. McAuliffe is a highly intelligent centrist who is the complete package, with good appeal for conservative voters. While his loss to Republican superstar Glenn Youngkin doesn't preclude him from running for president, it will make it a lot harder.

Glenn Youngkin himself could be another great hope for the Republicans. He delivered the first electoral blow to Joe Biden and the Democrats, and he did it largely without the help of Donald Trump. While it might be too soon for Youngkin to run in 2024, his victory does show that there is hope for Republicans who don't want to build their party around Trump.

* * *

Despite his dramatically different leadership style, I have been nothing but impressed by the consistent attitude President Biden has displayed towards the United States' alliance with Australia.

While Scott Morrison seems to have slipped in the order of the new president's phone calls to global leaders, this is because Biden's priority is reassuring other nations whose relationship with the United States had declined under Trump. Even if the first presidential phone call to Australia didn't happen until early February (leaving aside Morrison's congratulatory call after Biden was elected), at least there was no confrontation!

'President Joseph R. Biden, Jr. spoke today with Prime Minister Scott Morrison of Australia to highlight the strength of the U.S.–Australia alliance, which remains an anchor of stability in the Indo-Pacific and the world,' read the statement published by the White House on 3 February 2021.

In September, Biden made an online video address to the nation to mark the seventieth anniversary of the ANZUS Treaty. President Biden made it clear that ANZUS was 'as essential today as it has ever been', and noted that the only time the defence articles had been invoked was after the September 11 attacks. 'Our Australian friends stood with us in that darkest hour,' Biden said, 'just as our two nations stood shoulder to shoulder in every major conflict since World War I. Through the years, Australians and Americans have built an unsurpassed partnership and an easy mateship grounded on shared values and shared vision.'

When I heard these words, I was so glad that my focus on Australian–US *mateship* had apparently been embraced by the new leader!

Biden's handling of the US withdrawal from Afghanistan has been harshly criticised by both long-time supporters and critics of the war. I hold the unfashionable opinion that the withdrawal was unlikely to turn out much differently, whoever was in charge.

First, there needed to be an end to the war in Afghanistan. That had been a popular policy under Donald Trump, although he had run out of time to make it happen. Biden knew that keeping US troops in Afghanistan was completely unviable after what was now a twenty-year conflict. Americans would no longer tolerate the loss of life or the physical and psychological damage to veterans by the thousand. By the end of the war, America was sending young soldiers to fight in Afghanistan who had not even been born before the 9/11 terrorist attacks. American taxpayers were also exhausted, with the astounding cost of the war estimated at US$300 million per day, every day, for twenty years.

Second, it also needs to be recognised that a large proportion, if not a majority, of Afghans actually want to see the Taliban ruling their country.

The purpose of putting American, Australian and other allied troops on the ground in Afghanistan after September 11 was to stop terrorist attacks in the United States and its allies. I hold the view that ousting the Taliban after September 11 did make the world a safer place for that period. Despite the thousands of lives lost to the evil of radical Islamic terrorism, removing the Taliban from power removed the capacity for an unfettered terrorist state to flourish and carry out attacks of the scale of 9/11. Of course, the rise of Islamic State/Daesh replicated the model some years later, but it didn't end well for them either.

The unveiling of the AUKUS security pact by Joe Biden, Scott Morrison and Boris Johnson, based on an agreement by the nations to share nuclear submarine technology and intelligence, is the most significant national security development for Australia since the ANZUS Treaty itself. The AUKUS nuclear capability will change not just Australia's naval and defence capability but our standing in the world order – especially as it relates to China and its strategy for the Indo-Pacific.

It's a credit to Joe Biden that he saw fit to provide Australia with America's most sensitive security and intelligence technology. It also shows that Biden's administration understands the precarious security position that Australia and the rest of the Indo-Pacific finds itself in with the rise of China.

'We're taking another historic step to deepen and formalise cooperation among all three of our nations, because we all recognise the imperative of ensuring peace and stability in the Indo-Pacific over the long term,' Biden said the day the deal was announced.

During the Abbott government, there were discussions about nuclear-powered submarines when we were actively considering a replacement, long overdue, for the Collins Class submarines.

There was never any discussion at all about nuclear weapons, but there were occasional discussions about nuclear propulsion. There was some deep analysis of the various options, including acquiring Virginia Class submarines, but it was deemed politically unpalatable for Australia to even contemplate establishing a nuclear industry or opting for nuclear-powered submarines. At any rate, the Americans weren't having it. In fact, they even warned us off asking to share their nuclear-powered submarine technology.

Australia has a mixed history with submarines that dates back to World War I. An Australian navy submarine, HMAS *AE2*, ran the Turkish blockade through the underwater minefields of 'the Narrows' in the Dardanelles. *AE2* managed to 'run amok' until being captured and intentionally sunk by its captain, Irishman Dacre Stoker. It still lies there today.

Australians learnt a tragic lesson in World War II when we had no active submarines to protect our shores and a Japanese submarine was able to send three Type A Ko-hyoteki-class miniature submarines to cause havoc and death in Sydney Harbour.

Following World War II, we acquired Oberon Class submarines, which were small, noisy diesel subs made by the British. They were actually stationed at Neutral Bay in my electorate of North Sydney, at the naval base HMAS *Platypus*. The Oberon Class subs had an extended life, but were more useful for their deterrence value than anything else.

Of course, Australia then made its own submarine, known as the Collins Class. They were a modified version of a conventional diesel-powered Swedish submarine. Initially these were much maligned for cost blowouts and performance issues, but over time they have proved to be one of the most effective conventional submarines in the world. Despite the modifications, conventional submarines are slower and can be noisier than their nuclear-powered cousins. Given the immense territory of Australia's waters, we needed to travel further and faster than our most obvious adversaries.

When it came time to replace the Collins Class subs, the Abbott government thought the most obvious candidate was the Soryu Class, a Japanese submarine. It was the best conventional diesel submarine in the world. Prime Minister Shinzo Abe of Japan needed to change his country's laws to permit the sale of military hardware to another country – a legacy issue from World War II – and he was courageous in making that move.

Tony Abbott gave him every indication that if he was able to change those military equipment export laws, then Japan would win our submarine contract, which was the biggest military acquisition contract in the world. In the end the laws were changed; however, some domestic interests in Japan scuttled the big backed by Abe.

German subs were also proposed. When I was treasurer, I had a humorous conversation with the highly respected German finance minister Wolfgang Schäuble. He cornered me at the G20 and started lobbying for his country to build our submarines.

'But, Wolfgang,' I said in reply, 'Germany hasn't actually built the submarines that it's proposing.'

'Don't worry about that, Joe,' replied the German statesman, waving his finger around from his chair. 'All you need is a submarine to float around the Pacific and tell everyone, "It is German." That will be enough.'

Our selection committee, which had on it some leading American naval experts, then recommended the French proposal. In short, it had the equivalent of a *Hunt for Red October* propulsion system that was still diesel. It was an incredible design – in theory. The catch was that this design had never actually been built.

By the time we made the announcement that the French design had been selected, I was Australia's ambassador in Washington, DC, and so it was my responsibility to go to the Pentagon and let them know that we had gone with the French rather than the Japanese. They fully accepted that this decision was in Australia's best interests.

It's estimated that the Australian maritime program will be worth $2 trillion over the next one hundred years. Tony Abbott committed $90 billion to start building an entire new fleet for the Australian Navy, and in 2020 that amount was doubled. That was done in recognition of the threat to Australia's interests posed by China (and by Russia), which has been increasing its expenditure on its navy and has one of the best naval capabilities globally (not to mention a lot of nuclear subs with nuclear missiles on board).

The fact is that Australia's risk profile has fundamentally changed. Thirty years ago, we weren't the biggest exporter of energy in the Indo-Pacific region. We didn't have natural gas pipelines and ports around the entire country. Export terminals with massive new trains at Gladstone in Queensland or Karratha in Western Australia have changed our risk profile. We must have a naval presence that reflects our economic and strategic importance in the region. If that means having more submarines with more firepower, then so be it.

The biggest operational challenge is training submarine crews – especially given that no Australian expertise exists that has had access to the 'pointy end' of nuclear submarines. And we won't have Australian Navy nuclear submarines if they're not crewed by Australians.

Impressively, the Morrison government made an early decision to cancel the French submarine contract well before too much money was spent. All too often in defence matters, you're halfway through building the house when decide you need something different – and then you have to walk away having spent half your money on the wrong program. And the cost of maintenance is just as important as the original build, if not more important.

In the case of the French submarines, there's been less than 1 per cent of the total cost spent. The Australian government made a decision early that the French design was the wrong one for our navy. In my view, they have taken the right approach to what is by far our biggest, most complicated transaction.

President Emmanuel Macron of France has, predictably enough, been furious with Australia. But it's not as if the French weren't warned at every point that the program had real problems. They were also advised that they were too aggressive in promoting jobs in France rather than jobs and outcomes in Australia. Macron was more focused on the domestic politics of the transaction rather than on being a good supplier. The partnership was words, not deeds. At the same time, the strategic challenges with China were not only building, but accelerating. It became abundantly clear to me that this deal wasn't going to happen.

I suspect Macron's outrage is equal parts anger at the cancellation of the contract and frustration that France was not invited to join the AUKUS security alliance. No one likes a club being set up in their neighbourhood that they are not invited to join. Either way, we had to do what's best for Australia.

* * *

At the beginning of 2019, a rather flattering (albeit unrealistic) job offer was put to me by Mick Mulvaney. He asked me whether I would consider nominating for the presidency of the World Bank. Apparently, President Trump had thrown my name into the ring of candidates to head up the international body tasked with alleviating world poverty.

I was taken aback, and obviously flattered by the idea. I'll readily admit that the prospect of becoming only the second Australian to serve as president of the World Bank was enticing. Not since James Wolfensohn was nominated for the position by Bill Clinton in 1995 had an Australian served in the role, or in any other global role with as much status. (Strictly speaking, Wolfensohn had renounced his Australian citizenship by that point, so I would have been the first Australian in the role.)

Unfortunately for me, the prospect of 'Joe Hockey, President of the World Bank' lasted about one hot minute. I was informed a few days later by Steven Mnuchin, secretary of the Treasury, that it was impossible politically for the Americans to nominate anyone other than an American. Mnuchin then nominated his deputy at Treasury for International Affairs, David R. Malpass, for the role, and he was elected to the presidency from April 2019.

The experience of being suggested for the role did, however, give me pause for thought about my future. What was I going to do at the end of this? My tenure as ambassador concluded at the beginning of 2020, and I had no desire to extend it. As successful and extraordinary as my time as ambassador in Washington, DC had been, Melissa and I had decided it was time to move on from public life. Twenty-four years was enough.

Serving the Australian people and its government in Washington was an extraordinary privilege. Your home is the venue and meeting point for Australian interests not just in Washington, but throughout the United States and even North America. Melissa and I weren't the social king and queen of Washington, DC, and had no desire to be. We also wanted to take our children back to Australia. If they stayed longer in America during their formative teenage years, they might never want to live in Australia again.

When I was a government minister, I'd come within a phone call of taking up a senior role at Citibank in New York. While I'm glad I didn't take the gig at the time, the appeal of returning to the private sector had not left me. I am, at heart, an entrepreneurial person. I naturally focus on outcomes, and I suppose that's what made me a unique and successful politician. As blessed as I have been in politics and diplomacy, there was nothing left for me in public service.

My last conversation with Donald Trump took place in the Oval Office in mid-January 2020. He was genial and engaging. He was deeply concerned about the devastating bushfires raging in Australia at the time.

Typically, Trump threw a bunch of questions at me. 'Is this climate change, Joe?'

'Well, Mr President,' I began, but before I could answer, along came the next question:

'What about the koalas? Have any animals become extinct because of this?'

We talked about the parallels with California, about the build-up of fuel on the ground and the intensity of the fires. He offered Australia any help we might need or want.

Trump was fantastic with our kids, and insisted on having a photo at his desk with each of them. He signed lots of MAGA hats and gave us all the merchandise the White House could offer.

His charisma shone through when he was talking to my elder boy. 'Xavier, I have heard a lot about you,' he said. 'I hear you have a huge political career ahead. I'll be watching you all the way!'

The smile on my son's face at that moment was worth every bit of the pain of twenty-four years in public life. That the most powerful man in the world took some time to endorse my child's dreams made it all worthwhile.

I shook Donald Trump's hand and walked out of the Oval Office, leaving the president alone behind the Resolute Desk, a classic Trumpian grin on his face.

Leaving into the cold of a January night, I looked back at the White House, which was lit up like a battleship. I just stared at it for a moment, content in the knowledge that it was a remarkable journey from North Sydney to the Oval Office. Even more so, in one generation from an orphanage in Jerusalem to Washington, DC.

A couple of nights later, my farewell was held at Union Market. Amazingly, around four hundred family, friends and colleagues from across my political and diplomatic career were able to attend, some coming from as far away as Australia. Tony Abbott turned up fresh from fighting the bushfires, and gave a heartfelt and gracious speech. Greg Norman, as ever, was there to give a great speech as well. Anthony Pratt came along and even took care of the bill.

Mick Mulvaney came as the president's representative. Mick was put on the spot with a speech as well.

'Many people come to Washington and think they're surrounded by extraordinary people. Maybe they think they've become extraordinary themselves by the fact they're here,' President Trump's chief of staff said. 'But Joe Hockey understood these aren't extraordinary people. They're normal people with extraordinary jobs. Joe being Joe was his greatest asset.'

When it was my turn to speak, Melissa and the kids were by my side. Choked with emotion, I couldn't say too much. 'I'm the luckiest guy on earth,' I told the party.

Not a diplomat's speech, but honest as ever.

EPILOGUE

It's hard to resist an invitation for a late-night New York drink. After all, it is the city that never sleeps.

After suffering some confusion about the address, and being of portly demeanour, it seemed a good idea to jump out of the taxi and walk further up 5th Avenue, on the Central Park side of the street, to the rendezvous. After all, when you've only just turned fifty-seven years old, extra strides are always desperately needed. Then, in haste, while trying to cross the street, a near-fatal error was made.

Like so many who think they understand America after having visited a few times, Winston Churchill made the mistake of looking right for approaching cars rather than left. He was hit by a black car travelling at an estimated 55 kilometres per hour (35 miles per hour). It was 13 December 1931.

The robust Churchill escaped mostly unscathed, but was understandably shaken. As people often do in the United States, he then wrote his side of the story – titled 'My New York Misadventure' – and sold it for US$2500. A very large sum of money back then. It is quite a hilarious read.

The driver of the ill-fated vehicle, Edward F. Cantasano, an unemployed mechanic from Yonkers, of course also became a celebrity. Only in America. Wikipedia has a page dedicated to Cantasano. Even a video game has been made of the incident.

Churchill didn't suffer too much. Feeling the agony of abstinence from his much-needed alcoholic beverages in Prohibition-era America, Churchill convinced his doctor, Dr Pickhardt, to write the following prescription:

> *This is to certify that the post-accident convalescence of the Hon. Winston S. Churchill necessitates the use of alcoholic spirits especially at meal times. The quantity is naturally indefinite but the minimum requirements would be 250 cubic centimetres.*

God bless America. But Australia is the country I love.

The United States, with its population thirteen times larger than that of Australia, and its absolute devotion to freedom, liberty and enterprise, opens commercial doors that can remain selfishly shut in Australia.

There is a cost. Back in 1931, even Churchill was asked on his entry into hospital how he was going to pay for his treatment. There is a downside associated with unfettered capitalism.

But America is a great place to start a business, so on completion of my posting, after a lengthy discussion with Melissa, I formed the view that starting a new career in the United States was a no-brainer.

My ambassadorial chief of staff, Alex Tureman, a young and very driven Democratic operative from Jacksonville, Florida, had the same idea. He set up a small business and I travelled back to Australia to get my E-3 visa (which we'd saved from unwanted change), only to return to America to start the fourth career of my life: a small businessman.

It was obvious to me that the business needed a name that would resonate with everyone. When Dad had migrated to Australia back in 1948, he'd set up his delicatessen in Bondi. My beautiful mum, a Bondi Beach model, fell in love with the rather short and stumpy Armenian Palestinian behind the counter. Two cultures melded together. Thus, for me, Bondi Partners was a natural name. Two cultures coming together.

Of course, we didn't anticipate a pandemic. And when Alex and I sat opposite one another at a folding card table in the basement of my Washington rental, we were not only breaking the city's lockdown rules, we were looking at failure.

Kerry Stokes gave me some good advice when I told him we were setting up a new business: 'Burn your bridges behind you. You have to fear failure in order to succeed.'

When I spoke to Andrew Forrest not long after, he offered similarly useful advice: 'Don't be despondent, Joe – turn adversity into an opportunity.'

In less than two years, my firm has grown to have thirty employees in two countries. We have made a profit from year one, and now have three businesses.

The first is a strategic advisory business that helps companies expand into the United States and Australia. As Churchill found many years ago, they may think they know a country but the cost of looking the wrong way can be fatal. So we help with everything from HR and PR through to strategies navigating regulation, B2B engagement and government services.

Advising companies on major transactions is our second business. Investment bankers often don't understand politics, and these days every major transaction requires some navigation of government engagement. At the beginning of 2022, we were working on nearly $50 billion in transactions.

The third business is a patriotic duty. Together with the legendary Ashok Jacob at Ellerston Capital, I have established Australia's first National Security Investment Fund. We called it 1941 in memory of the famous year when the United States was brought into the major conflict in the Pacific, which was also the year in which Prime Minister Curtin declared that Australia would turn to America as its major ally in the battle for survival. We are investing in businesses that will help save lives today, and in the generations to follow.

Of course, setting up all that has come at a cost. Living through lockdowns and surviving multiple stints of quarantine has been tough.

Writing this book in partnership with the ever calm and persistent Leo Shanahan has been a form of COVID respite. He is a smart, sharp and engaging writer. It worked well that our seemingly hundreds of hours of Zoom calls were timed perfectly for a journalist's preferred late nights in Sydney and a small businessman's very early mornings in Washington, DC.

I have lived a fantastic life full of swings and roundabouts. No one has ever suggested that I am diplomatic, but diplomacy has served me well.

To all who have been a part of my story thus far: thank you.